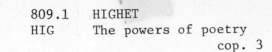
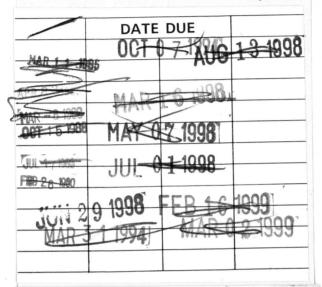

# THE POWERS OF POETRY

GILBERT HIGHET

The Powers
of
Poetry

*New York* / OXFORD UNIVERSITY PRESS / 1960

© 1960 by Gilbert Highet

Library of Congress Catalogue Card Number: 60-7062

Printed in the United States of America

Fifth Printing, 1970

© 1953 by Gilbert Highet (*People, Places, and Books*): Shakespeare in Love (original title 'An Autobiography of Shakespeare'); The Pessimist (original title 'An American Poet'); Mr. Eliot.

© 1954 by Gilbert Highet (*A Clerk of Oxenford*): Melody in Poetry; Rhythm in Poetry; A Poet and His Vulture; Professor Paradox; The Old Wizard; A Drinking Song; Seventeen Syllables; The Madness of Hamlet; What Use Is Poetry?

© 1954 by Oxford University Press (also in *Talents and Geniuses* © 1957 by Gilbert Highet): Death of a Poet.

© 1954 by Oxford University Press: Shakespeare in Italy.

© 1955 by Oxford University Press: Kicking His Mother; Could It Be Verse?; The Book of Miracles.

© 1956 by Oxford University Press: How Shelley Died; Diminuendo; The Poet and the Urn.

© 1957 by Oxford University Press: The Lady and the Poet; The Epic of a Crime.

© 1958 by Oxford University Press: A Mouse and a Louse; The Magic-maker; Propaganda and Poetry; A Little Latin Lyric; The Elegy in a Country Churchyard; Shakespeare's Dreams and Dreamers.

© 1959 by Oxford University Press: Obscurity in Poetry; Heir of the Whole World; The Aloof American (original title 'A Neglected American'); Memoirs of Heaven; Penetrating a Book; The Waste Land.

The author expresses his gratitude to the authors, publishers, and others in the following list who have kindly allowed him to quote from works in which they hold copyright. For the convenience of readers, the list is set out alphabetically under the names of authors.

W. H. AUDEN: an excerpt from "O Where Are You Going?" (copyright 1934 by The Modern Library, Inc.); "Mundus et Infans" (copyright 1942 by W. H. Auden); and Sonnet XII from *In Time of War* (copyright 1945 by W. H. Auden): all reprinted from *The Collected Poetry of W. H. Auden*, by permission of Random House, Inc. For permission to reprint these pieces in Canada, my thanks to Messrs. Faber and Faber, London.

MORRIS BISHOP: "Lines Prompted No Doubt by an Escape Mechanism" and an excerpt from "Railroad-Coach Seating Arrangement," from *A Bowl of Bishop*, copyright 1954 by Morris Bishop and used with the permission of the publishers, The Dial Press, Inc. "Lines Prompted No Doubt by an Escape Mechanism" appeared originally in *The New Yorker*.

E. E. CUMMINGS: the poem beginning IN) (from *no thanks*) on page 292 of *Poems: 1923-1954;* and the fog poem beginning un (from *New Poems*) on page 333 of *Poems: 1923-1954:* copyright, 1935, and 1938, by E. E. Cummings; reprinted from *Poems: 1923-1954* by permission of Harcourt, Brace and Company, Inc.

T. S. ELIOT: various excerpts from *The Waste Land;* five lines from "Ash-Wednesday" III; the first eight lines of "Five-Finger Exercises" V; one line from "The Rock"; and the whole of "Triumphal March": from *Collected Poems 1909-1935* by T. S. Eliot, copyright, 1936, by Harcourt, Brace and Company, Inc.

ROBERT FROST: "A Considerable Speck": from *A Witness Tree*, copyright, 1942, by Robert Frost; by permission of Henry Holt and Company, Inc.

A. E. HOUSMAN: excerpts (identified in the text of this book) from *Complete Poems*. Copyright, 1922, 1940, © 1959 by Henry Holt and Company, Inc.; Copyright, 1936, 1950, by Barclays Bank Ltd. By permission of Henry Holt and Company, Inc. For Canadian rights, my thanks to The Society of Authors, London, and Messrs. Jonathan Cape, Ltd.

ROLFE HUMPHRIES: an excerpt from his translation of Ovid's *Metamorphoses*, by permission of the Indiana University Press.

ROBINSON JEFFERS: "Summer Holiday," from *Roan Stallion, Tamar, And Other Poems*, copyright 1925 and renewed 1953 by Robinson Jeffers. Reprinted by permission of Random House, Inc.

DAVID McCORD: "A Hex on the Mexican X" and an excerpt from "Nightmare in a Museum," from *Odds without Ends;* copyright, 1945, 1954, by David McCord, by permission of Little, Brown & Co.

PHYLLIS McGINLEY: "The Old Philanthropist," from *The Love Letters of Phyllis Mc-Ginley;* by permission of the author and of The Viking Press, Inc.

LOUIS MACNEICE: "River in Spate" (originally entitled "A Cataract Conceived as the March of Corpses"), from *Poems 1925-1940*, copyright 1937, 1939, 1940 by Louis Mac-Neice. Reprinted by permission of Random House, Inc.

MARIANNE MOORE: an excerpt from "Propriety," from her *Collected Poems*, by permission of the author and The Macmillan Company.

OGDEN NASH: "The Middle" and an excerpt from "Epilogue to Mother's Day." "The Middle" was originally published in *The New Yorker* and is copyright © 1946 by Ogden Nash; "Epilogue to Mother's Day" is copyright 1935 by Ogden Nash, and is used by his kind permission and that of Little, Brown & Co., who published it in *I'm A Stranger Here Myself*.

KARL SHAPIRO: the opening stanza of "The Fly," from his *Poems 1940-1953*, copyright 1953 by Random House, Inc.

DAME EDITH SITWELL: the opening of "Sir Beelzebub," reprinted by permission of the publishers, The Vanguard Press, from *The Collected Poems of Edith Sitwell*. Copyright, 1954, by Edith Sitwell.

DYLAN THOMAS: excerpts from "The force that through the green fuse," "Should lanterns shine," "Poem in October," "On the marriage of a virgin," "Fern Hill," "Over Sir John's hill," and initial lines from other poems identified in the text of this book: all from *The Collected Poems of Dylan Thomas*. Copyright 1952, 1953, by Dylan Thomas. Reprinted by permission of New Directions and J. M. Dent & Sons. The Wild Welshman was published in the 16 March 1960 issue of *Vogue*.

W. B. YEATS: "Politics," "Youth and Age," and part of "Why Should Not Old Men Be Mad?", from the definitive edition of his *Collected Poems*, copyright 1956 by The Macmillan Company.

My thanks are also due to the editors and publishers of *The Antioch Review*, for granting me permission to publish here, revised and rewritten, a version of my essay on Carl Spitteler which appeared first in *The Antioch Review*, vol. 12 (1952), as "A Neglected Masterpiece: *Olympian Spring*."

For KEITH HIGHET

— himself a poet

Tout passe. — L'art robuste
Seul a l'éternité,
      Le buste
Survit à la cité,

Et la médaille austère
Que trouve un laboureur
      Sous terre
Révèle un empereur.

Les dieux eux-mêmes meurent,
Mais les vers souverains
      Demeurent
Plus forts que les airains.

                    — Gautier, 'L'Art'

This is a book of essays on poets and poetry.

First come three studies of poetic technique: the uses of rhythm in poetry, the various types of sound-effect which poets employ, and poetic language, which is sometimes clear and sometimes (for different reasons) obscure.

Next is a group of essays on individual poets, from Shakespeare to Dylan Thomas, discussing their characters, problems in their lives, and some of the experiences which profoundly affected their work. To be a poet is a difficult and exhausting career. Some eminent poets have been utterly worn out by the effort it entails; some have found it so distracting that it jeopardized their personal happiness; others, again, have found that poetry was the only consolation for some bitter grief of their own, their only solution for problems otherwise insoluble. To appreciate poetry thoroughly, we should know the men who write it.

In the third part there are twenty-one studies of poems, of special groups of poems, and of certain interesting aspects of well-known poetic works. In order to understand any poem whatever, we must first know to which type of poetry it belongs: whether it is a lyric, an elegy, an epic, a satire, or what. Therefore I have arranged these studies in four groups by pattern. This is particularly revealing in two cases: trying to explain T. S. Eliot's 'Coriolan' and his even more obscure *The Waste Land*, I found that, even although they contain no stage directions, no cast of characters, and no regular exchange of dialogue, they can best be classified as 'dramatic'; and this classification really helps in understanding them.

Finally, there is an essay which discusses some of the answers to the question 'Why does anyone write poetry, and why do we read it?'

Most of these pieces were written especially for this book. A few have been reprinted (with corrections and expansions) from my three earlier collections of essays, *People, Places, and Books* (1953), *A Clerk of Oxenford* (1954), and *Talents and Geniuses* (1957). In principle, I do not like reprinting, in one volume, matter which has already appeared in another; but I have had so many requests for a single book dealing with poets and poetry that I thought it might be forgivable to break the rule in this case.

*East Hampton, New York*                                        G.H.
*August 1959*

# CONTENTS

## POEMS

# Techniques

# Melody in Poetry

A GOOD POEM has many different approaches, many different methods of exerting power over its readers. Or should we say — over its readers, speakers, and hearers? We lose a great deal nowadays because we seldom read poems aloud, even to ourselves. Yet most poems in the enormous treasury of the world were meant to be spoken, or chanted in chorus, or sung to music. Much of their meaning is in their sound.

Two of the strongest powers of poetry are melody and rhythm. Rhythm is the pulse which, through its regularity, enhances our interest and sustains our excitement, and, through its variations, emphasizes the meaning. Melody is the music of vowels and consonants, syllables and words, which delights the hearer and emphasizes the meaning in a different way. In our own language and in others, much of the best poetry has a powerful rhythm. Some of the best poetry also has a subtle and delightful melody. This is one of the many strong ties between poetry and music. Poets know that there are many words which sound ugly but have interesting meanings, and many beautiful noises which have little or no meaning, at best only a vague significance. One of the problems of the poet's art is there-

fore to use such sounds in order to help the total effect of
a poem.

The most obvious of the poetic devices based on sound is
the regular echo which we call rhyme. Here the chime of repeated sounds gives us pleasure, just as we enjoy a piano and a
violin playing in concord and echoing one another. But beyond the pleasure of the ear, there is in rhyme a pleasure which
is connected with the mind. Two lines that rhyme seem to have
a secret kinship: their meanings are somehow closely allied,
and support one another, either by contrast or by similarity.
For instance, here is Pope describing one of his many enemies,
Lord Hervey, the effeminate courtier. Notice how the rhymes
sometimes stress a contrast, and sometimes play on a resem-
blance, since the man himself was a conglomeration of op-
posites.

> Yet let me flap this bug with gilded wings,
> This painted child of dirt, that stinks and stings . . .
> Eternal smiles his emptiness betray,
> As shallow streams run dimpling all the way . . .
> His wit all see-saw, between that and this,
> Now high, now low, now master up, now miss,
> And he himself one vile antithesis.
> Amphibious thing! that acting either part,
> The trifling head, or the corrupted heart,
> Fop at the toilet, flatterer at the board,
> Now trips a lady, and now struts a lord.
> Eve's tempter thus the Rabbins have expressed,
> A cherub's face, a reptile all the rest:
> Beauty that shocks you, parts * that none will trust,
> Wit that can creep, and pride that licks the dust.†

Without the sound effects that splendid description would have
lost much of its energy and its clarity. The brisk clear rhymes,
following in relentless pairs, sound like the double knock of a
hammer driving nails into a coffin.

---

* parts = talents
† *Epistle to Dr. Arbuthnot* 309-10, 315-16, 323-33

Sometimes again rhyme helps the sense, by being odd. If the poet is describing something absurd, he will amuse his hearers by adding ridiculous noises: by putting in unimaginable and almost impossible rhymes. W. S. Gilbert was good at this: you recall the Major-General's song in *The Pirates of Penzance,* which rhymes *gunnery* to *nunnery* and *strategy* to *sat a gee.* In English, the most successful such rhymester was probably Samuel Butler, the seventeenth-century satirist. Here is his description of the power of imagination stimulated by terror — with suitably ridiculous rhymes:

> Fear does things so like a witch,
> 'Tis hard to unriddle which is which;
> Sets up communities of senses
> To chop and change intelligences;
> As Rosicrucian virtuosi's
> Can see with ears and hear with noses;
> And when they neither see nor hear,
> Have more than both supplied by fear,
> That makes them in the dark see visions,
> And hag themselves with apparitions.*

Since nearly every rhyme here is unexpected, the subject sounds unnatural and absurd.

But beyond rhyme there is a much older device, both to make the sound echo and to improve the sense. This is alliteration: the echo of a single sound (vowel or consonant) from one word to another within a line or two. This can be used either for emotional emphasis or for the actual imitation of natural sounds. If you study how our best poets use it, you soon find that the various letters have quite different emotional connotations — *s* shows hatred, *t* disgust, *l* and *v* soft affection, and so forth. In this, we are getting very close to the mysterious and still unknown origins of language.

Let us look at some examples.

---

* *Hudibras* 3.3.11-20

First, a short and striking one from W. H. Auden, using *s* to show horror. In a description of a nightmare, he says

> Behind you swiftly the figure comes softly,
> The spot on your skin is a shocking disease.*

The same letter *s*, the letter of disgust and sinister cunning, the letter which begins the words *snake* and *serpent* and *Satan*, occupies one of the great scenes in Milton's *Paradise Lost*. The devil has returned from a successful mission: he has partly ruined God's newly created world, corrupted mankind, and established a bridgehead into the otherwise happy and virtuous universe, a bridgehead on this earth. Satan announces this to his comrades in hell; and then

> A while he stood, expecting
> Their universal shout and high applause
> To fill his ear; when, contrary, he hears
> On all sides, from innumerable tongues,
> A dismal universal hiss . . .†

He and his accomplices have all been transfigured into snakes; and in a few moments the poetry itself begins to hiss:

> Now were all transformed
> Alike, to serpents all, as accessories
> To his bold riot: dreadful was the din
> Of hissing through the hall, thick-swarming now
> With complicated monsters, head and tail,
> Scorpion, and Asp, and Amphisbaena dire,
> Cerastes horned, Hydrus, and Ellops drear,
> And Dipsas . . .

A little later in the same scene, *s* spits with the very sound of disgust, as the defeated fiends fill their mouths with the apples of Sodom, and then

> instead of fruit
> Chewed bitter ashes, which the offended taste
> With spattering noise rejected . . .‡

---

* *Songs and Other Musical Pieces* XXV
† *Paradise Lost* 10.504-8
‡ *Paradise Lost* 10.519-26, 565-7

Now let us take a gentler sound. The letter *f* is quiet, almost mute, like a tiny breeze blowing: so it can echo the soft activities of nature in springtime. Here is a stanza by Swinburne almost entirely based on *f*; notice how the repetition of the sound makes you think of the rustle of zephyrs and the almost audible movement of growth:

> The full streams feed on flower of rushes,
>   Ripe grasses trammel a travelling foot,
> The faint fresh flame of the young year flushes
>   From leaf to flower and flower to fruit.*

There are some *s* sounds in this stanza too; but they are nearly all softened down into *sh*: *rushes*, *flushes*; that sound is less bitter and makes us think rather of the gush of rain-filled brooks. The *t*'s in the second line somehow reflect the complicated growth of fresh vegetation, crossing and interlocking.

> Ripe grasses *t*rammel a *t*ravelling foo*t*.

And further, notice the skillful and delightful broadening of the vowels in the last line, to show the passage of spring into summer:

> From l*ea*f to fl*o*wer and fl*o*wer to fr*ui*t.

There is a good natural effect of this kind in Tennyson. In two lines he contrives to describe a stormy sky overcast by thunderclouds, some of them already breaking. To do this, he uses the rolling letter *r*, two soft *s* sounds, broad open vowels for the thunder, and narrow vowels for the rain: and here is the result:

> The ragged rims of thunder brooding low,
>   With shadow-streaks of rain.†

Without doubt, Tennyson was the master of this kind of thing in English. His teacher was the Latin poet Vergil, who is simply superb, probably the greatest poet of sound effects in

---

* *Atalanta in Calydon*, first chorus
† 'The Palace of Art' 75-6

all Western literature. Here are two lines from an early poem about country life in which Vergil imitates not only the sound but actually the rhythm of cooing doves and pigeons:

> Nec tamen interea raucae, tua cura, palumbes,
> nec gemere aeria cessabit turtur ab ulmo.*

That is only one of a thousand such brilliant effects in Vergil. Tennyson tried very hard to rival them, often adding his own sense of quaintness and fun. For instance, here is his half-humorous imitation of the music of a little brook: first two lines full of *t* and *r,* to show the grinding of gravel:

> I chatter over stony ways
> In little sharps and trebles...

And then two lines full of *b, p,* and *d,* to sound like bursting foam:

> I bubble into eddying bays
> I babble on the pebbles.†

Here is an even more amusing effect, also by Tennyson, describing an explosion; you can actually hear the separate stages: first the detonation, then the harsh rip of the torn air, then the waves of sound expanding and growing duller:

> High above, I heard them blast
> The steep slate-quarry, and the great echo flap
> And buffet round the hills from bluff to bluff. ‡

Different consonants have different powers. *W* sometimes sounds like the wind; hard *c* and *g* clatter like ice. Shelley describes a bitter frost mainly through these three letters:

> For Winter came: the wind was his whip:
> One choppy finger was on his lip:
> He had torn the cataracts from the hills
> And they clanked at his girdle like manacles.**

* *Bucolics* 1.57-8
† 'The Brook'
‡ 'The Golden Year' 74-6
** 'The Sensitive Plant' 3.86-9

The explosive initials, *t*, *d*, and *p*, can be used to suggest disgust and derision. This is splendidly conveyed in Macbeth's famous speech:

> Tomorrow, and tomorrow, and tomorrow
> Creeps in this petty pace from day to day
> To the last syllable of recorded time;
> And all our yesterdays have lighted fools
> The way to dusty death.*

We have been talking about consonants, because the effects they produce are clearer at a first hearing. But the best poets also work with vowel effects, although English is less well endowed with resonant vowels than Latin or Greek or Italian or French. One of the most exquisite lines in French poetry is a little masterpiece by Verlaine, describing a children's choir, with its music echoing round the hollow of a dome:

> Et, ô ces voix d'enfants chantant dans la coupole! †

Many poets have built astonishing descriptions of nature upon musical vowels and eloquent consonants. Here is an evocation of a thunderstorm, in only seven lines. Of course it is by Shakespeare. It is made of four sentences, each with a different tempo and different types of sound. The first evokes brief and violent gusts of *wind*. The second (built on *r* and *s*, with plunging and splashing rhythm) makes us hear a deluge of savage *rain*. The third, filled with immensely varied vowels and clashing consonants, shows us multiple flashes of *lightning*; and the fourth booms like *thunder*.

> Blow, winds, and crack your cheeks! rage! blow! /
> You cataracts and hurricanoes, spout
> Till you have drenched our steeples, drowned the cocks! /
> You sulphurous and thought-executing fires,
> Vaunt-couriers to oak-cleaving thunderbolts,
> Singe my white head! / And thou, all-shaking thunder,
> Strike flat the thick rotundity of the world! / ‡

* *Macbeth* 5.5.19-23
† 'Parsifal'
‡ *King Lear* 3.2.1-7

Tremendous; magnificent. But here are three lines from Tennyson which image the exact reverse: the peaceful sound of water, the cooing of doves, and bees humming somewhere out of sight:

> Myriads of rivulets hurrying thro' the lawn,
> The moan of doves in immemorial elms,
> And murmuring of innumerable bees.*

* *The Princess* 7.205-7

# Rhythm in Poetry

WHEN the poet Goethe first went to Italy, he found new experiences in love and new impulses in poetry and art. He also found that the two were closely connected. He wrote a fine book of poems about his visit, called *Roman Elegies*. In one of these he says that he found himself making love and making poetry at the same time. He would have his arms around his sweetheart, and be playing a little tune with his fingers on her back. She thought he was caressing her. He was caressing her: yes; but he was also working out the rhythm of a new poem. It is an amusing little picture; but it is very revealing to people interested in the work of creation: for it shows that one of the things Goethe felt to be essential in poetry was rhythm.

Most of the good poetry in English and other Western languages is strongly rhythmical. There are some fields in which poetry links up with logic, and religion, and metaphysics, and rhetoric; but in this particular field, it is close to music, and the rhythms of poetry give us the same sort of psychical excitement and satisfaction as the swing and the percussion of an orchestra.

The reasons for this are clear. Our love for rhythm is part of our subconscious and emotional endowment. It springs from one of those mysterious regions in which the mind and the body are interlinked: it is possible to read a poem in silence to oneself, and, by sympathy with its pulsations, to feel one's heart beating more rapidly and strongly.

The importance of rhythm in poetry is understood; but the methods poets use in producing and employing it are not obvious. They are worth discussing, for one of the ways in which good poetry differs from trash is in its rhythmical subtlety.

Let us take a simple case — the best-known meter in English, the heroic line. It is the verse of Shakespeare's dramas, of Milton's epics, of most of Tennyson and Browning and Keats and Shelley and Byron, of Dryden and Pope and scores of lesser men. Sometimes it rhymes, sometimes it is blank. But the basis of it is always the same.

It is built on one simple fact. English is a stressed language, in which nearly every word and every group of words have one or more stresses, and in which we use stress for emphasis. Normally we say

$$\text{\'English is a str\'essed l\'anguage}$$

with three stresses; and for emphasis we can also say

$$\text{\'English \'is a str\'essed l\'anguage}$$

with four. Every sentence we utter in English contains stresses; when these stresses form a regular pattern, we are speaking verse.

Now, the heroic line contains five more or less regularly spaced stresses, separated by five weak syllables which are not stressed. The two alternate, like this:

$$\text{And \'one, and tw\'o, and thr\'ee, and f\'our, and f\'ive.}$$

And here are two typical lines from Tennyson, both quite regular:

> Come down, O Maid, from yonder mountain height:
> What pleasure lives in height? the shepherd sang.*

The basis is clear and simple:

> And one, and two, and three, and four, and five.

That is the iambic pentameter, sometimes called the heroic line because it is used for heroic subjects.

But if a poet wrote every line in a long poem on that same rhythmical pattern, it would become intolerably monotonous. Therefore he exerts himself to vary it: delicately, for if he varies too widely, he will get away from the feeling of regularity altogether, and his readers will lose the sense of controlled and sustained excitement; but still, within a wide range of rhythmical values, he varies it so as to express more sensitively the varying emotions and ideas with which he is dealing.

The first way of doing this is to take the five beats, the five equal stresses, and make one of them a little weaker than the others. This gives our inner ear a short rest, and also imposes a slightly stronger emphasis on the two neighboring beats. You remember the beautiful prologue to the fourth act of Shakespeare's *Henry V*, where the Chorus describes the night watch before the decisive battle, with the young king walking among his soldiers to encourage them. It is a splendid piece. Now, some of the lines in it are perfectly regular:

> The hum of either army stilly sounds...
> The country cocks do crow, the clocks do toll...

But in one inimitable line Shakespeare says that all shall see

> A little touch of Harry in the night.

---

* *The Princess* 7.177-8

Now, this cannot be spoken in five exactly equal beats:

A líttle tóuch of Hárry ín the níght.

Instead, it must be this:

A líttle tóuch of *Hárry* ... in the níght.

And so, from the weakness of the word *in,* the poet gains time to make a little pause before it, and gains energy to provide some extra strength for the affectionate and gallant name *Harry.*

Another variation on the regular pattern of rhythm is equally simple and equally valuable. It is to add one weak syllable at the end of the line. Instead of

And óne, and twó, and thrée, and fóur, and fíve,

this gives us

And óne, and twó, and thrée, and fóur, and fíve, and ...

Obviously, this is a change and a rest for the ear; but it can also convey doubt or hesitation or wonder, for it makes the line end not with a definite final stress, but with a weak syllable trailing away into silence. So in the most famous monologue in English poetry, Hamlet's meditation on suicide, there are many lines which close on the strong stress, like these:

To sleep; perchance to dream: ay, there's the rúb.

For in that sleep of death what dreams may cóme

When we have shuffled off this mortal coíl

Must give us pause.

But the opening lines of the same speech all have an extra syllable, hanging in hesitation, drifting away into doubt: not this:

To be or not to be, that is the choíce—

but this:

> To be or not to be, that is the que′stion:
> Whether 'tis nobler in the mind to su′ffer
> The slings and arrows of outrageous fo′rtune,
> Or to take arms against a sea of tro′ubles,
>
> And by opposing end them? *

English is particularly fortunate in this: our poets can end a line either with a strong, stressed syllable or with a light, unstressed syllable, as they wish. In Italian it is almost mandatory to end with the weak syllable:

> Nel mezzo del cammin di nostra vi′ta
>
> mi ritrovai per una selva oscu′ra.†

And in French poetry written in couplets it has become compulsory to end one couplet with heavy syllables and the next with light syllables, like this:

> Non: vous avez beau faire et beau me raisonner,
> Rien de ce que je dis ne me peut détourner:
> Trop de perversité règne au siècle où nous sommes,
> Et je veux me tirer du commerce des hommes.‡

But to make a variation so rigidly regular as that really destroys the beauty of variation: the verse of poetic drama in French has therefore a smaller emotional range than that of English drama.

Now, take a third type of variation. The basic flow of rhythm in this kind of verse is a regular alternation of weakly and strongly stressed syllables, evenly balanced. Good poets often invert the succession in one pair of syllables, so as to bring two

---

* *Hamlet* 3.1.56-60
† Dante, *Comedy* 1.1-2
‡ Molière, *Le Misanthrope* 5.1.3-6

weak syllables together and two strong syllables together. This produces surprise and extra emphasis. Consider the opening of Milton's *Paradise Lost*. Milton is announcing his subject, which is the Fall of Man; and he is praying for the help of the Holy Spirit in writing on this great theme. He begins:

> Of Man's first disobedience, and the fruit
> Of that forbidden tree, whose mortal taste
> Brought death into the world, and all our woe,
> With loss of Eden, till one greater Man
> Restore us, and regain the blissful seat,
> Sing, Heavenly Muse!

You hear the steady pulsation of the alternating weak and strong syllables. But you also hear telling variations on the regular succession of weak and strong. In the very first line there is an eloquent change of emphasis: for we cannot say

> Of Mán's first disobédience, ánd the frúit ...

Instead, we must say

> Of Mán's *fírst* disobédience, ánd the frúit ...

Then in the fourth line, with its reference to Jesus as the Redeemer, we are not intended to say

> With lóss of Éden, till one gréater Mán
> Restore us,

but rather

> With lóss of Éden, till *óne* gréater Mán
> Restore us ...

Milton is particularly good at this kind of thing, almost as good as his master Vergil. A hundred lines later in the same book, we hear the fallen archangel Lucifer speaking. He recalls how he fought against God

In dubious battle on the plains of Heaven
And shook his throne. What though the field be lost?
All is not lost...*

Here it would be impossible for us to say:

And shóok his thróne. What though the field be lóst?
Áll is not lóst.

Instead, we are compelled to echo the bold self-confidence of Lucifer, as he shouts

And shóok his thróne. Whát though the field be lóst?
*Áll* is not lóst.

You can hear the same use of variation throughout Shakespeare. So Hamlet's soliloquy does not begin:

To be or not to be, that ís the quéstion.

No, it begins

To be or not to be, *thát* is the quéstion.

So, in Macbeth's wonderful speech of remorse, made just after he has murdered a sleeping man, he begins with a regular rhythm:

Methought I heard a voice cry 'Sleep no more!
Macbeth does murder sleep, the innocent sleep...'

And then twice, for emphasis, he inverts the stresses of the opening: first this:

Sléep, that knits up the ravelled sleave of care,

then a regular line

The déath of each day's life, sore labour's bath,

* *Paradise Lost* 1.104-6

and then another emphatic inversion:

Bálm of hurt minds, great nature's second course...*

so that we can hear his mounting excitement in the urgency of the rhythm.

We have been talking only of inverting the stresses in a single foot of the line. But good poets can carry this much further, and invert several different stresses, so that we — as it were — feel the regular pulse working backward, and get additional excitement from the strangeness of the rhythm. *Hamlet* is full of such effects. When the young prince is in his mother's room reproaching her, and his father's ghost appears, you remember she cannot see it. In wild excitement and irregular rhythm, he cries

Why, loók you thére! Loók, how it steáls awáy!

Next, a slow regular line, in which two weak words are stressed in order to make them powerfully emphatic:

My fáther ín his hábit ás he líved,

And then a passionate double inversion:

Loók where he goés, even nów, oút at the pórtal! †

As soon as an actor speaks one scene of Shakespeare, even a page, we can tell whether he understands its meaning or not.

Now consider a truly astounding rhythmical effect, from Milton's *Paradise Lost.* It comes from the climax of the primal war in heaven, describing the fall of the rebel angels. In battle they have defeated the loyal angels, but now the Son of God himself goes forth to war against them, and drives them in rout

* *Macbeth* 2.2.36-40
† *Hamlet* 3.4.133-5

to the frightful gulf at the edge of heaven. And see how the
violence of their overthrow is imaged in three inversions:

The monstrous sight

Stroók them with horror backward; but far worse

Úrged them behind; headlong themselves they threw

Dówn from the verge of heaven: eternal wrath . . .

And then, to describe their catastrophic fall down through
space into hell, a wonderful line which is all distorted and
chaotic:

eternal wrath
Burnt after them to the bottomless pit.*

Impossible, utterly impossible, to read this as

Burnt áfter thém to thé bóttomless pít.

Instead, the line crashes down like the dizzy plunge of the out-
cast spirits, its rhythms altered and unnatural like the angels
changing into devils, and its terrible pace ending only in the
last, lowest, terrible syllable:

Búrnt áfter thém to the bóttomless pít.

Only good poets can venture on such tremendously daring
effects. That is why we not only read the best poetry but reread
it and study it. It never suffers from being better understood.
The first time we hear one of Shakespeare's great speeches, we
are moved. The fiftieth time we hear or read it, we understand
it better, and are far more deeply moved. Even such a simple
thing as the rhythm of ten syllables can make us hear the thud-
ding of a tormented heart, or open up the utmost gulfs of space.

Ten syllables: five iambics: the simplest and best-known meter
in all our literature, yet by far the most versatile, the most ex-

---

* *Paradise Lost* 6.862-6

pressive, the most powerful. Some poets have written almost all their poetry in this one measure alone, exploring thousands of its potential variations. Shakespeare composed some passages in longer lines, a few in shorter, and many songs; but he spent most of his effort on the five-beat iambic line. Between the clipped, neat, conventional rhythm of his early plays and his sonnets —

> And other strains of woe, which now seem woe,
> Compared with loss of thee will not seem so *—

and the sumptuous and appalling eloquence of his later plays —

> You fools of fortune, trencher-friends, time's flies,
> Cap and knee slaves, vapours, and minute-jacks † —

there is as vast a difference as between a Lully minuet and a Beethoven concerto, although both are played on the same four strings.

However, the heroic line is only one meter. There are dozens, scores of others in English alone, and many more in the other European languages. To savor the varieties of rhythm is one of the keenest pleasures of poetry. Most of us have been reading the flaccid measures of 'free verse' for so long that we have almost forgotten the power of energetic rhythm, whether simple or complex. Most bad poetry written today is quite obviously moribund: it has lost both its color and its pulse.

Many poets in the last century and a few in this have enjoyed experimenting with unusual rhythmical forms, to evoke vivid scenes, or to echo in words the driving vigor of a strong emotion. Robert Browning was once aboard ship on a long voyage. He was a restless, energetic man, hated being deprived of exercise, felt the ship as a slow-moving prison. He thought with affection of his favorite horse chafing in its stable at home, and he imagined how wonderful a long gallop on its back would be. A ride on a real horse was out of the question: so Browning

---

\* Sonnet 90
† *Timon of Athens* 3.6.107-8

sat down with a pencil and wrote a poem about a gallop on an imaginary horse. To make it more exciting, he invented an urgent reason for the ride, gave himself two gallant companions, placed the adventure in a dramatic period of history (the seventeenth century, when the Dutch were fighting the Spaniards), and thought out the whole geography of the gallop, from excited start to exhausted finish. He called the poem 'How they brought the good news from Ghent to Aix.' It is a wonderful experience to ride a fine horse which is strong, and brave, and loyal, and steadily paced: the rhythm is so pervasive that it seems to raise one's life to a higher intensity. Both the emotions and the rhythm have never been better described than in Browning's steady anapaests, one two thrée, one two thrée.

> I sprang to the stirrup, and Joris, and he;
> I galloped, Dirck galloped, we galloped all three;
> 'Good speed!' cried the watch, as the gate-bolts undrew;
> 'Speed!' echoed the wall to us galloping through;
> Behind shut the postern, the lights sank to rest,
> And into the midnight we galloped abreast.
>
> Not a word to each other; we kept the great pace,
> Neck by neck, stride by stride, never changing our place;
> I turned in my saddle and made its girths tight,
> Then shortened each stirrup, and set the pique right,
> Rebuckled the cheek-strap, chained slacker the bit,
> Nor galloped less steadily Roland a whit.

Browning wrote another remarkable poem about riding horseback. (Perhaps he composed it on the same voyage, while he looked out on the rolling hills and long sands of North Africa.) This one is more eccentric, but almost equally effective. It describes the thoughts of an Algerian tribesman as he rides across the waste to join the leader of the Algerian rebels fighting the French. Such a journey would not be a breakneck gallop, but a steady canter. Therefore Browning devised a brief recurrent cantering rhythm to image it. Also, the journey through those treeless waterless endless rocks and sands would be monotonous:

the horseman's spirit would have to brace itself against that monotony by unflinching resolution. Browning shows both the monotony and the resolution by using only one single rhyme for a poem of forty lines in length, by repeating the rhyme in the middle of five lines in every eight, and by framing each stanza inside a recurrent refrain.

> As I ride, as I ride
> To our Chief and his Allied,
> Who dares chide my heart's pride
> As I ride, as I ride?
> Or are witnesses denied —
> Through the desert waste and wide
> Do I glide unespied
> As I ride, as I ride?
>
> As I ride, as I ride,
> Ne'er has spur my swift horse plied,
> Yet his hide, streaked and pied,
> As I ride, as I ride,
> Shows where sweat has sprung and dried,
> — Zebra-footed, ostrich-thighed —
> How has vied stride with stride
> As I ride, as I ride! *

Browning's contemporary Victor Hugo accomplished an even more amazing feat of technique in describing a rider on horseback. His poem, 'Le pas d'armes du roi Jean,' gallops on and on for nearly a hundred lines, with its rhymes clashing and clattering like hooves; but each line is only three syllables long.

> Çà, qu'on selle,
> Écuyer,
> Mon fidèle
> Destrier.
> Mon cœur ploie
> Sous la joie
> Quand je broie
> L'étrier.

---

* Browning, 'Through the Metidja to Abd-el-Kadr'

Par saint-Gille,
Viens-nous-en,
Mon agile
Alezan;
Viens, écoute,
Par la route,
Voir la joute
Du roi Jean. . . .

La cohue,
Flot de fer,
Frappe, hue,
Remplit l'air,
Et, profonde,
Tourne et gronde,
Comme une onde
Sur la mer.

Take something much lighter and subtler. How does one evoke, in poetry, the broken babbling utterance of a singing bird? Marianne Moore can show us.

### PROPRIETY

Is some such word
    as the chord
        Brahms had heard
        from a bird,
sung down near the root of the throat;
it's the little downy woodpecker
            spiralling a tree —
                up up up like mercury.*

Words could scarcely be arranged more daintily than that, nor rhythm used more deftly.

Graceful and intricate Miss Moore's poems always are, and they are always controlled. Dame Edith Sitwell has — and this is very unusual for a woman writing poetry — sometimes expressed emotions so disorderly and excitements so frantic as to be all

---

* Marianne Moore, 'Propriety'

but unintelligible. I remember what a yell of scorn and anger went up from the commonsensical British in 1923 when she published *Façade*. This is the beginning of one of the poems they found most objectionable.

> When
> Sir
> Beelzebub called for his syllabub in the hotel in Hell
>          Where Proserpine first fell,
> Blue as the gendarmerie were the waves of the sea
>
>     (Rocking and shocking the bar-maid.)
>
> Nobody comes to give him his rum but the
> Rim of the sky hippopotamus-glum
> Enhances the chances to bless with a benison
> Alfred Lord Tennyson crossing the bar....*

Here, quite apart from the alcoholic words (*syllabub, bar-maid, rum*), and the irreverent parodies of an eminent poet and an ancient myth, and the deliberate illogicality of the sentences, it is surely quite clear that the hiccupping staggering burbling lurching rhythm, together with the compulsive but meaningless rhymes, is meant to image the excitements of drunkenness. Just as Coleridge's 'Kubla Khan' is a fragmentary monument to the powers of laudanum, so this poem is a dream filled with the fumes of 151-proof alcohol.

Alfred Lord Tennyson was no stranger to the delights of drink and the temptations of manic excitement. One of his finest poems describes a graver and grimmer madness, the madness of war. In the reign of the Roman emperor Nero, the British queen Boadicea † after many sore provocations raised a terrific revolt against the Roman occupying forces, massacred many thousands of them and their supporters, and burned Roman colonies in Britain to the ground. Although, technically, she was supposed to be an 'ally' of the Romans, and although she

---

* Edith Sitwell, 'Sir Beelzebub'
† Her name was Boudicca, but it was misread by early scholars as Boadicea, which is, to our ears, more euphonious.

was a queen, she had been flogged and her daughters raped by Roman bullies. The speech in which she roused her tribesmen to rebellion and the upsurge of their fury are described by Tennyson in a meter which is unlike anything else I know in English poetry: * long racing trochaic lines, one two, one two, one two, one two, kill them, kill them, kill them, kill them— which, instead of pausing at the end of each measure, dash off into a frenzy of excitement:

'Burst the gates and burn the palaces, break the works of the statuary,
Take the hoary Roman head and shatter it, hold it abominable,
Cut the Roman boy to pieces in his lust and voluptuousness,
Lash the maiden into swooning, me they lash'd and humiliated,
Chop the breasts from off the mother, dash the brains of the little
    one out,
Up my Britons, on my chariot, on my chargers, trample them under
    us.'

So the Queen Boadicea, standing loftily charioted,
Brandishing in her hand a dart and rolling glances lioness-like,
Yell'd and shrieked between her daughters in her fierce volubility,
Till her people all around the royal chariot agitated,
Madly dash'd the darts together, writhing barbarous lineaments,
Made the noise of frosty woodlands, when they shiver in January,
Roar'd as when the rolling breakers boom and blanch on the
    precipices,
Yell'd as when the winds of winter tear an oak on a promontory. †

For many thousands of years before we could think, we — like the other animals — heard and felt rhythms. Therefore there are some poems where almost all the meaning is the rhythm — just as there are some pictures where almost all the meaning is the color. One of my favorite poems is a piece of surrealist imagination by the Anglo-Irish poet Louis MacNeice. It comes from his first published book, *Blind Fireworks,* and I have never seen

---

* Perhaps he was inspired by the meter of Catullus' terrible poem 'Attis,' which also describes madness and mutilation and savagery.
† Tennyson, 'Boadicea'

it reprinted or mentioned in discussions of modern poetry. Yet it is a brilliant sequence of pure rhythms, which, like blazing tints and twisting shapes, make us almost believe a nightmare. It is called 'A cataract conceived as the march of corpses.' What could be more disparate than a living waterfall and a mournful funeral? The poem is a combination of contradictions: the slow movement of a burial-procession with the rapid rush of water, the somber melancholy notes of a death-march with the gay surge of a cascade, the permanence of death and the continuity of time.

The river falls and over the walls the coffins of cold funerals
Slide deep and sleep there in the close tomb of the pool,
And yellow waters lave the grave and pebbles pave its mortuary,
And the river horses vault and plunge with their assault and battery.
And helter-skelter the coffins come and the drums beat and the waters flow,
And the panther horses lift their hooves and paw and shift and draw the bier,
The corpses blink in the rush of the river, and out of the water their chins they tip
And quaff the gush and lip the draught and crook their heads and crow,
Drowned and drunk with the cataract that carries them and buries them
And silts them over and covers them and lilts and chuckles over their bones;
The organ-tones that the winds raise will never pierce the water ways.
So all they will hear is the fall of hooves and the distant shake of harness,
And the beat of the bells on the horses' heads and the undertaker's laughter,
And the murmur that will lose its strength and blur at length to quietness,
And afterwards the minute heard descending, never ending heard,
And then the minute after and the minute after the minute after.

## Obscurity in Poetry

MOST Americans do not like poetry. We may respect it, but we do not enjoy it. Some day, this may change. Fifty or sixty years ago, Americans did not like complex music, and went to the opera or to a symphony concert only because it seemed to be a social event; now we are a nation of music-lovers, who stand in line and pay good money for seats at concerts, collect records of fine music, and have high standards of composition and performance. Perhaps fifty or sixty years in the future we shall appreciate poetry in the same way; but now we do not.

I hear shrill voices cry 'Boors! Vulgarians! Materialists!' No. The voices are wrong, or at least unfair. People who dislike poetry can give good reasons for their dislike. Most often they say that they cannot understand poetry. It cannot be read continuously, they say; when spoken, it is unsystematic, illogical, an empty pattern of words, an insoluble theorem, a crossword puzzle without clues.

This is true for some poetry, but not for all. Many poems can be understood at first reading. Many can not. Both easy and difficult poetry can be good, each kind in its own way. Poems are trying to resemble the experiences of life — some of which we can accept and enjoy at once, while on others we must spend months, years, decades of thought and emotional assimilation. A poem *need* not be easy to grasp at first. It is not prose — just as a painting is not a photograph and a statue is not a plaster cast. Prose is logical, and ought to be orderly. A poem need not be logical, and often is not. Poetry is halfway between prose and music: it is sometimes like an intimate conversation, in words and phrases which need not be fully uttered, and sometimes almost like dancing and wordless music.

You know how infuriating it is to listen to a child sitting at a piano and hitting notes for fun, without any connection, without a trace of sequence or development. Suppose you were tone-deaf, you would probably feel the same irritation whenever you heard real music. A short march or a hymn would be a mild annoyance. A symphony in four movements would be absolute torment, because you would be totally unable to grasp any links between all these meaningless noises which the conductor was extruding from the orchestra and sending through the air in a perfectly arbitrary pattern. In the same way, a poem-deaf man, who thinks that all words should be used only to express logical connections between ideas and facts, will be profoundly irritated if he is forced to read a poem in which there is a structure that is not logical, not explicable in words, and perhaps perceptible only when it stirs deep and powerful emotions which he prefers to leave unstirred, far beneath the surface. Shelley's friend and biographer Hogg illustrates this by a story about a famous Cambridge mathematician who had never read *Paradise Lost*. A friend told him it was a great poem which everyone ought to read. So he went away and read it, and came back saying it was a waste of time.

'I have read your famous poem. I read it attentively: but what does it prove? There is more instruction in half a page of Euclid! A man might read Milton's poem a hundred, aye, a thousand times, and he would never learn that the angles at the base of an isosceles triangle are equal!'

Is there any way of explaining the serial noises to a tone-deaf listener, the word-jingles to a poem-deaf reader? In poetry, many books have attempted to do so — especially in the forty years since the end of the First World War, when poetry (like prose fiction and music and painting and sculpture and other arts) became audaciously experimental and often unconscionably difficult to comprehend. The first of these books which genuinely impressed me, a book which opened the eyes of many puzzled readers of my generation, was William Empson's *Seven Types of Ambiguity*. This came out first in 1930, and has now reached a third edition (Meridian, 1955). One of the newest attacks on the problem is *The Chequer'd Shade,* by John Press (Oxford, 1958), which goes thoroughly into many of the types of difficult poetry written in English during the last four hundred years, with many beautiful and enigmatic quotations.

The first type of difficult poetry is that which was perfectly clear when it was written, but has now turned into a puzzle — because some of its words have changed their meanings or gone dead. There is a lovely medieval carol about the Virgin Mary, which begins

> I syng of a mayden
>     that is makeles,
> Kyng of alle kynges
>     to here sone che ches.

Here you have to know that 'makeles' means 'matchless' and that 'ches' means 'chose' before you can even penetrate to its surface beauty. So it is with many poems written long ago — or even composed quite recently in obscure dialects. There are some charming lyrics in William Barnes's *Hwomely Rhymes* (published in 1859), but they are in a Dorsetshire patois which is as thick as clotted cream and almost as indigestible.

Customs also grow obsolete. Therefore a poet who uses symbols drawn from some well-known social practice will become hard to understand once it is forgotten. Nowadays very few of us know anything about the sport and skill of falconry. Therefore we cannot feel the emotions we should when Othello uses the special language of falconry to say that, if his wife is wild and disloyal, he will untie her from his heart and let her go, to hunt and live at random.

> If I do prove her haggard,
> Though that her jesses were my dear heart-strings,
> I'd whistle her off and let her down the wind,
> To prey at fortune.*

Such a set of symbols was once widely understood and powerfully meaningful. Now it is obsolete. But in all ages some poets have used symbols which only they themselves and a little coterie of their admirers could understand, because the symbols were taken from a small, limited, eccentric, private world. In our own time W. B. Yeats and W. H. Auden and other eminent poets have deliberately chosen to construct private universes from which the majority of their fellow-beings are to be excluded. Yeats hated and despised democracy, preferred the cold aristocratic tower to the cozy little cabin or the Dublin barroom, and with enormous effort built up a system of religion and philosophy which was almost wholly his own.

Here we strike a really refractory problem in the understanding of poetry. Some of those who write about difficult poems tell us that, if we only try, we can understand and enjoy every one of them. They imply that the poets truly want us all to enter the sanctuary and make ourselves at home. 'Seek,' they say, following a higher authority, 'and ye shall find; knock, and it shall be opened unto you.' But there are some poets who never want to admit the general public. Yeats, and Mallarmé, and Rilke, and Valéry, and others would no sooner expect the average man to read their poems than they would look for aesthetic response from a dog or a horse. Auden is a self-created enigma, a man who believes that he can live fully only if he lives eccentrically, a secretive, nonconformist, wary, determinedly original thinker and writer. Like Yeats, he uses symbolism which is intended to baffle and even to discourage his readers. Unless you have studied Yeats's complex transcendental dog-

---

* *Othello* 3.3.260-63

mas and given them at least a modicum of acceptance, you cannot understand many of his later poems; and you are not invited to do so. Be an initiate, or stay outside: shut the door, and leave the great spirit in peace. Auden has inhabited not one but a succession of these little worlds surrounded by spiritual barbed wire. Without knowing a good deal of his psychical and social background and even of his special languages, it is often scarcely possible to understand what he is talking about; or even, sometimes, to know whether he is being bitterly humorous or gloomily serious.

> Pardon the studied taste that could refuse
> The golf-house quick one and the rector's tea;
> Pardon the nerves the thrushes could not soothe,
> Yet answered promptly the no-subtler lure
> To private joking in a panelled room.

This is the opening of Auden's *Birthday Poem,* addressed to a very intimate friend, Christopher Isherwood, with whom he shared certain worlds no outsider could ever enter. Auden begins by mentioning three special kinds of upper-middle-class English happiness: a 'quick one,' a short drink downed in a few minutes, with the chaps in the golf-club; a tea party with the Anglican clergyman and the best people of the parish; love of mild nature, as expressed in the singing birds of the garden and the hedgerow. He goes on to say that he chose 'private joking in a panelled room,' the gossip of a small group, meeting in an exclusive school, an Oxford or Cambridge college, or a fine eighteenth-century house. He shrank from the more conventional fulfilments as too robust or too prissy, but chose another form of exclusiveness which, however, is itself also an affectation. A poem such as this would be almost unintelligible to anyone living outside Britain, and would have only a limited meaning for many native-born Englishmen. Most people exist outside those narrow borders of language and social convention; and Auden does not speak to them.

There is another kind of poetry where the symbols are not private, and where the poet is describing emotions which many other people have felt. Yet here too the poetry is difficult to understand because the images are tightly tangled, squeezed together, combined into confusion: it is meant to be exciting through its very complexity and rapidity, like closely textured music. Shakespeare loved doing this. Rather than hunt one poor metaphor to death, he would leave it panting, and gallop after three or four others. In calm and measured passages, his characters use only one image, and develop that magnificently. The Duke of Burgundy, wishing to make peace between victorious young Henry V and the beaten French king, says that France is the garden of the world, but now lies neglected: Peace, who once cultivated the garden, has been expelled,

> And all her husbandry doth lie on heaps,
> Corrupting in its own fertility.
> Her vine, the merry cheerer of the heart,
> Unpruned dies; her hedges even-pleached,
> Like prisoners wildly overgrown with hair,
> Put forth disordered twigs; her fallow leas
> The darnel, hemlock and rank fumitory
> Doth root upon, while that the coulter rusts
> That should deracinate such savagery;
> The even mead, that erst brought sweetly forth
> The freckled cowslip, burnet, and green clover,
> Wanting the scythe, all uncorrected, rank,
> Conceives by idleness, and nothing teems
> But hateful docks, rough thistles, kecksies, burs,
> Losing both beauty and utility.*

But when Shakespeare's characters are excited, then their thoughts move too rapidly to allow them to dwell upon one single symbol, they leap from metaphor to metaphor with exuberant illogicality. So Cleopatra, after her Antony has died, will not mourn him in sober phrases, but breaks out into a splendid panegyric of the man who dominated the world as a hero and a god.

---

* *Henry V*, 5.2.39-53

His legs bestrid the ocean; his reared arm
Crested the world; his voice was propertied
As all the tuned spheres, and that to friends;
But when he meant to quail and shake the orb,
He was as rattling thunder. For his bounty,
There was no winter in't, an autumn 'twas
That grew the more by reaping; his delights
Were dolphin-like, they showed their back above
The element they lived in; in his livery
Walked crowns and crownets, realms and islands were
As plates dropped from his pocket.*

First, she compares her Antony to a deity, in the majestic posture of the Sun God straddling the harbor of Rhodes, but far outdoing that colossus; † to this picture she adds the all-powerful arm of conquering Jove. Then she likens his voice to the two loudest sounds of nature: in peace, to the music of the spheres; in war, to thunder. His generosity was so rich, it was like a season of harvest never ended by winter; his pleasures, as exuberant as the dolphins that leap out of their natural element. And lastly, his power was so superb that kings and princes were like servants in his suite, kingdoms like coins overflowing his rich pockets. Gods, celestial spheres, harvests, dolphins, servants, coins — the images are incongruous, but they blend into one picture of superhuman nobility. In our own time, Dylan Thomas was the master of this type of emotional compression; and it is strange to hear recordings of him reading his own poems, to be hypnotized by the opulent flow of his voice, and then to turn to reading them and analyzing those meanings which suddenly seem to become confused and obscure. The two experiences are both parts of understanding his poetry.

Again, it is possible for a poet to think in a fairly straightforward way, without employing confused images; but to distort

---

* *Antony and Cleopatra* 5.2.82-92
† 'Why, man, he doth bestride the narrow world / Like a Colossus.' *Julius Caesar* 1.2.134-5

his language in order to give it a sound and rhythm unlike the sound and rhythm of ordinary speech. He does this so as to make his words more intense and memorable. What is easily read may be easily forgotten. Gerard Manley Hopkins, the English Jesuit poet, thought much about the spiritual despair to which religious converts are often exposed. In one fine poem, he said that within the soul there were heights and depths like the peaks and crevasses of the Alps, and that a man in spiritual agony felt as though he were about to fall from the summit to the gulf. This is not a new thought, and it is a fairly clear one, but it should not be spoken too quickly or assimilated too rapidly: so he said it thus —

> O the mind, mind has mountains; cliffs of fall
> Frightful, sheer, no-man-fathomed.   Hold them cheap
> May who ne'er hung there.*

Not only is this memorably expressed; but the distortion of the syntax, the slow effortful movement of the meter, such subtleties as the gap between the noun and its adjective in 'fall/Frightful,' image the tortured state of the mind that has to endure such a crisis.

Last, the poet may be expressing some thought which is truly obscure, so complex that he cannot put it into normally shaped and regularly cadenced language. There are such experiences, and they are among the highest subjects for poetry, but they cannot and should not be described in simple stanzas and easy syntax. The poet who knows them must be difficult; he must compel his readers to pause, reflect, and study. When at last they do grasp his meaning, they will find it a revelation. Gerard Manley Hopkins wrote to a friend saying that in poetry there were two different types of clarity: 'either the meaning to be felt without effort as fast as one reads, or else, if dark at first reading, when once made out *to explode.*' The first of these types of clarity is the pure candor of simple ideas and common

---

* Hopkins, *Poems* 65

poems: 'Oh, what a beautiful morning!' 'Crabbed age and youth cannot live together'; 'The wan moon is setting behind the white wave.' The other is the blinding brightness which is attained after long meditation on recondite but valuable truths. It is both expressed and exemplified in a few words of the mystic Henry Vaughan:

> There is in God (some say)
> A deep, but dazzling darkness.*

The most arduous difficulties in poetry are attempts to express truths or to ask questions which are never otherwise stated or asked, although they stand in the very center of our lives.

---

* 'The Night' 49-50

# Poets

SHAKESPEARE


## Shakespeare in Love

———————————

LET US look for a little at Shakespeare's Sonnets. We all know
the opening lines of some of them — this:

> When to the sessions of sweet silent thought
> I summon up remembrance of things past . . .*

or this:

> Like as the waves make towards the pebbled shore,
> So do our minutes hasten to their end . . . †

or this, the best-known of all:

> Let me not to the marriage of true minds
> Admit impediments.  Love is not love
> Which alters when it alteration finds,
> Or bends with the remover to remove:
> O, no! it is an ever-fixed mark
> That looks on tempests and is never shaken . . . ‡

———————

* Sonnet 30
† Sonnet 60
‡ Sonnet 116

Yes, we all know *some* of Shakespeare's Sonnets. You remember the story about the old lady who was taken to see *Hamlet* for the first time. After it was over, she said she didn't like it much: the play was good enough as a play, but it was too full of quotations. Everything Shakespeare wrote (even the terrible plays like *Cymbeline* and *The Winter's Tale*) is full of quotations; and there are many in the Sonnets. But although we remember these, very few of us know the Sonnets as a whole, and very very few of us love them. They are not often sold as specially printed gift volumes. Young men seldom buy them and carry them about. When I was eighteen and went for long solitary midnight walks, I had *A Shropshire Lad* in one pocket and Omar Khayyam in the other; but it never crossed my mind to carry the Sonnets of Shakespeare. (*Venus and Adonis,* perhaps; but not the Sonnets.) Critics who write books on the Bard usually play down the Sonnets, discuss them only in the by-going, quote from them less often than from his other works. And yet there are twenty-one pages of them (the same length as *A Midsummer-Night's Dream*); and they contain some of Shakespeare's autobiography, his passions, his weaknesses, the sound of his voice.

But they are difficult to read, and difficult to admire. We cannot follow them closely, we cannot fully understand even the publisher's inscription which opens them, and half the time we can scarcely tell what Shakespeare is talking about.

That is the chief reason why they are so hard to read and enjoy. They are fascinating, but they are enigmatic. In 150 sonnets, all almost exactly the same size and shape, Shakespeare covers more ground than many a modern novel. Dimly, cryptically, he describes, not a continuous adventure, but a succession of complex situations, terribly hard to understand and yet deeply moving.

They start off unexpectedly enough, with Shakespeare's love for a young man. It is an idealizing love: for, as the Sonnets open, Shakespeare is urging his friend to settle down, get married, and have children. Nevertheless, he talks in terms of passionate admiration, praising the youth's looks, and longing to see him and be near him. Who was the young man? Shakespeare could easily have told us; but he did not mean us to know.

Then there are some peculiar poems about a rival poet — someone (says Shakespeare) of far more talent than he, someone who addresses poems to the same youth, and, by attracting his interest, strikes Shakespeare's own poetry dead. This is very odd, isn't it? Did Shakespeare really think that any other poet was more gifted than himself? If so, when? and who was the other, the ship

> Of tall building and of goodly pride? *

Spenser? or Marlowe, whom Shakespeare was to parody in his plays? or Chapman, who was working on a translation of Homer? It sounds like Marlowe ... but we are not meant to know.

And then, a little later, comes in a woman: a dark woman, the unfashionable color in an England which has always preferred blondes. She had black eyebrows, and 'mourning eyes.' †
And she was dark also in mind and heart. Shakespeare says he did not especially admire her looks and could not idealize them.

> My mistress' eyes are nothing like the sun;
> Coral is far more red than her lips' red. ‡

And very soon he knew that she was treacherous, a liar, proud, and cruel; still, she had a magical, a haunting power over him, to drive him nearly mad:

> O! from what power hast thou this powerful might,
> With insufficiency my heart to sway? **

---

\* Sonnet 80
† Sonnet 132, cf. 127
‡ Sonnet 130
\*\* Sonnet 150

Who was she? Perhaps she was Queen Elizabeth's maid of honor, Mary Fitton. (There is a fine portrait of Mary Fitton in Carrol Camden's *The Elizabethan Woman*: she really looks bewitching.) Anyhow, she not only dominated Shakespeare, but apparently enchanted the youth whom Shakespeare had admired. Once friends, the two became rivals — or fellow-victims.

But there the Sonnets stop — with no conclusion, and no resolution, not even a crisis. The last important poem is a shout of bitter self-reproach in which Shakespeare calls himself a liar and perjurer. Then there are two saccharine sonnets about Cupid's losing his little arrows: so that the collection ends not with a pang but a simper. True to life; but unsatisfactory as art. The Sonnets have the fascination of an autobiography, without its clarity. It is like reading an important document in a cave by the light of matches which keep blowing out.

And then some of us are a little disgusted by their tone. It is mawkish. It is gushing. It is sentimental. In his plays, Shakespeare is always in control. His heroes rant madly sometimes, or make silly jokes; but he remains in command. Therefore it is a shock to see him, in the Sonnets, talking more foolishly than his most affected hero. Instead of sounding like Hamlet, or even like Romeo, he too often gabbles like Malvolio.

Like all Shakespeare's works, the Sonnets are full of splendid lines. True. But here is another snag. Unlike most of his work, they are also full of bad lines. Some of them are atrocious. They are so bad that they are embarrassing, and several scholars have suggested that inferior poets must have written them and foisted them in. Shakespeare could never resist a pun, and he went on punning all his life, with reasonable success; but the puns in the Sonnets are cruel and unnatural punishment. For instance, his first name to his friends was Will: so he writes stuff like this:

> Whoever hath her wish, thou hast thy Will,
> And Will to boot, and Will in over-plus.*

---

* Sonnet 135

It is even worse when he recalls how he first met his beloved:

> To me, fair friend, you never can be old,
> For as you were when first your eye I eyed,
> Such seems your beauty still.*

Elsewhere, he can make even such silly talk into poetry. When Rosalind prattles like that, it is delightful. In Shakespeare's own voice, it is painful.

But of course, we do not know exactly when he wrote the Sonnets. They were printed and published in 1609, when he was at the end of his career as a playwright. By that time he had become the magnificent poet of *Antony and Cleopatra,* the profound psychologist of *Hamlet,* the grim cynic of *Coriolanus.* But after you read the Sonnets two or three times, you see clearly that, when he produced them, he had never composed a single play. Leaf through his dramas. Read the gay, easy rhetoric of *King John,* the musical fireworks of *A Midsummer-Night's Dream.* Then turn back to the Sonnets. At once you see that they are the work of an amateur, a novice, a beginner. Often they repeat the same idea two or three times, as though the young poet's fancy were pouring out variations which his taste could not distinguish nor his art suffice to concentrate. They rhyme neatly, they scan, they balance; but they constantly fall into that dismal region lying between poetry and prose, where we are neither soaring on wings nor walking along firm earth, but jolting painfully along on a nervous and ill-trained horse. Here is the end of a sonnet to Time:

> This I do vow, and this shall ever be;
> I will be true, despite thy scythe and thee.†

And this is the close of a poem to his friend:

> Look what is best, that best I wish in thee:
> This wish I have; then ten times happy me! ‡

---

* Sonnet 104
† Sonnet 123
‡ Sonnet 37

You will ask: how could a gifted poet write such stuff, not once only, but again and again? No one knows the whole answer, because no one fully understands Shakespeare; and, because he was a very complicated character, the answer must be extremely complex. But certainly one part of the answer is the obvious one: when he wrote the Sonnets, he was *young, very young*. He possessed his talents, but he was not sure of them and had scarcely learned how to use them. He had written some non-dramatic poems, acted a little, perhaps; collaborated on a play, possibly; but never yet attempted to create a universe out of his own imagination.

Not long ago, the sharpest detective in contemporary English literary history wrote an essay on this problem. Mr. Leslie Hotson, in *Shakespeare's Sonnets Dated* (Oxford, 1950), gives good reason for believing that they were completed in 1589, when Shakespeare was only twenty-five. If this is correct, we can easily understand why the Sonnets embarrass us. They are like a very young man's love, passionate but awkward. And as literature, they are timid and conventional — whereas the mature Shakespeare was to become bold and powerful.

Once we are sure of this, we can return, and read the Sonnets with far more enjoyment. Even the silliest things in them are now seen to be not the blunders of a fine poet, but the first sketches for the masterpieces that were later to come from the same mind. For example, the pun on the words *eye* and *I*, so weak and forced in the Sonnets, reappears four or five years later in the mouth of a loving girl, and is now strengthened into fantastic hysterical poetry:

> Hath Romeo slain himself? Say thou but *Ay*,
> And that bare vowel *I* shall poison more
> Than the death-darting *eye* of cockatrice:
> *I* am not *I*, if there be such an *Ay*;
> Or those *eyes* shut that make thee answer *Ay*.*

---

* *Romeo and Juliet* 3.2.45-9

So, also, the bitter experiences through which the young Shakespeare was then living were later to be concentrated and reheated until they became the incandescent lava of Othello's passion, the acid fumes of Timon's world-hatred. In the finest of the Sonnets, we can see him practicing the inimitable eloquence of his mature life, the silver tongue fed by a golden thought:

> They that have power to hurt and will do none,
> That do not do the thing they most do show,
> Who, moving others, are themselves as stone,
> Unmoved, cold, and to temptation slow;
> They rightly do inherit heaven's graces,
> And husband nature's riches from expense;
> They are the lords and owners of their faces,
> Others but stewards of their excellence.
>
> The summer's flower is to the summer sweet,
> Though to itself it only live and die,
> But if that flower with base infection meet,
> The basest weed outbraves his dignity;
> For sweetest things turn sourest by their deeds;
> Lilies that fester smell far worse than weeds.*

Such lines could well be spoken in the greatest of his plays. And so, as we look at the Sonnets, and see them for what they are — a preparation for something better — we can understand the comparative failure of much modern poetry. The Sonnets are really a description of Shakespeare's private world: that is the chief reason why they are interesting; and it is also the reason why they are inferior to the rest of his work. So many modern poets prefer to inhabit their own narrow universe, and cannot or will not enlarge it. But, after the Sonnets, Shakespeare spoke no more in his own voice. It was too limited. Juliet says of Romeo:

> When he shall die,
> Take him and cut him out in little stars.†

---

* Sonnet 94
† *Romeo and Juliet* 3.2.21-2

In the same way, Shakespeare cut himself out into hundreds of men and women. Through his plays, he made his own distracted and eloquent heart into a huge and busy and delightful world, which we still are honored to inhabit.

## Shakespeare in Italy

SUPPOSE you were looking over the career of a distinguished author — someone with an ordinary middle-class background and education, but gifted with an extraordinary imagination, a fluent and infinitely various style, and a profound understanding of psychology; someone who started writing light pieces in his twenties, and went on producing deeper and stronger work nearly every year until his death; someone who was acclaimed as talented when young, became successful in middle age, and was universally recognized as a genius after he died. Let us say he spent most of his life in his homeland, and wrote many tales about its history. Let us say also that he wrote about foreign countries — some of them wholly imaginary (desert islands, never-never lands, Shangri La's) and some of them quite real. If you were trying to decide what countries he had actually seen with his own eyes, surely you would examine the books he set in foreign lands, with foreign characters, customs, names, and so on.

Now, if you saw that he started his career by writing, not about his homeland, but about Italy and France; if you found that his Italian stories were mostly about one small region of Italy, that his other Italian and his French tales had vague settings with little or no local color, and that his stories laid elsewhere (except, of course, in his native land) were decorated merely by conventional details, which were sometimes absurdly wrong — what would you think? Surely you would conclude that he had made a rapid visit to Italy and France, and that he had actually lived in only one district long enough to get to know it; after he came home, he used his memories to give his tales the appearance of actuality. That is what most authors do when they write about foreign lands. Some details they get from guidebooks or from friends or from sheer imagination; these may be right or wrong or distorted. Other details they take from their own personal experience — and about them there is usually a feel of authenticity which can scarcely be counterfeited.

If you look over the plays of William Shakespeare, you will be struck by a pattern just like that. Most of his dramas are historical. They are about the history of Britain, which he got from reading earlier plays and the records of his own country; or they are about the history of Greece and Rome, which he got chiefly from reading Plutarch's *Parallel Lives of the Greeks and Romans*. (There is a copy of North's translation of Plutarch in the Bodleian Library at Oxford, which has handwritten notes in it, and may have belonged to Shakespeare himself.) Nearly all his other plays are recent or contemporary dramas, some set in never-never lands, like *The Tempest*, and the rest chiefly in Italy and France.

Some time ago I spent several months in Italy: a unique experience, combining admiration and perspiration, art and indigestion. All the time I was in the southern and central regions, I scarcely ever thought of Shakespeare. True, two of his plays are laid in Sicily, *Much Ado About Nothing* and *The Winter's Tale;* there are some scenes in Florence in *All's Well That Ends Well;* but in none of these dramas is there anything in the way of a vivid description of places or local color.

But as soon as I reached the northern provinces of Italy, I was constantly being reminded of Shakespeare. One of his very earliest plays was called *The Two Gentlemen of Verona*. (It is a Spanish tale, which he transferred to Italy.) Soon after it came *Romeo and Juliet,* which is laid in Verona and Mantua. A little later he wrote that very funny comedy *The Taming of the Shrew*. The original story was set in Athens; Shakespeare moved it to northern Italy, to Padua (and Verona), and renamed its characters with good Italian names: Petruchio, Katharina, Baptista, Bianca, Biondello. One of his most famous early dramas is *The Merchant of Venice*. Years later he returned to Venice for the background of the superb tragedy, *Othello*. For anyone who remembers and enjoys Shakespeare's dramas, it is very difficult, walking through Verona and Mantua and Venice, to resist the impression that he also walked through some of those same streets, saw those same buildings, heard the same melodious Italian spoken, yes, and picked up some words and phrases of it himself. People either like Italy very much, or dislike it intensely. Shakespeare scarcely ever speaks of it without delight. Although he was horrified at some aspects of the Italian character — in particular, the treacherous cunning which we know from the Mafia, and which he personified in Iago and Iachimo and others — he was charmed by the beauty of the country, the splendor of its cities, its magnificent palaces and noble churches. The very first words of the play in *The Taming of the Shrew* express that warmth:

> Tranio, since for the great desire I had
> To see fair Padua, nursery of arts,
> I am arrived for fruitful Lombardy,
> The pleasant garden of great Italy...*

And the same feeling reappears in one of the very earliest plays of all, *Love's Labour's Lost*, where the schoolmaster cries:

> *Venetia, Venetia,*
> *Chi non te vede, non te pretia!* †
> ('Venice, Venice, you must be seen to be valued!')

That is not the only Italian in Shakespeare. Several times, particularly in his early plays, he throws in Italian phrases—

---

* *The Taming of the Shrew* 1.1.1-4
† *L.L.L.* 4.2.100-101

just like a young traveler recently returned who wants to show off a little. He makes people say *'Mi perdonate'* and *'Con tutto il cuore ben trovato'* and *'Alla nostra casa ben venuto'* and so on. He puts in Italian slang sometimes, even when it is not altogether appropriate. So the blustering English soldier Pistol shouts to Justice Shallow:

> Under which king, bezonian? Speak, or die.*

It sounds like a mysterious password, bezonian, but it is the Italian *bisognone* or *bisognoso,* 'dirty beggar.' And finally, can you imagine anyone talking modern Italian in prehistoric Troy? No? But Shakespeare, in *Troilus and Cressida,* set in the year 1180 B.C. or so, makes old Pandarus tease his naughty niece Cressida, calling her 'poor wretch, a poor *capocchia,'* † which means 'silly girl.'

Also, he loves giving his people Italian names. Sometimes he gets them wrong. Shakespeare was seldom exact, except in the observation of humanity and external nature, and he made terrible mistakes in all kinds of intellectual disciplines; thus he put the wrong accent on Roméo, Stepháno, Desdémona. But usually he gets them right, and he brings them in again and again. In the original story of *Othello* the Moor was not named. It was Shakespeare who first called him Othello. The name is unknown in history and literature, but it was a real family name in sixteenth-century Venice. So in *Hamlet* there are Danish soldiers called Bernardo and Francisco, and the young prince's best friend is called Horatio.

Besides all this, Shakespeare had a smattering of local north Italian history, which long remained in his mind. During his lifetime, Mantua was ruled by the powerful Gonzaga family. In 1592 (when Shakespeare was 28) one of the Gonzagas was murdered by his own nephew, in his country villa. Now, remember Hamlet, wild with excitement at the performance of

---

* *Henry IV Part 2.* 5.3.115
† *Troilus and Cressida* 4.2.32

the specially written murder-play-within-a-play. He points to
the killing on the stage, and shouts:

> He poisons him i' the garden for's estate. His name's Gon-
> zago; the story is extant, and writ in very choice Italian! *

Still, I think the link which convinced me Shakespeare had actually visited northern Italy while he was young and impres-
sionable is that he knew of an Italian artist who is not very
famous and whose chief masterpieces are in Mantua. In that
strange drama, *The Winter's Tale,* a courtier speaks of a statue

> many years in doing, and now newly performed by that rare
> Italian master, Julio Romano; who, had he himself eternity
> and could put breath into his work, would beguile Nature
> of her custom.†

The real Giulio Romano was a pupil of Raphael, began work
in Rome, moved to Mantua a generation or so before Shakespeare's birth. His house is still there. One of the most beautiful buildings in Italy is the palace he designed for the Gonzaga family, the Palazzo del Te. He was not only a painter, but
(as Shakespeare says) he designed sculpture, and in his paintings he strove to give the appearance not of a flat pattern but of
three-dimensional form indistinguishable from nature — even
exceeding nature in beauty and violence. Giulio Romano is the
only Italian artist whom Shakespeare ever mentions, and Shakespeare's own plays and poems are full of mythological pictures,
gods and goddesses, angry giants, nymphs and satyrs, in the
manner of Renaissance art — a manner never better represented
than in the work of the Mantuan artist Giulio Romano.

None of Shakespeare's plays set in other countries give such
an impression of reality and contain so many details, except

---

* *Hamlet* 3.2.276-8. It is odd that Shakespeare makes Hamlet say the
play is the image of a murder done in Vienna. But in another play he apparently confused Verona with Vienna: the duke of Vienna in *Measure for
Measure* bears the same name, Vincentio, as the Gonzaga duke who ruled
Verona in Shakespeare's day.

† *The Winter's Tale* 5.2.107-10

the English dramas. His Denmark is not much like Denmark. His Scotland is a heath and a castle. His eastern Europe is absurd — Bohemia with a seacoast! His France is charming, but quite vague. Only his England and his northern Italy seem genuine.

It is not difficult to conjecture when he visited northern Italy. There is far more Italian in his early plays, written from 1594 onwards (when he was in his late twenties and early thirties), than in all the rest of his work. Now the theaters in London were closed, because of the plague, for many months in 1592 and 1593. The murder of the Gonzaga marquis happened in Mantua in 1592. If Shakespeare ever was in northern Italy, it was probably then, on a quick but memorable trip. He was neither the first nor the last of a long line of English poets who have found that Italy gave them clarity of vision, renewed their sense of beauty, and deepened their understanding of the human heart.

But, but, there is a but. There is no proof of the Italian visit. Shakespeare may have got his Italian from friends and associates, for instance, the talented Anglo-Italian John Florio. Also, he got some important Italian names and geography wrong. In *The Two Gentlemen* someone takes ship at Verona to sail to Milan, which is impossible, and in *The Tempest* it looks as though Shakespeare thought Milan was near the seacoast, since Prospero, formerly the Duke of Milan, was kidnaped and sent out to sea in a boat without a sail.

Well and good: Shakespeare was wrong. He was often wrong. His imagination was so fertile that, if he had not actually read a book, he would invent its contents, and if he had not visited a place, he would describe it from his fancy. He would never trouble to check. Milan he had surely not visited. Mantua and Venice he almost certainly saw and remembered. As for Verona, he saw it briefly and remembered that it stood on a river and that it had canals around it; he invented the rest.

All that is characteristic of Shakespeare. He was a genius of fancy, not of exactitude. All the theorists who attempt to prove that the plays and poems must have been written by someone else, because Shakespeare came from a provincial town and had only a high-school education, can never have read his works with critical attention. The plays and poems which bear the name of Shakespeare are quite obviously not the work of an intellectual, not even of a highly educated man. Nobody so wise and well-informed as Bacon could possibly have brought himself to write down and publish one quarter of the painful and embarrassing mistakes that appear in Shakespeare's plays. No widely traveled and loftily educated nobleman like Oxford or Southampton could possibly have published works which contained so many elementary faults, not only in history and geography and language, but in ordinary good taste. Arnold, himself a good scholar, was right in saying to Shakespeare:

> Others abide our question. Thou art free.

The author of the plays of Shakespeare was not a university-trained scholar like Milton. He was not even a deeply-read and book-bound author like Ben Jonson. He was a smatterer; he made much out of little; he had a vivid observation, a sound if often distorted memory, and above all he had an astoundingly fertile, a magical Prospero-like imagination, which could call spirits from the vasty deep. It is for his fancy and his eloquence that we admire Shakespeare, not for his learning. Poetry needs some learning to clothe it, but its body is eloquence, and its spirit is the soaring imagination of which William Shakespeare from his earliest years was all compact.

# TRAHERNE

## Heir of the Whole World *

---

TOWARDS the close of the last century, in 1897, a book lover was
turning over the dirty, neglected, and usually worthless volumes
on a street bookstall in London. These institutions scarcely exist
in the United States; they are far below the level of regular
second-hand bookshops, and they are not even so ambitious as
the stalls along the Seine in Paris; usually they are barrows or
shacks containing old volumes of sermons, obsolete guidebooks,
much-used school and college texts, ancient volumes of handwritten poems or diaries. If a book stays on one of these rickety
wooden counters for a few months without being sold, it is
usually disposed of as waste paper, pulped, and forgotten. Still,
one can sometimes find curious and potentially valuable things
among all the trash. The English book lover did. His name was
Brooke. He was a specialist in religious poetry, and he came
upon two volumes of religious lyrics written by hand, poems
which he had never seen or heard of, and which (being un-

---

* 'You never Enjoy the World aright, till the Sea it self floweth in your
Veins, till you are Clothed with the Heavens, and Crowned with the Stars:
and Perceiv your self to be the Sole Heir of the whole World.' — Traherne,
*The First Century* 29

known to him although he was an expert) had apparently never
been published. The handwriting looked like the script of the
seventeenth century. Brooke bought the volumes for the equiv-
alent of a few cents, and read them carefully.

He found that they were full of delightful poems by one of
the happiest of men, a religious mystic who (unlike most
mystics) loved both God and the world, who, in sincere and
energetic stanzas, expressed the rapture of being alive, and
who, enjoying his life on this earth, enjoyed his link with God
as son to father. 'How like an Angel,' cried the poet, in the
same words as Hamlet but with a far holier continuation:

> How like an Angel came I down!
> How Bright are all Things here!
> When first among his Works I did appear
> O how their GLORY me did Crown!
> The World resembled his *Eternitie,*
> In which my Soul did Walk;
> And evry Thing that I did see,
> Did with me talk.*

That is the beginning of a noble poem in which the unknown
author spoke with infectious delight of his vision of this world
as the reflection of God's home illuminated by God's love. But
who was he, and why had his poems remained unknown for
over two centuries?

Brooke guessed that he was the Welsh physician and mystical
writer, Henry Vaughan. He passed the poems to an eminent
critic, who was convinced that they were Vaughan's. However,
before they could be published under Vaughan's name, the
critic died, and the manuscript was sold to a bibliophile called
Bertram Dobell. (Dobell was an intense lover of books. Born
in poverty, he worked as a delivery boy, collected old books
from the bookstalls with his scanty savings, set up as a book
dealer himself, and eventually became not only a critic but
something of a poet.) Dobell, after reading the poems with

* Traherne, 'Wonder'; *Hamlet* 2.2.326

eager enthusiasm, decided that they could not be by Henry Vaughan. Their subjects and metrical patterns were often the same as Vaughan's, but they were warmer than his calm, meditative lyrics, they accepted and welcomed where Vaughan was apt to criticize and even to doubt. Vaughan, as a medical man, shrank from excitement; this poet was an enthusiast. Who was the real author? Surely he had published something during his lifetime. There must be some poetry or prose issued in the time of King Charles II or thereabouts, which bore his name.

Brooke now remembered that, some time before, he had discovered in the British Museum a little old book of religious poems with a title almost as large as itself, *A Serious and Patheticall* (i.e. emotional) *Contemplation of the Mercies of God, in Several Most Devout and Sublime Thanksgivings for the Same,* and that the poems in it looked like some of those by the unknown author. Dobell read them, and agreed. But the book in the British Museum had no author's name, either. (In case this surprises you, remember that devoutly religious authors sometimes wish to remain anonymous: prostrate at the feet of God, they feel too humble to give their own private name to their songs of praise and of ecstasy.)

Still, there was one clue. The preface to the *Devout and Sublime Thanksgivings* said that they had been written by the private chaplain of a well-known statesman of King Charles II's time, Sir Orlando Bridgman. A contemporary book of gossip and backstairs history (Anthony à Wood's biographical dictionary, *Athenae Oxonienses*) identified the private chaplain. He was called Thomas Traherne, and he was quite unknown to fame, except that he had published two religious books in prose: a polemic work called *Roman Forgeries,* and a moral treatise called *Christian Ethics.* Brooke and Dobell now got *Christian Ethics* and read it. In it they found an unusual little poem praising the infinite power of God for having made things finite in size although not therefore finite in value. The same poem, with a few variations in phrasing, appeared in one of the manuscript volumes. Therefore the poems without the name were the work of Thomas Traherne; as such they were published by Bertram Dobell in 1903, and most recently in a sumptuous two-volume Oxford edition by H. M. Margoliouth.

Traherne was the son of a poor shoemaker from the Welsh borderlands. Born in 1637, he was sent to Oxford by a generous relative; became rector of a small parish in his native country of Hereford; served as chaplain to one of King Charles's chief officers of state; and died when he was 37, leaving most of his work still unpublished. His brother Philip survived him and edited his poems, but did not see them printed. They remained in manuscript (probably in the home of his family connections) until well within living memory; then the property was dispersed, and these volumes gradually found their way to the bookstall, where, partly by luck and partly by discernment, the book-detective William Brooke discovered them.*

Suppose he had not? Suppose the manuscript had been pulped and the poems forgotten? Should we have lost anything?

Yes, indeed. Traherne is a fine poet (some of his prose is almost equally distinguished) and he is a rare spirit. Mystical poets are not common. Few indeed are those who have true eloquence, as Traherne has. Fewer still are those who unite clear, natural, graceful words with a boldly original vision. We can see what is special about Traherne most easily in his descriptions of heaven on earth, that is, the heaven which children inhabit for a time.

> Certainly Adam in Paradice had not more sweet and Curious Apprehensions of the World, then I when I was a child. All appeared New, and Strange at the first, inexpressibly rare, and Delightfull, and Beautifull. I was a little Stranger which at my Enterance into the World was Saluted and Surrounded with innumerable Joys. . . . The Corn was Orient and Immortal Wheat, which never should be reaped, nor was ever sown. I thought it had stood from everlasting to everlasting. The Dust and Stones of the Street were as Pre-

---

* For a fuller account of this discovery see Richard Altick, *The Scholar Adventurers* (Macmillan, 1950), pp. 302-5

cious as GOLD. . . . The Men! O what Venerable and Reverend Creatures did the Aged seem! Immortal Cherubims! And yong Men Glittering and Sparkling Angels and Maids strange Seraphick Pieces of Life and Beauty! Boys and Girles Tumbling in the Street, and Playing, were moving Jewels. . . . The Skies were mine, and so were the Sun and Moon and Stars, and all the World was mine, and I the only Spectator and Enjoyer of it.*

So he says, in one of his prose meditations called *Centuries*. In poetry he reaffirms the same mystical, joyful, ecstatic awareness of childhood, that happiness which is lost (as he tells us) only when we grow up and before we turn again to the child's knowledge of God. Here is a vision from his poem 'The City.'

What Structures here among God's Works appear?
　　Such Wonders *Adam* ne'r did see
　　In Paradise among the Trees,
　　　No Works of Art like these,
Nor Walls, nor Pinnacles, nor Houses were.
　　　All these for me,
　　For me these Streets and Towers,
These stately Temples, and these solid Bowers,
　　　My Father rear'd:
　　For me I thought they thus appear'd. . . .
　　　They seem'd to me
　　Environ'd with Eternity.

As if from Everlasting they had there
　　Been built, more gallant than if gilt
　　With Gold, they shew'd: Nor did I know
　　　That they to Hands did ow
Themselvs.　Immortal they did all appear
　　　Till I knew Guilt.
　　As if the Publick Good
Of all the World for me had ever stood.
　　　They gratify'd
　　Me, while the Earth they beautify'd.

---

*Traherne, *The Third Century*, 1-3

> The living Peeple that mov'd up and down,
>    With ruddy Cheeks and sparkling Eys;
> The Musick in the Churches, which
>       Were Angels Joys (tho Pitch
> Defil'd me afterwards) did then me crown:
>       I then did prize
>       These only I did lov
> As do the blessed Hosts in Heven abov:
>       No other Pleasure
>       Had I, nor wish'd for other Treasure.*

Can you remember that happiness, the bliss of childhood? I do myself, very faintly at most times; only now and then — when I am happy, or see certain flowers or birds, or smell fresh grass, or look up through trees at the sky — can I recall it more strongly. But Traherne felt it far more keenly; and that although he was born in dire poverty, lived for ten years of his boyhood in a country torn by civil war, and grew up in a time of painful religious conflict and dangerous foreign threats to his own country's independence. All these things he felt, but he ignored them, and thought only of the positive facts that he was alive and that God had made a good world for him to live in.

It would be difficult, and perhaps it would be stupid or brutal, to summarize Traherne's mystical philosophy in a few propositions logically set out; certainly it would be impossible to analyze these basic beliefs by logic alone. Yet no one can read his fine poems for long without seeing through them to the vision which shine in Traherne's soul and irradiate his poetry. The first is the concept that a child in the world (before he is aware of sin, and before he begins to care about other dangerous things such as money, success, and fame) is like Adam in the Garden of Eden. It is natural for him to delight in everything he sees and touches, from the generous sun in the sky to the jewel-like green of the grass beneath his feet;

---

* Traherne, 'The City'

and he cannot enjoy it fully without seeing God in it all, and praising him for making and sustaining it. As the child grows and learns (and this is Traherne's second main idea), he learns sinfulness; the only way he can recapture and hold his first delight is (in the words of Jesus) to be born again and become as a little child.

In the first chapter of the Book of Genesis we are told that God created man in his own image: a difficult saying if examined by critical logic, a beautiful ideal for a mystic such as Traherne, who saw himself and all other spirits as parts of God.

> If I be like my God, my King,
>   (Tho not a Cherubim,)
>     I will not care,
>   Since all my Pow'rs derived are
>     From none but Him.
> The best of Images shall I
>   Comprised in Me see;
>     For I can spy
>   All Angels in the Deity
>     Like me to ly.*

It is a marvelous paradox. The poor cobbler's son is still a part of God, and through Him can apprehend the entire cosmos. This paradox is the third of Traherne's mystical ideas: that the infinite needs the finite, as the whole presupposes the parts; and that man — so small and worthless, so silly in mind and frail in soul and trivial in body — can still apprehend (through God) eternal time and infinite space. Only he must not live like an animal, eating, drinking, and copulating, without gratitude or awe. He must be aware.

> That Light, that Sight, that Thought,
> Which in my Soul at first He wrought,
> Is sure the only Act to which I may
>     Assent to Day:

---

* Traherne, 'The Image'

The Mirror of an Endless Life,
The Shadow of a Virgin Wife,
A Spiritual World Standing within,
An Univers enclosd in Skin.
My Power exerted, or my Perfect Being,
If not Enjoying, yet an Act of Seeing.*

Traherne often thought of the strangest of our bodily organs, the eye. Through a tiny instrument one sixth of an inch across, we can see a thousand square miles of land, together with the overarching sky. So through a weak soul inhabiting a rickety body, we can apprehend an illimitable universe, and, through it, the inexpressible and yet not unapproachable power which creates and directs it.

---

* Traherne, 'Fullnesse'

## *The Lady and the Poet*

---

THE LADY was a real lady; although her conduct was often eccentric, she was accomplished, witty, original, nobly born, and beautiful — really exquisite in her youth, to judge by several different portraits, which cannot all be lying. The poet was a real poet, but he had very few other advantages. He was a cripple; a Roman Catholic, at a time when Catholics were under severe handicaps, social and political; a commoner; and — as it transpired — not a gentleman. His defects helped him in his poetry rather than hindering him; but they nearly ruined the lady. If she had not been so brave and so fundamentally optimistic, she would have been utterly destroyed. As it was, she survived, though with a few ineradicable smears on her reputation.

The poet was the satirist Alexander Pope; the lady was Lady Mary Wortley Montagu. Most people who have not made a study of eighteenth-century society remember only two or three things about Lady Mary. One, perhaps the most important, is that it was she who invented inoculation for smallpox — or rather, had it introduced into Britain from Turkey, where she had seen it practiced. Another is that she was a brilliantly amusing letter writer. And the third is that, under various disguises, she appears in Pope's satiric poetry as a sloven, a Lesbian, a financial crook, and a miser — in fact, a repulsive monster. The malignant caricature drawn by Pope has often been the only portrait of the lady that exists in most people's minds. Not many men have injured a woman so deliberately and, on the whole, so effectively; and yet the essence of the bond between them is that Pope was, for years of his life, in love with her. The story illuminates some of the defects which certain kinds of poets seem to possess, ineradicably and ineluctably. (As I read it, I was strangely reminded of Dylan Thomas seizing Katherine Anne Porter in his big strong hands and lifting her up like a doll, till her head was an inch from the ceiling. Pope had never one-tenth of Thomas's physical strength, but he had all Thomas's spiritual energy.) It is almost a classic example of the miseries of love as felt by the intellectual with his nagging sense of inadequacy and frustration: see any early novel by Aldous Huxley, or the works of the French existentialists. And it is a striking case of the duel between a well-known pair of opponents: the positive, outgoing, courageous, determined woman, and the negative, critical, sickly, vindictive, determined man — the almost complete somatotonic and the perfect cerebrotonic, or the extrovert and the introvert.

Alexander Pope was a prodigiously clever writer who became famous at the age of twenty-three by issuing a poetic *Essay on Criticism,* and a little later by producing a delightfully fanciful mock epic called *The Rape of the Lock.* When he met Lady Mary he was about twenty-seven; he had enough money to live on, as much fame as any young writer needs, and the prospect of both more glory and more cash when he completed the translation of Homer on which he was at work. She was twenty-six, married to a cool, shrewd, selfish politician who cared little for her, or for any human being but himself. How they met, we do not know; but their first active contact was through the wit which they both possessed. In the autumn of 1715 she joined Pope and John Gay (the author of *The Beg-*

*gar's Opera*) in writing three satires on London society. Very sharp and original satires they were, too. The beaux and belles of the baroque age used to love dressing up as shepherds and shepherdesses, and calling one another by bucolic names such as Strephon and Phyllis. Pope and Gay and Lady Mary together produced three parodic poems in the bucolic manner, in which contemporary personalities were depicted in the throes of naïve countrified passion, but made utterly ridiculous. One of these was no less than Caroline, Princess of Wales. Naturally, the poems could not be published, but they were circulated in manuscript by the Whigs and drew on their authors much admiration and much hostility. Pope now began to fall in love with the first woman he had ever met who was nearly as intelligent as he himself.

Next year, Lady Mary's husband, Edward Montagu, was appointed British Ambassador to Turkey, and the family left for Constantinople. At this point Pope ventured to write something of his feelings for her:

> I find I begin to behave my self worse to you than to any other Woman, as I value you more. And yet if I thought I shou'd not see you again, I would say some things here, which I could not to your Person. For I would not have you dye deceivd in me....

In the eighteenth century, that was passion almost completely expressed in words.

While she was far away — almost at the other end of the world, it seemed, in Constantinople — Pope translated his love into poetry. He produced and published two graceful elegiac poems on the anguish of lovers separated forever. One of these, modeled on Ovid's letters of forsaken lovers, is the letter of Eloisa to Abelard; it is largely a translation into poetry of the actual letters of Heloise, but at the end of it there appears an evocation of Pope himself, as a 'future Bard,'

> Condemned whole years in absence to deplore,
> And image charms he must behold no more.

He sent a copy of the volume containing these poems to Lady Mary. We do not know how she acknowledged it, but she marked her copy to show that she knew what he meant.

This sounds moving. Yet we should recall that Lady Mary was popular, admired, and at least partly beautiful. (She had lost her eyelashes and her complexion in an attack of smallpox at the age of twenty-six. That was one reason why she was so keen on inoculation later, and compelled both her children to submit to it, with excellent results.) Pope was only four feet six inches high, with a permanent curvature of the spine — rather like that which afflicted the unhappy Leopardi some years later; he was unable even to sit up or stand erect without a metal brace. Was it possible for two such people to fall in love, mutually and reciprocally? Was it possible for such a woman to return the love of such a man? Perhaps it would have been if Pope himself had been only physically disabled — if, like many men who have suffered grave injuries from disease or accident, he had retained a good and kind and gentle spirit. But he did not; he was crippled not only physically but emotionally.

When he heard that Lady Mary's husband had finished his mission and was returning home, he wrote her more ardent letters than ever. 'I can't express how I long to see you, face to face.... Come for God's sake, come Lady Mary, come quickly!' The closer she got to England, the hotter poor Pope's letters became. In Dover she received a letter from him specially forwarded from Paris, which said (in part): 'Without offence to your modesty be it spoken, I have a burning desire to see your Soul stark naked, for I am confident 'tis the prettiest kind of white Soul in the universe.' And he followed this by telling her a story of two young lovers — Pope himself was still only twenty-nine — who lived in the Oxfordshire countryside, and had been struck by lightning at the same moment, so that they were united at least in death. He added three poems of his own, on this Pathetic Event.*

---

* 'Epitaphs, On Two Lovers Struck Dead by Lightning'

Lady Mary, however, grew colder as she approached the shores of Great Britain. (Most travelers do.) At least, so we can judge from a rather detached letter which she wrote as an answer to this effusive utterance of Pope's. However, when they met again, they were friendly. Next year Pope paid out some of his hard-earned and carefully saved money to have the finest portrait painter of the day, Sir Godfrey Kneller, produce a portrait of Lady Mary for his own home. It is a handsome, rather romantic piece, showing her with sensitive hands, a Turkish headdress, striking jewels, and the warm dark eyes which all her admirers mention. Pope had this portrait hung in the main room of his house, and seems to have kept it there for the rest of his life.

But it was bound to be a difficult relationship, in which one wanted more than the other could possibly give. Pope was becoming more and more the scholarly recluse, while Lady Mary was caught up in the controversy about inoculation, which she had to fight as hard as all medical innovators have always had to fight. She won in the end, but perhaps she came to see Mr. Pope as a little hermit in an ivory invalid-chair, while she herself was versatile, active, dominating, successful.

There was a pause of some years, until 1728, when Pope was forty and she thirty-nine. Then, apparently without any public warning, Pope attacked her in some of his new poems, most notably in a vile couplet of his satiric epic, *The Dunciad*. This is a very topical piece of spite, hard to understand nowadays; but it refers to a Frenchman whom Lady Mary is supposed to have defrauded of some money and infected with venereal disease:

> When hapless Monsieur much complains at Paris
> Of wrongs from Duchesses and Lady Maries *

This lampoon, although obscure today, had a powerful effect in a small narrow society where almost everyone knew nearly

---

* Pope, *The Dunciad* 2.135-6. 'Duchesses' is apparently slang for 'streetwalkers.'

everybody. It was difficult for Lady Mary's friends to look at her without the poisonous epigrams of Pope coming into their minds. The worst of it was that what he said of her began to come true, or at least to seem true. Some years later, in 1735, he characterized her in a few bitter lines of a satire on women. He contrasted her well-known wealth with her well-known dirt. Calling her by the Lesbian name of Sappho, he spoke of

> Sappho's diamonds with her dirty smock,

and compared her to a bluebottle or some worse vermin:

> So morning insects, that in muck begun,
> Shine, buzz, and fly-blow in the setting sun.*

She was becoming so careless about soap and water that later visitors reported her to be not only dirty but even smelly. A friend met her at the theater, and ventured to remark that her hands were rather dirty. Lady Mary, without blenching, replied, 'You should see my feet!'

That was the end of a love affair which began, at least on one side, with something like passion. Why did it so completely collapse into indifference and neglect and spite and hatred? No one knows. Lady Mary herself apparently referred to it only once: she told someone close to her that Pope had made a passionate declaration of love, and that, instead of temporizing or being kind, she had burst into a fit of laughter. For the little satirist to see himself made ridiculous in the eyes of a beautiful and witty woman was the last and worst insult; so he took his revenge.

But Love, or Fortune, was to provide a more terrible and suitable revenge. In her late forties, Lady Mary fell in love with a handsome young Italian nobleman only half her age — Count Francesco Algarotti. She pursued him to Italy; she even left her husband and family and settled down there so as to be in touch with the man she adored. Nothing happened. He

---

* *Moral Essays, Epistle 2,* 24-8

kept Lady Mary at a discreet distance, until at last, after some years, she retired to Switzerland. Now the conditions were reversed. She was unattractive, even repulsive; the beloved was noble and invincibly charming; she suffered all the pangs that she had inflicted on the miserable Pope. Pope's model, the Roman poet Horace, put the matter very well in one of his wittiest odes (1.33):

> Cruel Love always conjoins two inappropriate
> hearts, minds, bodies in one pair of unbroken chains:
>     Love does relish a savage joke.

BURNS

*The Unsigned Letters*

———————————————

THERE is hardly a better way to get to know a man than to read his letters. Many a scientist, or artist, or statesman has one face turned to the public, and another, which may be quite different, shown to his friends. A dramatic proof of this came in the year 1345, when a huge collection of letters written by Cicero to his best friend was discovered, after nearly a thousand years of oblivion. Then, for the first time since antiquity, a man who had been known as a powerful orator and a deeply read student of philosophy, serious and high-principled, was revealed as a very human being; more of an Italian than a Roman; excitable, vivacious, ready to weep copiously or laugh uproariously, a great worrier and something of a chatterbox. Yet, knowing Cicero better, most people liked him better. For another example of this, we need go no further than the Bible. We meet Paul of Tarsus first in the *Acts of the Apostles*. There we see many of his enigmatic actions, and hear him make fiery speeches; but it is not until we read his letters than we can begin to understand him.

Recently I went through a volume of letters written by a man whose work I admire and who would have made a delightful, if demanding, friend. I had never read them before.

They were full of surprises. Thinking over them afterwards, I wondered whether — if I had known nothing else about the man, his character, his achievements, his destiny — I should have been able to reconstruct the individual from the letters alone. With a weak and conventional personality, it is not possible to do this, except in the widest limits, when the man becomes Mr. Middleman of Middletown. But when the personality is strong, then it is easy, if we read his letters, to imagine his appearance and manner, divine his failings and see something of his merits. A good letter writer makes his sentences vibrate with rhythms of living speech.

The volume of letters is quite small, but varied. It is written by a man whom we shall call X. Who was he?

To begin with, we see that he was not rich, he had no privileges born with him, he was not an aristocrat. He was, nevertheless, proud and sensitive. Writing to a friend about his birth and origins, he says:

> I have not the most distant pretensions to being what the pye-coated guardians of escutcheons call a Gentleman. Last winter I looked through a long list of noble families, and there found almost every name in the country: but for me,
>
> > My ancient and ignoble blood
> > Has crept through scoundrels ever since the Flood.
>
> I was born a very poor man's son. For the first six or seven years of my life, my father was a gardener.

Proud and sensitive, X: far more sensitive than most of us. By the age of thirty, we have usually settled down to accepting the bad in life, together with the good; but not X. He sent a cheese to one of his friends, and with it an amusing but sincere letter recommending cheese as a cure for spiritual distress.

> Indigestion is the devil. . . . It besets a man in every one of his senses. I lose my appetite at the sight of successful knavery; sicken to loathing at the noise and nonsense of self-important folly. When the hollow-hearted wretch takes

> me by the hand, the feeling spoils my dinner; the proud
> man's wine so offends my palate that it chokes me in the
> gullet; and the perfumed ... pert coxcomb is so horrible in
> my nostril that my stomach turns. If ever you have any of
> these disagreeable sensations, let me prescribe for you
> Patience, and a bit of my cheese.

This letter tells us more about X. It shows a warm heart and
a strong (if slightly coarse) sense of humor. It breathes a sense
of social injustice, strongly developed, with an abiding wish
that prejudices and anomalies could be removed.

X does not write like the son of a poor man. He sounds
rather well educated. In fact, his father taught him history,
geography, and arithmetic when he was nine — which is rather
better than most of us do nowadays; and he attended good
publicly supported schools until he was taken away to help his
father on the farm. In one of his letters he says, reminiscently:

> The two first books I ever read in private, and which gave
> me more pleasure than any books I ever read again, were the
> life of Hannibal and the history of [a local patriot]. Han-
> nibal gave my young ideas such a turn that I used to strut
> in raptures up and down after the recruiting drum, and
> wish myself tall enough to be a soldier.

Even later, when X was working on the farm, he continued,
like young Abe Lincoln, to read and read. He says that by the
age of sixteen he was devoted to about a dozen special books
(including some famous classics), which he thought over while
'driving the cart or walking to labor'; and thereafter he read
the best books one by one as they came out, and thought over
them. Even a poor man can always get hold of books, if he
tries hard.

When he writes about religion, his bitterness surprises us;
but it helps us to place him in his age, and even his country.
Talking of the saddest story of the Bible, he says:

> Judas did not know, at least was by no means sure, what
> or who [his] Master was; his turpitude was simply, betraying

a worthy man who had ever been a good Master to him: a
degree of turpitude which has even been outdone by many
of his kind since. Iscariot, poor wretch, was a man of nothing
at all per Annum, and by consequence thirty pieces of silver
was a very serious temptation to *him;* but, to give but one
instance, [a distinguished statesman] the other day just
played the same trick to *his* kind master, though he is a man
of huge fortune, and come to that imbecile period of life
when no temptation but Avarice can be supposed to affect
him.

That bitterness reminds us of three different men, all great
writers and all (originally) generous hearts, who were shocked
and horrified by treachery and greed. It is like William Shakespeare, who thought a traitor was the worst type of scoundrel,
a being scarcely human; it is like Dean Swift; and it is rather
like the young Charles Dickens. X had some of their genius,
but he is none of them.

Whoever he was, he was highly sexed.

> *Vive l'amour* and *vive la bagatelle* were my sole principles
> of action till my twenty-third year.

So he wrote in his late twenties, and perhaps so he thought.
But he was not cured. At twenty-eight he wrote:

> In my conscience I believe that my heart has been so oft
> on fire that it is absolutely vitrified. I look on the sex with
> something like the admiration with which I regard the starry
> sky on a frosty December night. I admire the beauty of the
> Creator's workmanship; I am charmed with the wild but
> graceful eccentricity of their actions, and — wish them good-
> night.

To a sensitive emotional man like X, monotony and ennui
are fifty times harder to endure than they are for most of us.
Another of his letters shows that he sometimes chose a dangerous way of escaping them.

> To add to my misfortune; since dinner, a Scraper has been
> torturing Catgut in sounds that would have insulted the

dying agonies of a Sow under the hands of a Butcher — and thinks himself, *on that very account,* exceeding good company. In fact, I have been in a dilemma, either to get drunk, to *forget* these miseries; or to hang myself, to *get rid* of these miseries: like a prudent man, I, of two evils, have chosen the least, and am very drunk — at your service!

Drink, love, a sensitive nature, pride, and poverty. X suffered from all these a good deal. He was miserably poor throughout his life, though he worked hard. In one of his letters, to a man he respected, he says:

I might write you on farming, on building, on marketing, on planning, etc., but my poor distracted mind is so torn, so jaded, so racked and bedevilled with the task of the superlatively Damned — MAKING ONE [COIN] DO THE BUSINESS OF THREE — that I detest, abhor, and swoon at the very word Business.

In addition to his poverty, X had cruelly bad luck. At least two of his business ventures failed, simply through mischance; and then, still in the prime of life, he took a mortal illness which wrecked his usual courageous good spirits, and increased his bitter penury. His final letters are painful to read. This is to his cousin:

When you offered me money-assistance little did I think I should want it so soon. A rascal to whom I owe a considerable bill, taking it into his head that I am dying, has commenced a lawsuit against me, and will infallibly put my emaciated body into jail. Will you be so good as to accommodate me, and that by return of post, with ten pounds? Alas! I am not used to beg! The worst of it is, my health was coming about finely; you know and my physician assures me that melancholy and low spirits are half my disease, guess then my horrors since this business began. Forgive me for once more mentioning by return of Post. Save me from the horrors of a jail!

That desperate appeal was written nine days before X died, at the age of thirty-seven.

After reading these brief but brilliant extracts from his letters, you have no doubt placed him in his milieu and his period. Poor, a working-man — in fact, a farmer trying to make something of his life; educated, but without formal schooling; devoted to true art, and a hater of sordid money-making; a democrat, thinking aristocracy of blood to be artificial; low-born, but despising snobbery; a passionate lover and an enthusiastic drinker, with very little guilt about his passions and a coldly rational attitude towards religion. By the style of his writing and the style of his thinking, he should have lived towards the end of the eighteenth century, rather closer to Byron than to Pope.

But if you saw the letters as a whole, you would instantly know who X was. He keeps talking about his work. If he had been a surgeon, he would have described his operations; had he been a painter, he would have sketched little heads and landscapes in the margin; a musician, he would have discussed the opera or the quartet he was working on. X keeps quoting poetry, his own and others'. Once, after copying out an old poem he particularly admires, he says:

> Light be the turf on the breast of the heaven-inspired poet who composed this glorious fragment! There is more of the fire of native genius in it than in half a dozen of modern English Bacchanalians. Now I am on my hobby-horse I cannot help inserting two other old stanzas which please me mightily:
>
>> Go fetch to me a pint o' wine,
>>> And fill it in a silver tassie;
>> That I may drink, before I go,
>>> A service to my bonnie lassie.
>> The boat rocks at the pier o' Leith;
>>> Fu' loud the wind blaws frae the ferry;
>> The ship rides by the Berwick-Law,
>>> And I maun leave my bonnie Mary.

The letters were written by the greatest Scottish lyric poet, Robert Burns. He was born in a clay hut on January 25th, 1759, and died at the early age of thirty-seven. He was a splendid poet, and although he thought of himself as a 'Peasant,' he was in the truest sense a noble man.

## A Mouse and a Louse

Two of the most sympathetic poems in our language are about vermin. One is about a mouse; the other is about a louse. They are in the same pattern of meter, run to approximately the same size, and were written by the same author. In their own tiny way they are masterpieces of wit and charm. I think the poem about the little mouse might just conceivably have been composed by several other poets, but I do not believe that anybody else in the world at that time could have produced an address to a louse and filled it, in spite of its repulsive subject, so full of grace and sympathy.

The poet was Robert Burns. The pieces are his ode 'To a Mouse,' which he published when he was twenty-six, and his ode 'To a Louse,' produced in the following year. Not many of us know the complete poems nowadays, because they are written in southern Scottish dialect, and in old-fashioned dialect which is now opaque even to the Scots themselves. (I remember how terribly puzzled I was at school, when I first read the mouse lyric, by hearing Burns say, 'A daimen icker in a thrave 's a sma' request.' It means 'An odd ear of corn in a whole sheaf is a small request' from a mouse to a farmer; but it contains three obsolete words.) Still, everyone who is not

illiterate knows something of these poems: the two famous
quotations — 'The best laid schemes o' mice and men/ Gang
aft agley' (meaning 'go often awry') and 'O wad some Pow'r the
giftie gie us/ To see oursels as others see us!' To take subjects
so unpromising as a mouse and a louse, and to build them into
poems containing wisdom so memorably expressed as these two
sentences, was the work of a true genius.

True genius; but misunderstood, and despised. Burns was
writing in 1785, during the proud and pompous eighteenth
century, when a man scarcely dared to appear in decent society
without silver buckles on his shoes, and when only lofty subjects and elevated language were thought worthy of notice
either in conversation or in poetry. There is a ridiculous story
in Boswell's *Life of Samuel Johnson* about a hack poet of that
age who determined to compose an improving poem in the
manner of the great Roman Vergil. In his *Georgics* Vergil had
demonstrated that it was possible, with skill and taste, to write
fine poetry about a subject so simple and prosaic, and even
squalid, as farming. The eighteenth-century hack determined
to rival Vergil in English, and chose a subject which he
thought was both novel and important: the sugar industry of
Jamaica and the other British West Indian islands. He was
successful enough, no doubt, when he described the graceful
rows of waving sugar canes, the rich earth, the warm, glorious
sun. But then he had to deal with the various enemies of
sugar cane, and give directions for combating them. One of
the worst of these enemies is naturally vermin. The poet felt
bound to discuss this unamiable subject, and began a new
paragraph:

> Now, Muse, let's sing of rats.

When he read it to his friends, they could not keep from laughing: he altered it; and in the final version the rats are thus
eloquently periphrased:

> Nor with less waste the whiskered vermin race,
> A countless clan, despoil the lowland cane.*

* Boswell, *Life of Johnson* (Oxford, 1953), 698-9

Surely, he thought, that would be noble enough to make the rats poetical.

Burns was not a conventional hack. Revolution bubbled in his soul, and occasionally boiled over. He therefore chose subjects which were, as the critics of his time put it, 'low.' If he had written of princes leading their armies into battle on mettlesome steeds, or described the grandeur of a regal stag hunt, with dukes and duchesses galloping through mighty forests after the noblest of game, he would surely have been much respected in his own day. Since he wrote about mice and lice, he was admired by only a few, and snubbed by others.

To make things worse, he did not write in the 'pure' language of southeastern England, but in the southern Scottish dialect — and this at a time when even English itself was sometimes thought to be rather vulgar, and anyone who wished to be cultured larded his own language with phrases of French from time to time. Society preferred to speak and read southeastern English, and a poet who wrote in Scottish dialect was — almost by definition — not a poet. (This particular type of snobbery has persisted down to the present time. Many living Scotsmen and Scotswomen can remember that they were forbidden, at school, to use Scottish words and phrases, not because they belonged to a dialectal pattern different from southeastern English, but on the ground that they were 'wrong' and 'common' — as it *is* genuinely wrong and common in English to say 'the ryne in Spyne' rather than 'the rain in Spain.')

Burns had a further handicap. He did not usually write in the accepted English meters, the neat couplets of Mr. Dryden and Mr. Pope (which were ultimately derived from Greek and Latin via Italian and French). He liked to use Scottish measures, cheerful little lilts which did not sound like a rococo chamber orchestra performing a measured gavotte, but like a village fiddler batting out a jolly strathspey and reel. Many of his finest poems were set to the rhythm and music of old Scots folk songs, which meant that — although they were often cleaner and wittier than the original folk-song words — they still reeked of the soil. They wore not satin and buckled shoes, but hodden gray and muddy boots. They had the sweaty hair of a farmer, instead of the powdered wig of a gentleman. They were not Polite. They were Coarse. Some traces of that feeling still linger. It is still a little shocking to think of a poet writing about a piece of body vermin. Our ancestors had far more body vermin than we have; but they prided themselves far more upon their delicate spiritual feelings. That sensitivity made them look askance on Burns for his coarseness, even while they were admiring his poems for the fiery genius that glowed through every one of them. Though his contemporaries made him into a celebrity in Edinburgh, they did not accept him. Without putting the feeling into words, they knew that he was a revolutionary poet.

The poems that Burns wrote about the mouse and the louse are revolutionary poems. They do not preach the forcible overthrow of an established political order and the violent eradication of all those attached to it; but they are utterances which were, in the time of Burns, quietly new, gently shocking, and ultimately destructive of long-accepted aesthetic and social standards.

The poem on the louse is, I suppose, technically an ode: it is all addressed to the little insect, and it is in a lyric meter. But in fact it is a dramatic monologue, and should be imagined as a Breughel picture put into motion. Its title is:

'To a Louse, on seeing one on a lady's bonnet, at church.'

The old Scottish words sometimes sound puzzling, but they give it energy, while the general meaning of the poem is entirely clear. Burns is sitting at service in the little kirk of Mauchline. He is behind, and very close to, the prettiest girl in the neighborhood. Naturally. As he gazes at her, a louse slowly emerges from her dress at her neckline, walks up her hair, and climbs up her hat to the very top, where it sits, surveying the congregation, and inspiring Rabbie with one of his finest lyric poems.

Ha! whare ye gaun, ye crowlin ferlie?        *monster*
Your impudence protects you sairly;
I canna say but ye strunt rarely        *swagger*
   Owre gauze and lace;
Tho' faith, I fear, ye dine but sparely
   On sic a place.

Ye ugly, creepin', blastit wonner,        *oddity*
Detested, shunned, by saunt an' sinner,
How daur ye set your fit upon her,        *dare; foot*
   Sae fine a Lady?
Gae somewhere else, and seek your dinner
   On some poor body.

Swith, in some beggar's haffet squattle;        *Get away; temple; crouch*
There ye may creep, and sprawl, and sprattle
Wi' ither kindred, jumping cattle,
   In shoals and nations;
Whare horn nor bane ne'er daur unsettle        *comb of horn or bone*
   Your thick plantations.

Now haud you there, ye're out of sight,        *hold on*
Below the fatt'rils, snug an' tight;        *ribbons*
Na, faith ye yet! Ye'll no be right
   Till ye've got on it,
The vera tapmost, towering height
   O' Miss's bonnet.

My sooth! right bauld ye set your nose out        *bold*
As plump and grey as onie grozet;        *any gooseberry*
O for some rank, mercurial rozet,        *rosin*
   Or fell, red smeddum,        *powder*
I'd gie you sic a hearty dose o't,
   Wad dress your droddum!        *fix your wagon*

I wad na been surprised to spy
You on an auld wife's flainen toy;        *flannel cap*
Or aiblins some bit duddie boy,        *perhaps*
   On's wyliecoat;        *ragged vest*
But Miss's fine Lunardi, fye!        *bonnet*
   How daur ye do 't?

O Jenny, dinna toss your head,
An' set your beauties a' abread!                    *all abroad*
Ye little ken what cursed speed
    The blastie's makin'!                           *dwarf*
Thae winks and finger-ends, I dread,               *those*
    Are notice takin'!

O wad some Pow'r the giftie gie us                 *little gift*
To see oursels as others see us!
It wad frae monie a blunder free us
    And foolish notion:
What airs in dress an' gait wad lea'e us,          *leave*
    And ev'n Devotion!

It is a clever and charming poem. In particular, it is delightful to see how Burns, in stanza after stanza, traces the
steady, relentless movement of the louse from the first moment
when it emerges from the poor girl's dress and begins to make its
way up to the pinnacle of its Everest. It was a surprise to
Burns, and we hear his surprise echoed in his opening words:
'Ha! whare ye gaun, ye crowlin ferlie?' I suppose he would
have been still more astounded if the louse had looked around
and explained that it was going to climb to the very tip top of
the young lady's hat. Why? *Because it was there!* Nevertheless,
it is irresistibly comic to watch the horrid little beast making
its pedestrian, pediculous way through the complicated ribbons and lace and gauze of a fantastically fashionable Italian
creation, until it achieves the supreme pinnacle, high above
the pretty girl's head, where others in the congregation can see
it, while we must sit and watch it in civil, reverent silence. It
would be against religion to interrupt the church service by
speaking to a neighbor; and it would be frankly impossible to
say, 'Excuse me, Miss Jenny, but you have a louse on your
hat.' (She might reply, 'You have a bee in your bonnet.')
    But there is satire in the poem as well as outright comedy.
Burns addresses the louse, and explains to it that, on a well-
dressed girl with some social aspirations, it is quite out of

place. On a dirty, verminous beggar, it would be at home; or on a self-neglecting old woman, or on a badly reared child; but *not* on a member of good society. This is the same Rabbie Burns who wrote 'A man's a man for a' that.' He said, and he believed, that rank was but the stamp on the coin; what mattered was the metal, false or true gold, of which the coin was made. And the famous final stanza:

> O wad some Pow'r the giftie gie us
> To see oursels as others see us!
> It wad frae monie a blunder free us
>     And foolish notion:
> What airs in dress an' gait wad lea'e us,
>     And ev'n Devotion!

— that stanza reminds us that Burns wrote many of his most telling poems against the misuses of religion. He knew perfectly well that Miss Jenny, when she dressed for church that Sabbath morning, was thinking less about the psalms she would sing and the doctrinal content of the sermon she would hear than about the effect of her fine new hat on all the men and all the other women. In eight short stanzas, less than fifty lines, Burns has given us a brilliantly comic little drama, a gentle assertion of social equality, and a nipping satire on religious hypocrisy.

The other poem is as pathetic as the louse poem is comic. Burns was plowing on the farm which he and his brother Gilbert had rented. The soil was not good, the weather was wretched; the whole Burns family, poor already, could well be destitute in a year. As Rab drove the plowshare through the sour, wet earth one bleak November day, it smashed through the nest of a little field mouse. The homeless creature ran away in panic and despair. It was gone in a moment, soon to die of cold and wet; but it lingered in Burns's mind. In his poem he speaks to it from a heart full of love and sorrow and genuine sympathy. The conclusion is world-famous:

But, Mousie, thou art no thy lane         *art not alone*
In proving foresight may be vain;
The best laid schemes o' mice and men
   Gang aft agley;                *go often awry*
And lea'e us nought but grief and pain
   For promised joy.

Burns ends by saying that the tiny creature, miserable and terrified, is still less unhappy than he himself, with nothing but dreary memories and a grimly threatening future. Only a few months later, he was so desperate that he resolved to leave his home forever, and emigrate to Jamaica. In order to raise the nine pounds he required for the fare, he published a collection of his poems. Quite unexpectedly, it was successful, and brought him some money, and some temporary distinction. But it was not to last. In a few years, too few years, he died as pitifully as a mouse in a flooded ditch.

It is a true poem, Burns's address to a mouse; but it was also, in his time, a new poem. Very few other poets would have thought of writing a serious piece on such a trivial subject; and of all the hundreds of millions of men who have plowed the soil and disturbed small vermin, very few have ever felt much sympathy for them, none have expressed it as warmly as Robert Burns. The country tenant-farmer with the big heart and the eloquent voice — he belonged to a new age altogether, the age which was coming and which he did not live to see. I wish he had escaped from Britain, and crossed the Atlantic, not to Jamaica but to the newly independent United States of America. He would have had a longer and happier life, even if he had written no more poetry. And he might have done greater things than he did. The plowman with his head full of immortal eloquence, hating hypocrisy and loving liberty, was an elder brother of our seventh President, Andrew Jackson, and of a still greater man with a still nobler heart, who was born in a log cabin and went to his grave from the White House.

BYRON

*The Poet and His Vulture*

---

WE KNOW the faces of most poets only as stereotypes: the frail, earnest features of John Keats, Tennyson's dark beard and brooding eyes, the suave, enigmatic mask of Shakespeare. But there is one dramatic figure which, as we think of it, lives and moves. It stamped its appearance on the memory of a whole generation, and even set the style for young men's faces and young men's clothes and young men's manners. It still lives. It is Lord Byron.

Mention the name: at once the man appears. Slender; handsome, nobly, arrogantly handsome even in an age of fine-looking men; bold and unconventional, with collar open on a strong white neck; dark curling hair; intense gray eyes with dark eyelashes. And then the figure moves: we see that it is lame. Byron could ride a spirited horse, he could swim for hours in rough seas, he could even box if he did not have to move about much, but he could not walk normally, because one or both of his feet were deformed. This (he said) was due to his mother's behavior while he was being born; he could never forgive her; it worried him all his life, and he overcompensated for it. His lameness adds a touch of penetrating grief to our picture of him. Melancholy seems to surround Byron. No; something deeper: a gloom almost Satanic. Men and women were actually afraid of him. He created new characters, who lived in darker worlds: Manfred, the wizard of the high Alps, knowing more of spirits than of mankind and oppressed with a nameless guilt; savage Turkish pashas; daring rebels; lonely pirates whose names are

> linked with one virtue, and a thousand crimes.*

Byron wrote one splendid poem in which he addressed the Titan Prometheus — crucified on a remote mountain by an unjust god — as a fellow sufferer. And his life ended in bitter frustration. He died not as he would have chosen, on the battlefield, but of fever in a small Greek town, foreseeing no success for the struggling cause of liberation which he was endeavoring to keep alive, and leaving his finest, most ambitious poem forever incomplete. A somber destiny. Before he had worn his laurels long, their leaves were blackened.

When you first read Byron's poems, you are struck by their unrelenting pessimism. It is not hysterical, or revolutionary, nor is it the pessimism of the isolated intellectual. It sounds like the considered verdict of an educated, experienced, reflective man who has the gift of poetry. Here is a brief meditation on the heaped ruins of Rome, in a vision that evokes the pessimistic historian of a later century, Oswald Spengler.

> Cypress and ivy, weed and wallflower grown
> Matted and massed together — hillocks heaped
> On what were chambers — arch crushed, column strown
> In fragments — choked up vaults, and frescos steeped
> In subterranean damps, where the owl peeped,
> Deeming it midnight: — Temples — Baths — or Halls?
> Pronounce who can: for all that Learning reaped
> From her research hath been, that these are walls —
> Behold the Imperial Mount! 'tis thus the Mighty falls.

---

* Byron, *The Corsair* 1864

> There is the moral of all human tales;
> 'Tis but the same rehearsal of the past,
> First Freedom, and then Glory — when that fails,
> Wealth — Vice — Corruption, — Barbarism at last: —
> And History, with all her volumes vast,
> Hath but *one* page.*

That is the tone of most of Byron's poems. That is the tone which caught the ear of so many other young poets, and molded the minds of Heine, Lamartine, De Musset, Leopardi, Pushkin; yes, and Berlioz: lonely pessimism; heroic disillusionment; Promethean endurance; Titanic scorn. That is the dark vision that appears when we hear the name of Byron: proud face, lame foot, tragic gaze, tormented heart.

But look through his poems again; or, better still, open his letters and his diaries. At once a new Byron appears. Roars of laughter strike the astonished ear. A constant flow of epigrams, personal jokes, and nonsense rhymes gushes out. Byron turns out to be extremely good company, a loyal and cheerful friend, and a young man full of animal spirits, who would write a funny letter as readily as he would box five rounds with a visitor. That was the age of wits and eccentrics, when a reputation could be made by a brilliant talker. It was the age of Sydney Smith — who said that Daniel Webster was like a steam engine in trousers, and declared it required a surgical operation to get a joke into a Scotchman's head. Byron was brought up in Aberdeenshire, far in the northeast of Scotland, and that is where his strong character and his love of solitude were formed; but when he went to school at Harrow and then on to Cambridge, he was thrown into a rough but cheerful society, in which a man needed both wits and guts to make his mark. Byron made his mark.

Occasionally he hated it: society, and success, and his mother, and his wife, and the whole thing. But quite often he enjoyed it. When he did, out poured his gaiety and his fun.

---

* *Childe Harold's Pilgrimage* 4, stanzas 107-8

His letters are full of jollity. It must have been a cheerful fellow who described a stag party as 'all hiccup and happiness.' In his letters he kept improvising satirical poems like this:

> The world is a bundle of hay,
>     Mankind are the asses who pull,
> Each tugs it a different way, —
>     And the greatest of all is John Bull!

And in conversation he was equally amusing. Lady Blessington wrote down some of the epigrams he threw out to her:

> After a season in London, one doubts one's own identity.
> I have not quite made up my mind that women have souls.
> No man dislikes being lectured by a woman, provided she be not his wife, sister, mother, or mistress.

Really, Byron seldom became bitter unless when he spoke of the British climate, his own reputation, or his female relatives. It was a little naughty of him to describe his honeymoon as the treacle-moon (or we should say the 'molasses-moon'). There is a very funny letter, too, in which he talks about the poem that brought him fame, *Childe Harold*:

> I was half mad during the time of its composition, between metaphysics, mountains, lakes, love unextinguishable, thoughts unutterable, and the nightmare of my own delinquencies. I should, many a good day, have blown my brains out, but for the recollection that it would have given pleasure to my mother-in-law; and, even *then*, if I could have been certain to haunt her . . .

Yet Byron's humor goes deeper than that; it runs all through his work. His first poems were lyrical, and sentimental. When they were badly reviewed, he published a sharp, vigorous, and very funny satire called *English Bards and Scotch Reviewers*. (He still thought of himself, at that time, as an Englishman; he was cured later.) Thenceforward, although he was best known for his gloomy works, he kept producing poems of laughter also. Probably he is the last of the great satiric poets writing in English. The favorite of most readers who know Byron's satires is his *Vision of Judgment*, which pokes irresistible fun at the Poet Laureate's conception of George III's arrival at the pearly gates and his triumphal entry into heaven. And his final work, *Don Juan*, was a cross between epic, romance, and satire, in the manner of the gayest and most irreverent of Italian poets, Ariosto. It is full of good things. It specializes in one difficult but amusing art, which could be practiced only by a genuine humorist: comic multiple rhymes. Here is Byron's epitaph on Keats, whose death was partly brought on by bitter reviews of his poetry:

> John Keats, who was killed off by one critique
>     Just as he really promised something great,
> If not intelligible, without Greek
>     Contrived to talk about the gods of late
> Much as they might have been supposed to speak.
>     Poor fellow! His was an untoward fate;
>         'Tis strange the mind, that very fiery particle,
>         Should let itself be snuffed out by an article.*

From the same poem, here is a magnificent description of London, huge, fogbound as so often, and crowned by St. Paul's Cathedral. This is worth putting beside Wordsworth's sonnet on London:

> A mighty mass of brick and smoke, and shipping,
>     Dirty and dusky, but as wide as eye
> Could reach, with here and there a sail just skipping
>     In sight, then lost amidst the forestry
> Of masts; a wilderness of steeples peeping
>     On tiptoe through their sea-coal canopy;
>         A huge, dun Cupola, like a foolscap crown
>         On a fool's head — and there is London Town! †

In fact, the whole of *Don Juan* gives us a better impression of Byron's real character than any other of his poems. The

---

\* *Don Juan* 11 stanza 59
† *Don Juan* 10 stanza 82

tragedies and romances are pervasively somber. The satires are uproariously scornful. This poem contains love affairs, battles, shipwrecks, splendid descriptions of scenery, scornful vignettes of society, the love of travel, and fits of hearty laughter: all these, we know, were parts of Byron's life. Small but important details of his personality come out of it, usually illuminated by flashes of wit. There is recurrent anxiety about money, once pointed by an allusion to Machiavelli:

> Alas! how deeply painful is all payment!
>     Take lives — take wives — take aught except men's purses:
> As Machiavel shows those in purple raiment,
>     Such is the shortest way to general curses.
> They hate a murderer much less than a claimant
>     On that sweet ore which everybody nurses.
>       Kill a man's family, and he may brook it,
>       But keep your hands out of his breeches' pocket.*

There is some very acute observation of the psychology of women: for instance, this description of the Englishwoman, with a cold manner and a hot heart. Byron looks for a suitable image, and then cries:

> What say you to a bottle of champagne?
> Frozen into a very vinous ice,
>     Which leaves few drops of that immortal rain,
> Yet in the very center, past all price,
>     About a liquid glassful will remain;
>       And this is stronger than the strongest grape
>       Could e'er express in its expanded shape:
>
> 'Tis the whole spirit brought to a quintessence;
>     And thus the chilliest aspects may concentre
> A hidden nectar under a cold presence . . .
>     And your cold people are beyond all price,
>     When once you've broken their confounded ice.†

---

\* *Don Juan* 10 stanza 79
† *Don Juan* 13 stanzas 37-8

Besides this, there are several hangovers, and quite a lot of liver trouble;

> I think, with Alexander, that the act
>   Of eating, with another act or two,
> Makes us feel our mortality in fact
>   Redoubled; when a roast, and a ragout,
> And fish, and soup, by some side dishes backed,
>   Can give us either pain or pleasure, who
>     Would pride himself on intellects, whose use
>     Depends so much upon the gastric juice? *

Now, reading Byron's life and letters, and thinking over that last stanza, I believe I can suggest one reason for the extraordinary variations in his outlook and his personality. It is this. He was not naturally a slender, elegant, athletic, grave young man at all. Naturally, he was a plump, pleasant, pot-bellied person, and he spent tremendous, almost unremitting efforts on keeping down his natural fat. He was about five feet eight. When he was nineteen years old, he weighed 202 pounds. Because of his lameness and his difficulty in taking normal exercise, this corpulence would soon have become quite irremovable. Byron had a strong will. He resolved to get it off, and keep it off. He did so by painful exercises and a Spartan regime of dieting, which may well have wrecked his liver. He took exercise wearing seven waistcoats and a heavy topcoat; then he took hot baths; he ate hardly anything. By the time he was twenty, he had got down to 147 pounds. Only once or twice throughout the rest of his life did he rise above that. But it meant that he was constantly hungry. He would sometimes fast for forty-eight hours. In 1816 he lived on a diet of one slice of thin bread for breakfast, a dinner of vegetables, and green tea and soda water in between. To keep down his hunger, he chewed tobacco and mastic gum; sometimes he took laudanum. He was starving.

In *The Thousand and One Nights* there is a sinister story about a pretty young wife who would never eat dinner. Her

---

* *Don Juan* 5 stanza 32

husband would lie down to a hearty meal, but she would eat only grains of rice, picked out of a pilaff, one by one, on the point of a needle. At last he began to suspect her. He watched her, and found that she was a Ghoul: she stole out at night, and robbed graves and nibbled corpses. She had to compensate her protein deficiency. Perhaps she was simply trying to maintain a slim youthful line, in the Middle East, where so many women look like badly stuffed mattresses. Byron went through the same trial. The rich banker and patron of literature, Samuel Rogers, invited him to dinner when he was twenty-five or so, and later reported what happened.

> When we sat down to dinner, I asked Byron if he would take soup. No; he never took soup. Would he take some fish? No; he never took fish. Presently I asked if he would eat some mutton. No; he never ate mutton. — I then asked if he would take a glass of wine. No; he never tasted wine. — It was now necessary to inquire what he *did* eat and drink; and the answer was, 'Nothing but hard biscuits and soda-water.' Unfortunately, neither hard biscuits nor soda-water were at hand; and he dined upon potatoes bruised down on his plate and drenched with vinegar.

Rogers could not imagine any reason for this. He met Byron's friend Hobhouse later and said 'How long will Lord Byron persevere in his present diet?' He replied 'Just as long as you continue to notice it.'

> I did not then know, what I know now to be a fact, that Byron, after leaving my house, had gone to a Club in St. James's Street, and eaten a hearty meat-supper.

Rogers could only conclude that Byron had been shamming, in order to impress his host. In fact, he had been fighting his own appetite. He held the frontier for a time, and then was compelled to retreat.

The Anglo-Irish critic Cyril Connolly says that inside every fat man there is a thin man, screaming to be let out. The reverse is sometimes true, I think, and it was true for Byron.

He was a thin man, and inside him there was a fat man roaring to be set free. Or, to put it in scientific terms, Byron was by nature what Sheldon calls a viscerotonic, plump and jovial. He converted himself, by a terrible effort, into a muscular, balanced somatotonic with strong touches of the nervous, gloomy cerebrotonic. All three Byrons played their parts in his life and his poetry. The thin cerebrotonic conceived the grim otherworldly tragedy of *Manfred*; the tough athlete swam the Dardanelles, and wrote of pirates and duels and the storming of cities; the invisible fat man poured out the jokes and satires at which we still laugh. We can see now why Byron chose to compare himself to Prometheus, for that unhappy giant not only was crucified, but had a vulture tearing eternally at his flesh. Byron had several vultures with their beaks buried deep in his vitals; but the one which he felt most constantly, if not most painfully, was that haggard-eyed, sharp-clawed, tireless monster, a starvation diet.

*How Shelley Died*

WHEN a brilliant young poet dies, the world seems to have gone wrong. Not only has the young man disappeared, but the poems which he could have made are now abolished, and for ever. His death is usually sudden, sometimes violent, always painful.

One of the greatest English poets died at the age of twenty-nine, leaving much of his magnificent poetry still to be realized. He was Percy Bysshe Shelley, one of the greatest lyric poets in any language, and one of the few lyricists who have had any conception of the art of drama. Shelley was drowned on July 8, 1822, in the bay of Spezia in northern Italy, where he had been sailing with his friend Edward Ellerker Williams. His death was terribly sudden and terribly unexpected, and its horror was accentuated by the ghastly character of his funeral. His body, together with that of his friend, drifted for some days in the sea, and was partly eaten by fish. Finally it was cast up, miserably mutilated, and was temporarily buried on the shore where it was found. The bravest of Shelley's friends, Edward Trelawny, had it disinterred and, since it was impracticable to take it to a cemetery for burial, heaped up a funeral pyre on the shore and burned it. The burning was not a simple matter; it took several hours: Byron could not endure to watch, and swam out to sea in an effort to escape; Trelawny stood by to the end, and when Shelley's heart would not burn, snatched it out of the flames. That night Byron and Trelawny both got drunk, and sang, and laughed, and perhaps wept.

Shelley died so abruptly and strangely that most of his friends and admirers almost forgot the manner of his death. Was he drowned by accident? Or by some other means?

Perhaps no one will ever know now. But the man who burned his body and saved his heart, the man who loved him as well as any human being (that is, any male human being) loved him, thought he had been murdered. Trelawny may have been wrong; he himself was a melodramatic character, who led a life of danger and violence; but he was not a pathological liar, and we should consider his statements carefully. And Shelley's wife, or rather his widow, Mary, so far from contradicting the worst interpretation of the known facts, seems to corroborate them.

Shelley had been living for some time in La Spezia. (There he had managed to get some rooms of an old monastery made fit for normal habitation.) La Spezia is a seaport in a beautiful gulf in northern Italy, midway between Genoa and Leghorn. He loved sailing, and indeed the bay of Spezia is a most wonderful place for sailing. He and his friend Williams had a two-masted schooner built at Genoa on a British plan; * they called it, first, the *Don Juan* after Byron's ideal, then *Ariel* after Shelley's own. On July 8, 1822, they sailed from Leghorn (where Shelley had been visiting Leigh Hunt) about midday. During the afternoon a formidable Mediterranean storm came up, with strong winds, thunder, and lightning. All the ships

---

* The schooner was 24-26 feet long with a beam of 8 feet.

and small boats in the vicinity either ran for shelter or put out additional anchors and struck their sails. After the storm cleared, the *Don Juan* had disappeared: Shelley and his friend were never seen alive again.

It sounds like a simple shipwreck. The *Don Juan* was caught in a sudden violent squall with all sails set fast, was blown out to leeward and over, swamped, and foundered. Yet Shelley's friend Trelawny did not believe that. He thought there was another explanation. He thought Shelley's boat had been sunk, and he had some evidence to support his belief.

The first piece of evidence is painfully convincing. When the *Don Juan* was recovered, she was lying thirteen miles out from the nearest coast (Viareggio), at a moderate depth, with all her sails set. But she was stove in. Her timbers had been broken in on one side, by some external force. That force could not have been a submerged rock, for there are no rocks within many miles. Therefore the little ship was attacked by another ship, either accidentally or on purpose. Also, she was a good, seaworthy craft: after she had been salvaged she was repaired and used for sailing up and down the Italian coast for many months. This makes it less probable that she merely capsized, while other boats remained afloat.

Next to this come two more tenuous pieces of evidence. Trelawny said that on the day after the storm the mate of his own ship, who came from nearby Genoa, went ashore to ask about the Shelley schooner. Everyone in the port denied knowing anything about her; but the man from Genoa recognized, in a local fishing boat, an oar of British make, which he thought he had seen on board the *Don Juan*. He asked the fishermen about this, but they swore 'by all the saints' that it did not come from the doomed ship.

A similar statement comes from another source, through Shelley's widow, Mary Shelley. She wrote a description of the disaster a month after it happened, in a long letter to a friend, which still exists. She went to see another friend of Shelley, a naval officer named Captain Roberts. (He was the man who later had the unhappy boat salvaged and took it over for his own amusement.) Roberts had been watching the *Don Juan* through a telescope before the storm overtook her and hid her from sight forever. He seems to have made his own enquiries, and he told Mary Shelley that a fishing boat actually saw the *Don Juan* in difficulties and sinking. The crew of the fishing boat 'could not they said get near her — but 3 quarters of an hour after passed over the spot where they had seen her — they protested no wreck of her was visible, but Roberts going on board their boat found several spars belonging to her — perhaps they let them perish to obtain these.'

Against this is the fact that, as far as could be told from their corpses, neither Shelley nor his friend Williams appears to have been in physical fear. Shelley had been reading, as usual, and he had just had time to slip his book into his pocket — or his books: one was certainly a volume of the poetry of John Keats, and the other was a volume of Greek tragedy, the plays of Sophocles. His friend Williams had pulled his shirt half over his head and had taken off one boot. This looks as though the schooner had simply been overtaken by a heavy squall, and the two had tried to abandon ship. This reminds us of Shelley's character. Most of us, if we could neither swim nor navigate, would not dream of going out sailing in a small boat without a native steersman, on the Italian coast, where storms are frequent and dangerous. It is astounding to think that Shelley could not swim. All his poetry emphasizes the joy of escape from the earth into some freer and lighter element. Usually his imagery is drawn from flying; but the experience of swimming, being borne up on the calm liquid bosom of the sea or battling the strong masculine billows, would have appealed mightily to Shelley, as it appealed to Byron and later to Swinburne. Perhaps he never learned to swim because it was a thing expected of boys at his school, Eton College: he refused to be a 'wet bob.' In any case, some time before his death he explained to one of his friends that in case of an accident he would let himself sink like a stone, because he could not swim, and would not burden anyone else with the duty of trying to save him.

However, there is some further evidence. An old Italian fisherman who died over fifty years later was reported to have confessed on his deathbed that he had been one of the crew of a boat which had run down Shelley's schooner. He had kept silence about it ever since. He said that the crew had intended to highjack the *Don Juan* to get the money Shelley was supposed to have aboard.

Now, there are two explanations of this, both of which will fit. One is that Shelley was mistaken for Byron, or else associated with Byron. Byron was thought to be very rich indeed; he had been working for the liberation of Greece from the Turks, and he had collected a fair sum of money for use in the revolution. Shelley himself was a revolutionary and a strong partisan of the liberation of Greece, so that he might easily have been thought to have the same kind of money. The other explanation is that Shelley had just been foolish. A few days earlier he had gone to the local bank and — isn't this absolutely characteristic of that unworldly, innocent, optimistic, trustful man? — had drawn out a large sum in gold for current household expenses, and walked back through the streets, swinging the bag absent-mindedly in his hand: a bag from which there emerged a heavy and appetizing sound of chinking. Late in life Trelawny said he remembered that two fishing boats 'followed' Shelley's schooner because their crews believed the rich milord Byron was aboard. 'They did not intend to sink the boat, but to board her and murder Byron.' On this explanation, Shelley's death was caused by a brutal but explicable act of piracy.

On the other hand, the whole thing may have been a terrible mistake, a mistake exaggerated by a legal situation which is strange to modern minds. In the early years of last

century the various states and kingdoms of Italy were subject
to extremely stringent laws of quarantine. The principal purpose of these laws was to prevent the importation of epidemic
disease, and particularly of bubonic plague, into the Italian
peninsula; and they were administered with relentless strin-
gency. Nowadays every passenger entering the United States
of America has to produce proof that he or she has been successfully vaccinated within the past three years; but in Italy
last century the laws were far more rigid and complicated, and
among other things they subjected everyone who was even
suspected of carrying infection to confinement for at least fourteen days (nominally forty days) in restricted quarters between
a hospital and a prison. (If you recall the beginning of Dickens's fine novel, *Little Dorrit*, you will remember that its
second chapter takes us to the quarantine barracks off the
port of Marseilles, where every single traveler who has arrived
from the Middle East has been forced to wait in case the plague
may manifest itself.) Under these grim laws of quarantine
even the corpses of Shelley and Williams suffered. No one
would touch them. They were dragged ashore by hooks, and
buried on the beach under a light covering of sand. If a boat
picked up a living man at sea in the Mediterranean, within
the operation of these laws, its whole crew would be subject
to quarantine when it returned to port. It is possible, therefore,
that Shelley's boat was run down by accident, and that the
men who ran it down were afraid, because of the laws of
quarantine, to pick up the members of the crew. At the height
of a storm, in the darkness and high winds, a collision is only
too easy. If the *Don Juan* was struck on the weather quarter
by a fishing boat running before the wind, she would have
been driven over on her lee side, and begun to fill with water,
and soon foundered. Trelawny at first admitted this as a pos-
sibility. He added that if the fishermen had taken a drowning
man on board they would have been subject to 'the penalty of
18 or 20 days quarantine — which would ruin them.' If this
explanation is correct, then the death of Shelley was not caused

by a planned murder; it was the result of a hit-and-run collision.

There, then, are the three possible accounts of the death of Shelley: accident, culpable homicide, brutal murder.* No one will ever know the truth, on this earth at least. Yet it is strange to read the poem which Shelley wrote only the year before his own death — as a tribute to another young poet who had died quite as tragically — and to find, in the last stanza of his *Adonais*, these prophetic words:

> My spirit's bark is driven,
> Far from the shore, far from the trembling throng
> Whose sails were never to the tempest given;
> The massy earth and sphered skies are riven!
> I am borne darkly, fearfully, afar. . . .

* There is an acute analysis of the case by Leslie A. Marchand in an article called 'Trelawny on the Death of Shelley,' in the *Keats-Shelley Memorial Bulletin* 4 (1952) 9-34. See also H. J. Massingham, *The Friend of Shelley* (Cobden-Sanderson, London, 1930) 160-77, and Appendix II, 325-8.

EMERSON

## The Aloof American

---

We have passed the middle of the twentieth century. As Americans, we are nearly two hundred years old. We have always had a mind of our own, and from very early times we have had our own voice, in prose, and in poetry.

Who is the typical American poet of the nineteenth century? Not Edgar Allan Poe: few of us know and admire more than his Raven poem. Not Longfellow: although he wrote some charming poems, he now seems too conventional and even derivative. Not Emily Dickinson, in spite of her concentrated brilliance: she was a feminine poet, and this is a masculine country. Whittier and Lowell? They are almost forgotten nowadays, except by antiquarians, and specialists, and those delightful eccentrics who write in to the *New York Times Book Review* to ask whether anyone can identify a poem they learnt at school, seventy years ago, beginning

> Blessings on thee, little fellow,
> Barefoot boy, with hair so yellow.

I believe that just as everyone would say the great American statesman of the middle nineteenth century was Abraham

Lincoln, so the typical American poet was Walt Whitman. In many ways this is a right choice. Walt Whitman sang a new song for America. He proclaimed that sexual activity and sexual awareness were healthy, were necessary, were a sort of sacrament; and nowadays we follow this creed and practice it. He was friendly and openhearted and passionately democratic; he was boldly original and yet usually easy to understand; and the form of his poems was a winning compromise between the swinging rhythms and oracular phrasing of the Old Testament, and a modern free verse, with no nonsense about sensitive rhythms or elaborate rhymes. Yes, from our point of view at least, Walt Whitman is the American poet of the nineteenth century.

Yet there was at the same time another American poet, whom Walt Whitman much admired, and who was for many years much more famous both in the United States and in Europe. This was Ralph Waldo Emerson of Concord, Massachusetts. His volume of *Poems* came out in 1846, when he was forty-three years old. It had, and (for a book of poetry) it still has, one great merit: it was unexpected, it was unpredictable, it was startling. Many critics said that it was too difficult. Quite a number of readers objected to the philosophy which they could detect behind its cold stone verses. But the book stands up still, after more than a hundred years; and, unless our taste is much more drastically vulgarized, it will stand for another hundred.

Strange, the vicissitudes of destiny, in literature as in politics. Nowadays Walt Whitman seems to be a central, typical figure of American life, with his white beard and his genial sloppy life and his simple bold formless writing. Emerson, neat, clean-shaven, tall, thin, fragile, lissome, and clerical, looks like a remote eccentric, inhabiting a special glassed-in air-conditioned vivarium reserved for transcendentalists and other oddities. But it was just the opposite while the two poets were alive. Whitman was then wildly unconventional, almost crazy; Emerson, in the North at least, was a hugely popular figure, a voice of America, a character who might well have fitted into one of his most famous lectures, 'Representative Men.' It was a private letter from Emerson in praise of Whitman's first book, *Leaves of Grass*, saluting Whitman 'at the threshold of a great career,' that launched him towards his future fame: for (without Emerson's permission) it was sent to the *New York Tribune* in order to publicize *Leaves of Grass*; it was used in the second edition of the poems, and even stamped on the back of the volume. In spite of this barbaric yawping, Emerson continued to admire Whitman and his work, and took some trouble in writing to Salmon Chase in order to get Whitman a government job, saying that his poems 'showed extraordinary power and were more deeply American and democratic than those of any other poet.' Later, as the two men grew older, they drew further apart. Whitman became a sage, Emerson a quiet recluse. In his selection of great poems, called *Parnassus,* Emerson did not include a single poem by Walt Whitman. He was sadly conscious of the strong smell of gas that surrounded Walt whenever he was not writing his very best. He once said that he hoped Whitman would write the songs of a nation, and not simply make its inventories; but he had deeper desires and hopes for Whitman buried in his soul, which he never uttered and Whitman never fulfilled.

They are both fine poets, poets of whom America can be proud. Yet they wrote two different kinds of poetry — so different that they might almost have been speaking different languages, and were certainly thinking and feeling in utterly different spiritual worlds. They were Americans, contemporaries, allies in politics, spiritual friends in many things. But they spoke differently.

Throw open the poems of Walt Whitman, and you hear an exultant, confident, innocent shout:

> I am the credulous man of qualities, ages, races,
> I advance from the people in their own spirit,
> Here is what sings unrestricted faith.

> Omnes! omnes! Let others ignore what they may,
> I make the poem of evil also, I commemorate that part also,
> I am myself just as much evil as good, and my nation is —
>      and I say there is in fact no evil,
> (Or if there is I say it is just as important to you, to
>      the land or to me, as any thing else).*

Noble, is it not? Almost devoid of real meaning. Still, optimistic and noble. It gives us a simple thrill, like hearing a band playing a marching song in the very street where we are standing, we can hardly resist it, we cry 'Camerado!'

Then throw open the poems of Emerson — or rather open them warily, as though you were handling a hypodermic — and you become aware of a cool quiet voice, no less confident than that of Whitman, but far more restrained in meaning and in appeal.

> Good-bye, proud world! I'm going home:
> Thou art not my friend, and I'm not thine.
> Long through thy weary crowds I roam;
> A river-ark on the ocean brine,
> Long I've been tossed like the driven foam;
> But now, proud world! I'm going home.†

Home — away from the world which most of us inhabit: so the world is exile, or prison; and Emerson's home is elsewhere. This is the very reverse of Whitman's delighted acceptance of all the world as his home; *he* wants nowhere else, he is happy even in a noisy workshop or a common saloon. He desires to give himself to the world. Emerson wishes to reserve himself, to keep himself safe from the world. Yet both are Americans.

Turn elsewhere in the poems of Walt Whitman, and hear him set out on a mission to humanity.

Afoot and light-hearted I take to the open road,
Healthy, free, the world before me,
The long brown path before me leading wherever I choose.

---

* Whitman, 'Starting from Paumanok,' VII
† Emerson, 'Good-bye'

Henceforth I ask not good-fortune, I myself am good-fortune,
Henceforth I whimper no more, postpone no more, need nothing,
Done with indoor complaints, libraries, querulous criticisms,
Strong and content I travel the open road.*

Now turn to his friend Emerson, and hear a graver note. How
does he face the voyage through the world? (By the way, Emerson actually traveled widely, visiting many countries of Europe
and lecturing in nearly every one of the United States, while
Walt Whitman remained pretty close to his home through
most of his long life.) Emerson realizes that the outside world
is not necessarily the friend of every man or woman living:
that we need not stride out boldly into the unknown in order
to find adventure; and that we can often endure enough and
face dangerous enough adventures simply by staying in our
own circle and waiting for the future to invade our defences.
He said so in a short poem:

> Every day brings a ship,
> Every ship brings a word;
> Well for those who have no fear,
> Looking seaward, well assured
> That the word the vessel brings
> Is the word they wish to hear. †

All through their work it is the same. Whitman is outgoing,
free, confident, undisciplined. Emerson is withdrawn, controlled, wary, self-limited. If the two men had been totally
alien, if they had lived in separate worlds and seen disconnected visions, then it would be senseless to compare them. But
no. They had much in common. Neither of them was a Christian. Both were lovers of wild nature; each had a grand and
reassuring pantheistic confidence in the grace and vitality of
the physical universe. Both were optimists, Whitman an un-
qualified and strenuous optimist, Emerson a wary and hopeful

---

* Whitman, 'Song of the Open Road' 1
† Emerson, 'Letters'

optimist. Whether Walt Whitman ever lost anyone whom he loved nearly and dearly, I do not know, although I think not; but Emerson lost his first-born son, and was able to console himself with a beautiful and ultimately serene poem called 'Threnody.' Both of them were passionate patriots, and democratic idealists, and opponents of slavery; both had built their lives upon confidence in the noble future of mankind which was to be attained through liberty. Both of them were well-read, although Emerson, the Harvard graduate and polyglot, knew a great deal more about the literature of the world than Whitman, educated in Brooklyn schools; but both enjoyed talking to what Whitman called 'powerful uneducated persons' and what Emerson described, in a poem, as 'rude poets of the tavern hearth, Jake and Reuben.'

The fundamental difference between them is not simply the difference of two minds. It is the difference of two Americas. There are many scores of Americas, but there are two vitally important spirits which both inhabit this country and which are never quite at ease together. One is the cool, calm, orderly, inventive spirit which has inspired New England for many generations: one of its voices was Emerson. The other is the warm, excitable, disorderly, enthusiastic spirit which explored the West, and climbed the Rockies, and pioneered first over half a continent and then, now, over half the world. Of that spirit, Whitman was an early voice; there are others, which are still sounding in our ears; but perhaps we need still more confident and patriotic voices, to express its hopes and aims. We are living now in a period of courageous expansion. We feel more sympathetic to the bold, outgoing Whitman than to the wary, critical, outwardly conventional Emerson. Yet both speak for America, and both are recognized by foreigners as characteristically American poets.

Here, in two short poems, are the two Americas, as Whitman and Emerson saw them. One is the optimist, the liberal, the expansionist, who cries:

My comrade!
For you to share with me two greatnesses, and a third one
    rising inclusive and more resplendent,
The greatness of Love and Democracy, and the greatness of
    Religion.

Melange mine own, the unseen and the seen,
Mysterious ocean where the streams empty,
Prophetic spirit of materials shifting and flickering around me,
Living beings, identities now doubtless near us in the air
    that we know not of,
Contact daily and hourly that will not release me,
These selecting, these in hints demanded of me.

Not he with a daily kiss onward from childhood kissing me,
Has winded and twisted around me that which holds me to him,
Any more than I am held to the heavens and all the spiritual
    world,
After what they have done to me, suggesting themes.
O such themes — equalities! O divine average!

Warblings under the sun, usher'd as now, or at noon, or setting,
Strains musical flowing through ages, now reaching hither,
I take to your reckless and composite chords, add to them,
    and cheerfully pass them forward.*

The other poet is the ultimate optimist and immediate
pessimist, who believes that most people are not persons full
of energy and will, but clay; and that, in order to be a Wash-
ington or a Lincoln or a Roosevelt, it is not enough to be one
of the common men. Here is Emerson's picture of the hero
who almost becomes a god, a god of this world.

    This is he, who, felled by foes,
    Sprung harmless up, refreshed by blows:
    He to captivity was sold,
    But him no prison-bars would hold:
    Though they sealed him in a rock,
    Mountain chains he can unlock:

---

* Whitman, 'Starting from Paumanok' X

Thrown to lions for their meat,
The crouching lion kissed his feet:
Bound to the stake, no flames appalled,
But arched o'er him an honoring vault.
This is he men miscall Fate,
Threading dark ways, arriving late,
But ever coming in time to crown
The truth, and hurl wrong-doers down.
He is the oldest, and best known,
More near than aught thou call'st thy own,
Yet, greeted in another's eyes,
Disconcerts with glad surprise.
This is Jove, who, deaf to prayers,
Floods with blessings unawares.
Draw, if thou canst, the mystic line
Severing rightly his from thine,
Which is human, which divine.*

Emerson and Whitman, one neglected nowadays, the other much admired, if little read. Did they merely live, and write, and die? Or have they left followers and friends? Surely they have. The most famous living poet born in the United States is T. S. Eliot. Is he not, in his aloofness, his elegant control, his pessimism, a descendant of Emerson? The most famous living novelist born in America is probably Ernest Hemingway. In his energy and his naïve idealism and his sprawling simplicity, is he not a son of Walt Whitman? Even more neglected than Whitman during his life was a prose writer who is now much admired, Herman Melville: does he not belong in the same tradition as Walt Whitman, and are Thomas Wolfe, and Sinclair Lewis, and Carl Sandburg, not part of the same generous tradition? But Emily Dickinson, and Robert Frost, and John Marquand, and E. E. Cummings, and Thornton Wilder — are they not the friends and pupils of the dry and cool artist, Ralph Waldo Emerson, the aloof American?

* Emerson, 'Worship'

# The Fourth of July

---

I DOUBT if any European ever understands Walt Whitman until he comes and lives in the United States. When I first read *Leaves of Grass* I was nineteen. It was — especially at that age — an electrifying experience, a revelation; but there was much that remained unrevealed. The mysticism, the pantheism, the energy, the eroticism so strangely sublimated or so universally merged with other emotions — these I could comprehend. And through other channels I already knew the American optimism, the sense of vigorous exploration that fill Walt Whitman's poetry. At the time I loved his rhythms, so powerful and irregular — like the sculptures of Rodin, I thought, or like the half-improvised expansion of the American people over their continent. Still, there was much of Walt Whitman which, before I came to live in America, looked alien to me, and incomprehensible. Sometimes he seemed willfully grotesque, as though he enjoyed his own clumsiness, like a lazy cowhand slouching on the back of an ill-cared-for horse. Often he seemed artificial and pedantic, with his snatches of French and Spanish stuck on like false eyebrows. His little poem 'To a Western Boy' begins

Many things to absorb I teach to help you become eleve of mine.

The sentence is distorted and clumsy, and it is not improved by the intrusion of the French word. What on earth has a French *élève* to do with Whitman from Brooklyn and a boy from the West? No, such things are hard for any European to understand.

And there is one other force in Whitman's poetry which I now enjoy and admire, but which was unsympathetic or meaningless to me, as long as I was a European. This is his genial humor, his power to laugh at his own country and his institutions, while at the same time revering them profoundly and naturally.

Would you think it possible for an American President with high moral standards to tell dirty stories at his Cabinet meetings? Mr. Lincoln did it. Would you think it possible for an American patriot to make fun of Independence Day? Whitman did it, in a queer and delightful poem written for the Fourth of July 1854. He calls it 'A Boston Ballad.' He begins by describing the Fourth of July parade: he watches the troops and the bands and the flags . . . and then he sees something else. He sees something which, for most poets in most other countries, would bring tears, and horror, and a nameless gloom. Marching along with the living troops there are the phantoms of the dead soldiers who fought in the War of the Revolution. Yet, instead of shrinking from that terrible sight, Whitman makes a joke. He laughs at the old ghosts. Or perhaps he laughs with them at the calm, peaceful, satisfied faces of their descendants, marching along so proudly without realizing that they are accompanied by the spirits of '76. Finally, he thinks of centering the procession on a corpse, a skeleton with a grinning skull. This is surely a hideous idea; and yet Walt makes it funny, understandable (at least to Americans), and natural.

His Independence Day poem has three parts.

*First, the parade.*

To get betimes in Boston town I rose this morning early,
Here's a good place at the corner, I must stand and see the show.

Clear the way there Jonathan!
Way for the President's marshal — way for the government cannon!
Way for the Federal foot and dragoons, (and the apparitions copiously
    tumbling).

I love to look on the Stars and Stripes, I hope the fifes will play
    Yankee Doodle.

How bright shine the cutlasses of the foremost troops!
Every man holds his revolver, marching stiff through Boston town.

*Then, the procession of ghosts.*

A fog follows, antiques of the same come limping,
Some appear wooden-legged, and some appear bandaged and bloodless.

Why this is indeed a show — it has called the dead out of the earth!
The old graveyards of the hills have hurried to see!
Phantoms! phantoms countless by flank and rear!
Cock'd hats of mothy mould — crutches made of mist!
Arms in slings — old men leaning on young men's shoulders.

What troubles you Yankee phantoms? what is all this chattering of
    bare gums?
Does the ague convulse your limbs? do you mistake your crutches
    for firelocks and level them?

If you blind your eyes with tears you will not see the President's
    marshal,
If you groan such groans you might balk the government cannon.

For shame old maniacs — bring down those toss'd arms, and let your
    white hair be,
Here gape your great grandsons, their wives gaze at them from the
    windows,
See how well dress'd, see how orderly they conduct themselves.

Worse and worse—can't you stand it? are you retreating?
Is this hour with the living too dead for you?

Retreat then — pell-mell!
To your graves — back — back to the hills old limpers!
I do not think you belong here anyhow.

*Finally, a macabre suggestion for improving the parade.*

But there is one thing that belongs here — shall I tell you what it is, gentlemen of Boston?

I will whisper it to the mayor, he shall send a committee to England,
They shall get a grant from the Parliament, go with a cart to the royal vault,
Dig out King George's coffin, unwrap him quick from the grave-clothes, box up his bones for a journey,
Find a swift Yankee clipper — here is freight for you, black-bellied clipper,
Up with your anchor — shake out your sails — steer straight toward Boston bay.

Now call for the President's marshal again, bring out the government cannon,
Fetch home the roarers from Congress, make another procession, guard it with foot and dragoons.

This centre-piece for them;
Look, all orderly citizens — look from the windows, women!

The committee open the box, set up the regal ribs, glue those that will not stay,
Clap the skull on top of the ribs, and clap a crown on top of the skull.

You have got your revenge, old buster — the crown is come to its own, and more than its own.

Stick your hands in your pockets, Jonathan — you are a made man from this day,
You are mighty cute — and here is one of your bargains.

So it ends, this strange poem, with a crack like a bullwhip, with a dry Yankee chuckle, almost with a jet of irreverent tobacco-juice on the old bones of that old bonehead, His Majesty King George III. And yet, next to that comical and boldly irreverent poem, in the same collection, and on the same page, there comes another fine poem which nearly all Europeans could understand. It is called, simply, 'Europe.' It is an evocation of the European revolution of 1848 which failed where the American revolution had succeeded. It describes the rebellions of country after country, crushed out under cavalry hoofs, blasted to pieces by shells, drowned in blood, buried under the re-established privileges of kings and oligarchs throughout the European lands. It personifies Liberty,

> Its feet upon the ashes and the rags, its hand tight to the throats of kings.

That bitterness, that sense of heroic and tragic failure, many Europeans could comprehend. What they would find difficult would be the nonchalant optimism of the 'Boston Ballad.' They would find it hard to understand the almost cynical realism with which it dismisses the old heroic ghosts, and at the same time satirizes the purblind cheerful descendants of those ghosts, the heirs of the liberty they fought for. And the final few lines, in which the spirit of the United States appears, not as a majestic demigod, a Winged Victory, but rather as a Yankee business man who put across his first and smartest deal when he traded an old spavined king off for a spry young colt of a republic —

Stick your hands in your pockets, Jonathan — you are a made man from this day,
You are mighty cute — and here is one of your bargains...

that optimistic dismissal of the past and confident trust in the present, that almost cynical informality, would, for most Europeans, be shallow or clumsy or even repulsive. I wonder whether Whitman himself could have written such a poem after the outbreak of the Civil War.

But it is a truly American tone, that blend of realism and idealism, that half-deliberate awkwardness. We see it in the bearlike pawing and roaring of Thomas Wolfe, and in the hard bull-like energy of Ernest Hemingway. The same angularity, the same ostentatious naïveté, comes out in much of the best American art: for instance, in the dancing of Martha

Graham (think of her *Appalachian Spring* and *Frontier* and *American Provincials*), and in the music of Aaron Copland — still more, in that of Charles Ives, who has a fine orchestral piece very much in the same spirit as Whitman's poem, where two raucous and amateurish brass bands blend in a discord which is crude and yet inexpressibly touching. It is in the painting of Grant Wood and Andrew Wyeth. It is essential in the novels of Herman Melville and William Faulkner. Whitman does not feel ashamed of his awkwardness: he boasts of it:

Not youth pertains to me,
Nor delicatesse, I cannot beguile the time with talk,
Awkward in the parlor, neither a dancer nor elegant,
In the learn'd coterie sitting constrain'd and still, for learning inures
    not to me,
Beauty, knowledge, inure not to me — yet there are two or three
    things inure to me,
I have nourish'd the wounded and sooth'd many a dying soldier,
And at intervals waiting or in the midst of camp,
Composed these songs.

(Even the misuse of the odd word *inure* is deliciously appropriate to Walt.)

It is in all of Whitman's poetry, this strange simplicity which Europeans would see as clumsiness. It fills his superb elegy on the memory of Lincoln — the poem which is set in springtime and graced by the perfume of flowers and the song of a bird. A non-American poet would surely have used the lovely word *April*, evoked spring and the cool aristocratic fragrance of a pleasure-garden. Not Whitman. With his Quaker ancestry, he will not even say *April*. Instead, he recalls

the Fourth-month eve at sundown.

His flowers grow not in a garden, but in the half-neglected space in front of a working farm:

the dooryard fronting an old farm-house near the white-wash'd
    palings.

And his bird is not the elegant, almost mythical nightingale, but something more native to America, a Thoreau of birds:

> In the swamp in secluded recesses,
> A shy and hidden bird is warbling a song.
> Solitary the thrush,
> The hermit withdrawn to himself, avoiding the settlements,
> Sings by himself a song.

Gazing at that picture, which might be by Thomas Eakins, we see that one of Whitman's truly American qualities should not be called awkwardness, but realism, complete realism. He saw the beauty of ordinary things. Very few men who try to write poetry can do that. Sometimes, for a whole generation or more, poetry is apparently determined to ignore the beauty of ordinary things. Distinguished poets do not see it, do not care about it, or perceive it only in flashes. It was only when W. B. Yeats was growing old that his eye began to turn away from visions of the remote past and dreams of the elusive occult, to look at the cold rough stone of an Irish wall, and to hear with delight the nesting jackdaws chatter and scream.

Whitman's rough-handed bluntness is enjoyable when it is a form of fun. But it rises to a higher level of poetry when it voices the delight of the farmer in growing things and the daily earth. In one of his finest poems, which scarcely any other poet could have written, he looked at the land, and saw it as *compost*. Compost means death and decomposition; but it also means new life. For Whitman the new life was not merely the cherry blossom and the daffodil, but the young onion and the cornstalk.

So he says, in 'This Compost,'

The grass of spring covers the prairies,
The bean bursts noiselessly through the mould in the garden,
The delicate spear of the onion pierces upward,
The apple-buds cluster together on the apple-branches,

(and now a wonderful mythopoeic line)

The resurrection of the wheat appears with pale visage out of its
    graves,
The tinge awakes over the willow-tree and the mulberry-tree,
The he-birds carol mornings and evenings while the she-birds sit
    on their nests,
The young of poultry break through the hatch'd eggs,
The new-born of animals appear, the calf is dropt from the cow,
    the colt from the mare,
Out of its little hill faithfully rise the potato's dark green leaves.
Out of its hill rises the yellow maize-stalk, the lilacs bloom in the
    dooryards.

There is much nonsense in Whitman, there is a great deal of
sentiment which now seems rather mawkish, there is some ob-
trusive eroticism, but there is also one of the finest qualities
of the American artist — the power to look at people, and the
earth, and the trees and the crops and the animals, just as they
are, and to love them all.

## *Professor Paradox*

---

ON THE WALL of my study there hang two portraits of classical scholars. One shows a kindly figure with a huge domed head and peaceful eyes, gazing off into the distance as though he were listening to music. That is Gilbert Murray. From the frame of the other there looks out an unpleasant but intelligent person, who might well be an English country lawyer. Behind him there are a table heaped with books and a packed bookcase. He wears an old-fashioned suit with a single collar and a broad ascot tie. He is a gray-headed man with black eyebrows. A bushy white mustache, trained downward at the ends, curls around and does something to conceal a firm mouth. There is a permanent frown between his eyebrows, and he gazes steadily, not to say rigidly, at the onlooker with an expression of hostility and rejection. This is A. E. Housman.

Housman was a paradox. I have been thinking about him, off and on, for nearly thirty years, and I still cannot understand all his character and all his work. There are some things about him which no one will ever understand now. And yet

I have not been able simply to dismiss him from my mind, and to stop wondering what made him tick. His portrait confronts me every day — as unsympathetic and repellent as Gilbert Murray's is attractive and encouraging; there is much to admire in his career as a scholar, for he was at one time the best Latinist in Britain, one of the three best in the world; and then there is his lovely poetry — three tiny volumes, *A Shropshire Lad, Last Poems*, and the posthumous *More Poems*. A distinguished man, but a difficult one.

That long and busy life, 1859 to 1936, produced three small collections of short lyrics, about 150 in all. They are nearly all about youth and love and youthful sorrow; some about soldiering; some about crime and death and suicide — all treated in a manner which breathes youthfulness, which is filled with images of youth (spring flowers, folk music and country dancing, sport and hill-climbing) and empathy with nature; they are not about men and women, but about lads and girls; and their very rhythms are the rhythms of the ballad and the folk song, unsophisticated and uncomplex. They are charming. But is it not a paradox that the man who wrote them was, to the world, a cold, bitter, touchy, taciturn professor, who seemed to have been born elderly, whose best friends were afraid of him, whose brother was accustomed to receiving woundingly cruel letters from him, and who kept a personal notebook full of savage epigrams (with the names of the victims left blank) to be introduced into reviews or conversations whenever he found a suitable opportunity for giving pain?

His work in the classics also was rather paradoxical. If you heard that a professor of the classical languages had written a collection of original poems which made his name famous throughout the English-speaking world, you would expect that he would devote himself to sympathetic literary appreciation in Greek and Latin; that he would use his understanding of poetic creation to penetrate further into the minds of the great classical poets; and that his books would contain elucidations of their artistic technique, their rich vocabulary, their multiple meanings, all the most human but most difficult part

of their work. Not so Housman. His chief achievement as a
classical scholar was an edition of the five volumes of Manilius,
an obscure Latin poet who wrote a poem about astronomy and
astrology. Housman spent thirty years on this work, and his
major effort was directed toward two things, both unpoetic —
explaining the complexities of Greco-Roman astrological theory, and removing the corruptions introduced into the text by
medieval scribes.

His poems present a further paradox, particularly when they
are read all through from beginning to end. The paradox is
this. They are all apparently straightforward and direct, like
this:

> Loveliest of trees, the cherry now
> Is hung with bloom along the bough,
> And stands about the woodland ride
> Wearing white for Eastertide.*

In this stanza the meter is ordinary ballad rhythm, the rhymes
are simple couplets, the words (although charged with poetry)
are not unusual, the entire stanza is a single calm sentence, and
the thought is simply a description plus a metaphor. And so
it is with nearly every stanza, nearly every poem, in Housman's
lyrical works.

They are clear and easy to understand — separately. But it
is not easy to see what they are about, all together. We can
understand one poem by itself; then a second; and then a
third. But when we try to understand them as a whole, we fail.
Yet Housman published them in carefully arranged groups.
The poems were intended to be understood, but they cannot
be. They are both explicit and obscure. They are frank, but
limited, utterances. They represent both the betrayal and the
concealment of a secret. This ambivalence becomes still clearer
when we read some of the poems which Housman's brother
discovered and published after his death: for these are much

---

* *A Shropshire Lad* 2

more candid than the earlier poems, as though he had grown tired of keeping his secret.

I hope no one will think that we *ought not* to discuss what lies behind these poems. Anyone who publishes a book is saying something to the world. He wishes to be heard. He wants his words and his thought to be discussed and remembered. Housman was a professor of Latin. He knew well how minutely scholars will examine the models, the techniques, the inspiration, and the philosophy of any poet who is worth reading. He knew this well, for on the title page of one of his prose works he put the phrase from Horace, *nescit uox missa reuerti*, 'a word once spoken cannot return.' If he had not wished to betray something of his own life, he need only have kept his poems unpublished, or circulated them privately among a few friends; and, since he was a distinguished classicist, he would still have made a name for himself in other ways. But he published *A Shropshire Lad* at his own expense, after several publishers had refused it. Therefore his poems and their meaning were meant to be discussed.

Both his poetry and his life were public, and yet secretive. They illuminate each other.

A. E. Housman was born in 1859 — not in Shropshire, but in a neighboring county. At Oxford, where he attended St. John's College, he went out for various university prizes, but won none of them. There are two stages in the degree at which he was aiming. In the first stage (the classical languages and literatures) he got first-class honors. In the second part (philosophy and history) he failed absolutely, and left Oxford with far poorer prospects than he had had when he entered the University. This bitter disappointment darkened his entire life.

He spent the next ten years or so atoning for it. To support himself he got a minor job in the civil service, worked at it daily, and spent the late afternoons and evenings in the British Museum, where he did specialized research on problems of classical poetry, particularly textual criticism. Gradually he made a reputation by publishing learned articles which marked him out as one of the most promising scholars of his day. In 1892, at the age of thirty-three, he became professor of Latin at London University. There he studied hard and taught a little, publishing more and better studies in the technical areas of classical scholarship, until in 1905 he was appointed Kennedy Professor of Latin at Cambridge. There he remained until his death in 1936.

He brought out *A Shropshire Lad* in 1896, when he was thirty-seven. His *Last Poems* appeared when he was sixty-three, in 1922, followed by a still smaller group published posthumously and edited by his brother, Laurence Housman.

One further paradox appears in his poetry. The lyrics in these three volumes are usually melancholy, and sometimes painfully sad. Personally Housman appeared to be a glum and disagreeable man, who seldom smiled. But he also wrote very funny poems, parodies, and squibs. His 'Fragment of a Greek Tragedy' is one of the most brilliant and penetrating poetic parodies ever written. And consider this epigram, which he thought of one morning while shaving. He had just been reading of the election of a new Pope — always a long and oppressive ceremony — and he wrote:

> It is a fearful thing to be
>   The Pope.
> That cross will not be laid on me,
>   I hope.
> A righteous God would not permit
>   It.
> The Pope himself must often say,
> After the labours of the day,
> 'It is a fearful thing to be
>   Me.'

In fact, Housman was two people, a professor and a poet. As a professor, he wrote a lot and lectured regularly. As a poet, he wrote little and was seldom seen. That second side of him was scarcely known to those who survived to talk about him — including his brother Laurence, his publisher Grant Richards, and Fellows of his own College. They could not understand him fully. They gave differing accounts of his character. But they all knew him later in life, after he had had the experiences which (as he himself declared) created his poetry. These acquaintances (or friends?) speak of him only as he was after the age of thirty-five or so.

Now, nearly all his poems are about youth. Therefore they refer to something that happened to him in his youth. The great public tragedy of his youthful life was his failure to use his brains properly and to make his way directly into a distinguished career as a scholar. It might appear that his debacle in Oxford was the disaster which created most of his poetry — the wish for death, the hatred of the world, the incurable loneliness, all these are the accompaniment of failure.

But no. It was not that kind of failure. As one reads his poems one sees that the failure had something to do, not with ambition, but with love. Again and again he speaks of lost love, love misunderstood, love ending in bitter separation, love ending in death or the wish for death. And so one wonders whether he had been in love with some girl who mistreated him: especially when one hears that he usually spoke of women with hatred, and detested meeting them. But then one rereads his three volumes of poetry. The love in them is sometimes, but not always, love for a girl. It is more often love for a friend, who did not understand or who would not listen, and who went far away — enlisting in the army, or dying abruptly, or vanishing in the illimitable distance. This is such a poem:

> Because I liked you better
> Than suits a man to say,
> It irked you, and I promised
> To throw the thought away.
>
> To put the world between us
> We parted, stiff and dry;
> 'Good-bye,' said you, 'forget me.'
> 'I will, no fear,' said I.\*

But he did not forget; he could not.

---

\* *More Poems* 31

Two or three times we find poems — especially among those published after Housman's death — in which he says that the laws of God and man can scarcely be kept and are meaningless to the poet. There is one strange lyric about a youth who is hanged simply 'for the colour of his hair' although he has tried to conceal it by dyeing it.

And when we look more closely into Housman's biography, we see that he had one special friend, from whom he later parted, and of whom he could never speak without emotion. This was a young scientist called Moses Jackson. With Jackson he shared rooms when he was at Oxford; apparently it was from Jackson that he learned how to be idle and to miss his first-class honors; even after that, in London, he lived with Jackson and with Jackson's younger brother. Now, the crisis which Housman's poems describe happened to him when he was twenty-four or twenty-five. In real life, at the age of twenty-seven, Housman moved away to another house, where he settled down to live alone. A year afterward Jackson got a job in India, and departed.

> Such leagues apart the world's ends are,
> We're like to meet no more.*

They seldom did. A few years later the younger Jackson died of typhoid.† But Housman never forgot them. His greatest work, the edition of Manilius, was dedicated 'To M. J. Jackson, who despises these studies,' with an exquisite elegiac poem in Latin by Housman; and among his papers after his death, his brother found Jackson's last letter, written to him when he was about sixty, with every faintly penciled word gone over in ink, to make it last a little longer.

Somewhere in those early years lies the secret which Housman wished both to reveal and to conceal. All that was left to him — after Jackson went to the other side of the world and his young brother died — was a cold heart, filled with bitterness increasing year by year; a memory of friendship,

---

* *A Shropshire Lad* 22
† See 'A.J.J.': *Last Poems* 42

inextricably mixed with suffering and a sense of undeserved
guilt; warm emotions which were allowed to appear only now
and then, always with embarrassment and constraint and remorse; occasional kindness to a young man with a frank face
and an open heart; much cruelty about women, coupled with
a certain taste for indecency which appeared now and then in
his specialist articles (one of them, sent to the chief British
classical periodical, was so revolting that the editors rejected
it even though it was in Latin; Housman was furious and had
it published in a German magazine); a determinedly selfish
gourmandise; an acknowledged preference for Epicureanism
over Stoicism, and for Cyrenaicism, the cynical philosophy
which teaches that nothing matters but the pleasure of the
moment, above them both; of course no trace of Christian
religious feeling; and, behind it all, what he himself called

> The mortal sickness of a mind
> Too unhappy to be kind.*

That was what created the hard, bitter, silent face that
looks out from his portrait. If he had not written so well,
thought so hard, and sung so sweetly, I should take the picture
down. And yet, when I look at those harsh eyes, I seem to
see courage, and pain, and a soft heart which was hardened by
some evil fortune as well as by its own folly. Although Housman denied that he was a Stoic, there is a Stoical courage in
one of the poems he conceived in his worst time: the poem of
the spoiled spring and the rain ruining the young flowers
which ends

> The troubles of our proud and angry dust
> Are from eternity, and shall not fail.
> Bear them we can, and if we can we must.
> Shoulder the sky, my lad, and drink your ale.†

Housman once said that poetry was intended to harmonize our
sufferings. Without his poetry, both his sufferings and ours
would be more difficult to understand, and far less easy to
endure, or to forgive.

---

* *A Shropshire Lad* 41
† *Last Poems* 9

## *The Old Wizard*

———————————

A WIZARD; a seer; a mystic; an explorer of the unknown. All these descriptions would suit one of our greatest modern poets.

I saw him once, and spoke with him, when he was nearly seventy years old. I recall him as tall, and proud, and grim; he was wearing a baggy gray suit and a woolly tie, and high boots, up to his knees. They looked adventurous, as though he were about to set off on a dangerous voyage, and they made it clear that he did not relish being shut up within four peaceful walls and a quiet roof. Our host told me that the wizard had some malady which the boots were meant to alleviate; but they looked characteristic of him as a ruffian, a buccaneer, what he himself called 'a wild old wicked man.' He was harsh to me when we talked, and he was brusque to our host. At the time I put this down to my own youth and inadequacy; but now I know the wild old wicked man was terribly unhappy, and found it difficult to be kind, even to himself. He was the poet William Butler Yeats: he hated old age, and his old body, and most of the life that surrounded him.

He said so himself, in a pathetic poem written in the last few years of his tormented life.

Some think it a matter of course that chance
Should starve good men and bad advance,
That if their neighbours figured plain,
As though upon a lighted screen,
No single story would they find
Of an unbroken happy mind,
A finish worthy of the start.
Young men know nothing of this sort,
Observant old men know it well;
And when they know what old books tell,
And that no better can be had,
Know why an old man should be mad.*

He himself, in those years, was very nearly mad. The madness
of youth is painful but endurable. The madness of old age is
unbearable: for it is a struggle between the principle of life
and the principle of death, the vigorous spirit and the decaying body, public reputation and private passion, duty and
personality, decorum and spontaneity, the finite necessity and
the hope of infinity. That was the madness which Yeats was
grappling with toward the end. Violent echoes of the struggle
come out in his final poems: there is a good study of them by
Vivienne Koch, called *The Tragic Phase*; but the poems themselves outrun any analysis.

Yeats was born nearly a century ago, in 1865, and died in
1939. His parents were Protestants; and apparently his ancestry was, like that of Swift and Shaw and other Anglo-Irish
authors, a painful and difficult mixture of English and Celtic,
poverty and riches and learning and ignorance and orthodoxy
and eccentricity and duty and rebellion. Yeats himself said his
immediate kinsmen bore the Cornish name of Pollexfen and
the English name of Middleton. He recollected hearing stories
about some of his ancestors who had fought for the British
crown — one of his uncles was killed in the Battle of New
Orleans — and about others who had been the friends of Irish
patriots; his nurses and playmates in childhood were Celtic
Irish, but his father and mother felt their cultural home was

* 'Why should not old men be mad?'

London, where Yeats was brought up and lived for some of his most active years. He wrote in English; I doubt if he ever managed to learn Irish Gaelic. And he spent much of his energy trying to bridge the gulf between the English and the Irish theater. The Irish have always been wonderful story-tellers, but they had never had wholly native plays and play-wrights until Yeats and his friends got to work. Yeats and a few others determined to add something new to Irish litera-ture: a collection of plays on heroic and fantastic subjects from Irish myth and history, written in the English language. Such a thing was bound to have only a limited success. To begin with, most of the themes Yeats chose were shaped not for spoken drama but for storytelling. How can anyone stage a play whose climax is a battle between a warrior prince and the waves of the wild sea? Such things are essentially epic, and undramatic: they must happen off stage and merely be de-scribed: this means that the drama must change back into the story from which it was drawn. And Yeats's poetic plays were not clearly understood by the English-speaking world; not only people living in England but audiences in Toronto and Edinburgh and New York were bound to be puzzled and even estranged by those wild stories that stemmed from the remote pre-Christian world of the Celtic Iron Age. On the other hand the Irish nationalists could not wholly admire them either, since they were written in English and recognizably belonged to the English poetic tradition. Yeats says himself that the first poems to move him were a group of Orangemen's rhymes and Macaulay's *Lays of Ancient Rome*; * from these he went on to Scott and Shakespeare, then to Byron, Shelley, Tennyson, Browning, and Spenser; much of his mature work echoes the cadences of Swinburne. His dramatic work was bound to cre-ate, or rather to express, a conflict that proved to be insoluble.

Yeats was a man of conflicts; and no one is quite clear to this day what he was trying to do, what he hoped to make of

---

* On these poems see p. 197 of this book.

his own active life and unusual talents. He did not know himself. Sometimes he thought it was his duty to write only for a small community of spiritual aristocrats, without caring for the opinion of the mob; and yet, when his work was unsympathetically received by the general public, he was bitterly offended. Later, when he was given the Nobel Prize and almost universally acclaimed, he was often astonished and often ill at ease. As he himself wrote,

> Much did I rage when young,
> Being by the world oppressed,
> But now with flattering tongue
> It speeds the parting guest.*

Once the Irish Republic had been established, he worked hard to strengthen its culture; and yet he despised the whole business of states and republics and governments: he thought it was all bosh compared with the life of the individual and the experience of the spirit. Among his later poems there is a strange little lyric which expresses some of that dissatisfaction and reveals something of his trouble. It is called 'Politics'; and it is headed by a rather pompous and shallow remark from the pen of Thomas Mann:

> In our time the destiny of man presents its meaning in political terms.

Now, Yeats hated abstract statements like that, and broad universal conclusions; he despised political activity as such; and he was a sensual man with a roving eye; so here is what he thought of a political discussion:

> How can I, that girl standing there,
> My attention fix
> On Roman or on Russian
> Or on Spanish politics?
> Yet here's a travelled man that knows
> What he talks about,

---

* 'Youth and Age'

> And there's a politician
> That has read and thought,
> And maybe what they say is true
> Of war and war's alarms,
> But O that I were young again
> And held her in my arms!

Poor Yeats. In such a mood he sounds like the aging Tolstoy. Of course the two men differed in many vital ways. Yeats became a nationalist. Tolstoy ended by ignoring nationalism. Tolstoy was deeply concerned about Christianity, and tried to become like the saints, while most of Yeats's religious thinking was centered on the pagan cults of prehistoric Ireland and the esoteric philosophies of Asia. Tolstoy worried about the peasants, and endeavored to imitate their simplicity; Yeats did not care how the ordinary farm laborers lived, and retreated into a tower to avoid them: can you imagine his working all day in the fields and coming in for dinner, like Tolstoy, sweaty and barefooted? Yeats had a miserably unsatisfactory love affair with a proud, beautiful lady, whereas we are told that Tolstoy's temptations were gypsy women and the pretty peasant girls, so much so that when he was quite old his wife would disguise herself in peasant clothes and follow him into the forest, just in case... Yeats began in the middle class and became more aristocratic, while Tolstoy began as a nobleman and tried to end as a muzhik. But they were both visionaries, they were both strongly sexed, and they were both tormented by their own bodies and tempers. Toward the end of their lives they were both 'wild old wicked men': like King Lear, with the storm raging in their own hearts.

Such storms can be calmed only by religion or by philosophy: so we find that, throughout much of his life, Yeats was occupied by philosophical meditation. In particular, his letters to Sturge Moore are full of closely argued discussions of complex questions in philosophy. There is one interesting exchange on a single problem which sounds crazy, but is really valuable. Yeats explains that Ruskin once picked up a ghost cat and threw it out of the window; and he says he himself once saw a real picture and a ghost picture side by side. The problem is to define in what sense both pictures can be called real. Of course this problem can scarcely be solved: it is the problem of *appearance and reality*. But it is fascinating to watch Yeats grappling with it — since he, much more than most of us, was aware that there are different orders, or levels, of existence, and that he (like ourselves) lived in two worlds at the same time.

In politics also, Yeats lived in one world but belonged to another. He never, I think, believed that democracy was a reasonable and admirable way of life. His letters show him reading Spengler with sympathy, and the English philosopher Wyndham Lewis with enthusiasm. Wyndham Lewis is not much read now, partly because his style is so crude, partly because his tone is so repellent, partly because his thought is terribly uneven; but he is a convinced and bitter critic of many principles of democracy. Yeats followed him — not as far as fascism, but certainly toward admiration of the Superman, and the belief that our world is sustained and made meaningful chiefly by the work of noble families and exclusive groups. Most of us live in a crowd and the present moment. Yeats was solitary, gave himself only to a few friends, existed chiefly in the past and the unseen.

But it was neither his philosophical discussions nor his political thinking which really filled his mind and strengthened his poetry. Yeats felt that many conflicts which beset him, both within his own self and throughout his world, could never be solved by reason alone. And so, it seems, he regarded himself not chiefly as a poet but as a magician. Much of his best poetry is about magic; and some of his best poetry almost *is* magic. If you read his life history, you soon see that he thought far less about the techniques of literature than about the techniques of magic. I do not mean simply mysticism, which is a special kind of meditation upon the nature of the divine and an effort to enter a new relationship with it: I mean actual magic, practices and utterances which evoke and control supernatural forces. Yeats's wife sympathized with him and assisted him, for she was a medium; and it was largely from revelations obtained through her that he wrote the strangest, most consistent, and deepest of all his works, the mysterious panorama of the spiritual world called *A Vision*.

Now, most of us are not magicians, and are not mystically inclined. We find it difficult to take this kind of thing seriously, or at best to tolerate it only because it helps to produce good poetry. But there is another way to understand it and even to approve it. It is to regard Yeats's magical activities through the eyes of the psychologist Carl Jung. In a remarkable analysis of the handbooks of medieval alchemy,* Jung points out that the alchemists (and by implication many of the magicians) of the Middle Ages were in fact engaged in a *spiritual* exploration. Their aim was not solely, perhaps not even chiefly, to obtain wealth or any material success; but rather to reduce the conflicts in the human soul to a final harmony. One of the deepest lessons of Jung is that in order to become great one must accept the necessity of suffering. That is what Yeats would never accept; and it is because he rejected the full understanding of tragedy that he never managed to produce a single great work of poetry. Through poetry, Yeats could only express the conflicts that tormented him. It was through *magic* that, for a time at least, he could transcend them.

---

* C. G. Jung, *Psychology and Alchemy* (translated by R. F. C. Hull), Bollingen Series XX, Pantheon Books, New York, 1953

## The Pessimist

---

IT IS SAD that the word *romantic* has been so misused and vulgarized. If it had not been, we could call this American poet a romantic figure. Most of the many meanings implied in the word would fit him: unorthodox, strongly individual, imaginative and emotional, daring, careless of routine success, a lover only of the material things which can be loved without desire (not money and machines, but mountains, waters, birds, animals); lonely, too, lonely. Yes, he is a romantic figure.

His name is Robinson Jeffers. He lives in Carmel, California, in a house which he and his sons built, stone by stone. He is past seventy now. When he first settled in Carmel, it was a small windswept village smelling of trees and the sea, inconveniently simple, unfrequented, unfashionable, a good place for a man to be himself and nobody else. Now — at least in the summer — it is a bright and busy seaside town, with a beach, cocktail bars, branches of very chi-chi metropolitan stores, and a rich flow of traffic from the rest of California. In those quaint narrow streets there is hardly room for all the Cadillacs. This is the same kind of change which, in our own lifetime, has infected many other places: Montauk, Acapulco, Oxford, Provincetown, the list grows every year. Mr. Jeffers does not enjoy the change. He did not expect it when he built his home there on the lonely peninsula near Point Lobos. But he is a pessimist, and he has long been convinced that mankind spoils nearly everything it touches. He does not, therefore, see much of the beauties of prosperous, expanding California. He prefers to watch the ocean which is full of life but which is too cold and powerful for us to swim in, the rocky hills which will not grow grapefruit but have a superhuman dignity of their own.

Mr. Jeffers is not a popular poet. He never wished to be a popular poet, he has shunned every device which leads toward popularity, he avoids publicity, he will not lecture and give readings and play the guitar, he has no immediate disciples, and has formed no school. It is not that he is deliberately obscure. You can understand all his poetry, if you read it with care: far more easily than the work of his contemporaries Eliot and Pound and Valéry. It is not that he was once ambitious, and is now soured by lack of recognition: far from it. His poetry is not meant to be liked. It is meant, I think, to do people good.

But it is very remarkable poetry, and he is a very distinguished man. America has produced great statesmen, soldiers, engineers, explorers, civilizers, inventors, and actors. It has produced — in nearly two centuries — very few great poets. Robinson Jeffers may prove to be one of those great poets. I say *may*, because I honestly do not know whether he will or not. But if he does, he will be like some other solitary artists who were recognized during their lives as odd, provocative, masterful, self-sufficient, and eccentric; and whose work turned out to be as durable as stone. Such was Euripides, whom Mr. Jeffers admires and somewhat resembles; such was Lucretius; such was Dante; such were Breughel, and Monteverdi, and Poe. It takes time for a good work of poetry to prove what it is.

There is a handsome one-volume edition of Mr. Jeffers' *Selected Poetry*, published by Random House. It contains about six hundred pages. Not much for a life's work, you may think; but many of these poems are the result of thirty or forty years of thought, and they are intended to live ten times as long.

Mr. Jeffers writes three different types of poem. Some are meditative lyrics, anywhere between ten and forty lines long — a thought, a brief description of something seen, a memory, or a vision. Some are long narrative poems — that is a good form which we are foolish to neglect nowadays: a story told in verse is harder to do, but often far more effective, than a story told in prose. There are about a dozen of these exciting, lurid, visionary poetic tales set in the wild hill-country of central California near Monterey. They are about bitter loves, and about hatreds more satisfying than love. Crime, sensuality, madness haunt them. Brothers kill each other. Fearful illicit passions rage through them like forest fires.

In the same form Mr. Jeffers has also written several dramas, and poems partly narrative and partly dramatic, most of them on plots from Greek tragedy. The best known is his adaptation of the *Medea*, which was (he says himself) inspired by Judith Anderson's art and personality, and which showed us her magnificent acting in New York during the winter of 1947-8. These pieces also move among the grim ideas which have long filled his mind and which are the basis of his poetry.

Both the lyrics and the stories are written in large, muscular, unrhymed lines, with an irregular pulse which is basically a new sort of blank verse, with a long rhythm (about ten beats to the line) which reminds me irresistibly of the Pacific Ocean hammering at the rocks. It is intended to echo the ebb and flow of excitement, the interchange of narrative and speech. For my taste it is usually too irregular, because I can remember poetry only when it has a fairly steady pattern; still, it is free and powerful and eloquent, anything but monotonous and conventional.

Now, if I try to explain what Mr. Jeffers' themes are, I shall risk distorting them, oversimplifying them, making them too naïve or brutal, breaking up their subtle interrelations, vulgarizing a poetic statement by changing it into a Message. And yet his work is very cohesive, so that one can bring out its leading motives, as one could not do with a wayward poet like Yeats; and his ideas are so strange that unless we are boldly introduced to them, we may not comprehend them at all. He is a tragic poet; and tragedy is a truth which is hard to understand.

First, let us look at one of his short poems. Through it we can see his manner and a few of his leading thoughts. It is called 'Summer Holiday.'

> When the sun shouts and people abound
> One thinks there were the ages of stone and the age of
> bronze
> And the iron age; iron the unstable metal;
> Steel made of iron, unstable as his mother; the towered-up
> cities
> Will be stains of rust on mounds of plaster.
> Roots will not pierce the heaps for a time, kind rains
> will cure them,
> Then nothing will remain of the iron age
> And all these people but a thigh-bone or so, a poem
> Stuck in the world's thought, splinters of glass
> In the rubbish dumps, a concrete dam far off in the
> mountain. . .

Now, there is no sex in this, while there is a great deal in Mr. Jeffers' long poems. There is no clash of personalities, while his major works are boldly dramatic. But the strong pessimism is characteristic; so is the sense of history; so is the peculiar blend of deep, long thought and deeply felt but controlled emotion; so is the sense of the earth — our mother, our home, and our grave.

You may not think this an attractive poem. But you will agree it is memorable. You will remember it. Through remembering it, you may come to admire it, and to understand more of an eminent but deliberately isolated American writer.

Mr. Jeffers, you see, believes a number of terrible things. They are not all true for Christians, who believe in redemption; but they are true for many other inhabitants of this world.

First, he believes that men and women are animals. For him, there is *no difference* between a delicatessen, or a fur store, and a pack of coyotes hunting down a deer: except that the coyotes hunt and devour in hot blood, whereas we breed the meat-cattle and slaughter them and trap the furry animals and skin them with a cold greedy purposefulness which is more disgusting. Many animals are cruel and noble. Their cruelty contains style and courage, the cougar and the hawk. Men and women are usually cruel. When they are cruel and mean, they are loathsome animals. When they are cruel and noble, they may be noble animals.

Then, Mr. Jeffers utterly abominates war, modern war. He sees it as a symptom and a cause of what he considers the decadence of our civilization. He believes that growing populations and multiplying machines all over the world have distorted the balance of nature, and that war is now the greatest of all such distortions. His last book was full of violent isolationism. One might expect him to regard the whole of warfare as an understandable activity like the ferocity of animals: to think of the shark when he sees a submarine, to admire the flight of bombers as much as the flight of the hawks; but he cannot.

Third, he is unlike most of us in his view of happiness. Most people, I think he would say, want easy pleasure and drowsy happiness. But real fulfillment is not pleasure: it is something more powerful. Effort and suffering are more natural than rest and enjoyment. Pain lasts longer and is more real than pleasure.

Fourth — the fourth of Mr. Jeffers' themes is the grandest of all, and the most wretched, and the most difficult. It is this. *The human race is not needed.* It is an infestation from which the planet is suffering. Look at a wooded mountainside, with the bear and the deer in the forests, the badger and the fox in the brush, birds and their cousins the reptiles crawling and flying above and below. Can you truthfully say that it would

improve that scene to drive a six-lane motor-highway across it?
Or to put a town in the middle of it? And when people say
that it would be a terrific disaster if another war blotted out
the human race, do they mean it? Do they mean that the
mountains would weep, the rivers run backward with grief,
and the animals and the birds go into mourning? Or would
the earth begin its peaceful work of purification, covering up
— with falling leaves and drifting dust and sifting earth and
growing plants and moving hillsides and encroaching forests —
our cities, our factories, and our prisons? And then would the
whole planet, with its other children, heave a single, long,
unanimous sigh of relief?

These are some of the ideas which — unless I have gravely
misunderstood him — Robinson Jeffers holds. He also has an
extremely complex and difficult conception of sex, and the
family, as a source of tragedy. He has made these themes into
fine poetry. He does not think they are pleasant ideas. But
he thinks they are true. He thinks that they have the truth of
nature; that they are somehow part of nature. And he loves
nature, wild nature. In this he is more like a primitive American than a modern man — like the Indians who climbed Chief
Mountain to be alone and see visions, or the early white
hunters who went out into the West because they loved land
and animals without humanity. But he is also like several distinguished American artists: Thoreau; Melville; Martha Graham, and Ernest Hemingway. Most of nature, he knows, is not
pleasant; but what is a thunderstorm? What is a forest fire?
What is a north wind bringing bitter snow over the mountains?
or the ocean surging against a rocky cliff? The sound, the
power, the terror, and the nobility of these things make the
truth of Robinson Jeffers' poetry.

## Mr. Eliot

---

> How unpleasant to meet Mr. Eliot!
> With his features of clerical cut,
> And his brow so grim
> And his mouth so prim
> And his conversation, so nicely
> Restricted to What Precisely
> And If and Perhaps and But.
> How unpleasant to meet Mr. Eliot! . . .

So says T. S. Eliot himself, in a sweet-and-sour parody of Edward Lear, the eccentric, aesthete, and humorist of a century ago. It is a funny poem — one of a series called *Five-Finger Exercises*, which are full of parodic allusions to Shakespeare and Keats and Tennyson and Lewis Carroll and Sherlock Holmes and who knows what else?

> How unpleasant to meet Mr. Eliot!
> With his features of clerical cut,
> And his brow so grim. . .

However, it is not true. I have never met him myself. I have been in the same room, at least twice, with a host who wanted to introduce me to him; but someone always came up and shook Mr. Eliot's hand and said, 'You know I *loved* your play, the one about the cocktail party,' and he smiled politely and said he was glad. My wife met him later, though, and says he was quite charming. He is a tall, slender man, sometimes bent into the shape of a question mark. He looks like a senior British civil servant; or an eminent surgeon visiting a convalescent patient; or a retired diplomat ... He is at the other extreme from the professional romantic, like Walt Whitman with his flying beard, or Carl Sandburg with his healthy open face and boyish hair, the Scandinavian troubadour. He looks distinguished, almost ageless, certainly younger than his years: no heavy wrinkles, no superfluous flesh, even his stoop apparently due to politeness rather than fatigue — although that may be a good disguise, and perhaps he really is very weary.

He is a puzzle. He is a strong character: a powerful personality. He must be. Most literary-minded people of my age have been thinking about him (off and on) for a quarter of a century. And yet he has produced this impact not by self-advertisement and frequent public appearances; he is rather retiring, both in America and in Britain, and rarely makes speeches or gives lectures; nor by writing a great deal, for his entire works could be printed in three or four volumes, and he seldom contributes to magazines or anthologies. No; no. He is a reticent man. He is an enigmatic poet; he wishes to remain a mystery.

In 1952 Mr. Eliot's collected poems and plays were published by Harcourt, Brace in a single volume. The book is already a classic. All over the United States, and in Britain and France and Germany and Italy and Japan and elsewhere, students are working over these cryptic and fragmentary poems, writing essays on them, producing technical and sociological interpretations of them, imitating them in their own compositions, and inevitably converting a living man into a myth. But he and his works are still a puzzle. Nobody fully knows what Mr. Eliot's poetry means, except Eliot himself. And, oddly enough, that is part of its power. That is part of the guarantee that it will last. Long after we are dead, people will be arguing about the meaning of Eliot's poems, music will be composed and pictures will be painted and more verse will be written, under the inspiration of a few score pages of poetry by Thomas Stearns Eliot, born in St. Louis, Missouri, educated at Harvard and Oxford, naturalized a British subject, self-described as a royalist, an Anglo-Catholic, and a classicist.

It is a surprisingly small body of work to be so powerful. Just over half the volume is a group of plays, *The Cocktail Party*, *The Family Reunion*, and *Murder in the Cathedral*. The total of Eliot's serious non-dramatic poetry comes to about a hundred and fifty pages. One hundred and fifty pages, for a life's work.

That situates him at once with the mystics, the difficult poets, who have spent many years approaching some truth almost too great for understanding, and trying to say something of what they saw. Such have been St. John of the Cross in Spain; and Hölderlin in Germany; and Vaughan and Donne in England; and Mallarmé and Valéry in France; and, in this country, perhaps Poe. These people had a certain experience of life which they found so complex, so dangerous and alarming, so much profounder than normal thought and living, that they could not communicate it in ordinary speech — not even in ordinary poetic speech: only in poetry which was deliberately fragmentary and inadequate and symbolic, in just the same way as language itself, compared with the full richness of certain great experiences, is fragmentary, inadequate, and symbolic. (That is why Dante is such a superb writer. He was one of the very few men in the world's history who have had such a vision and have been able to communicate it as a coherent whole. The effort of doing so, the suffering it cost him, are still visible in the portraits of his strong but tormented face. Most others cannot even think of making a complete exposition of such experiences. So all Eliot's poems about this central adventure are indirect, symbolic, incomplete.)

Now, it is hard to understand why a man should spend much of his life on writing, and publishing, and re-publishing a relatively small collection of poems which do not tell the whole truth about the world clearly and single-mindedly. Say the truth, or keep silent; do not confuse us with puzzles. Why trouble to write and print what is only partly intelligible — what is not *meant* to be fully intelligible?

Let us see how it looks. Much of it is in foreign languages; much of it is quotations lifted from other poets, from the Bible and the Prayer Book; much of it is in broken phrases, which do not form complete sentences and paragraphs. It is as though we overheard a musician not playing, but picking over a piano, trying a new harmony here, recalling a favorite phrase there, passing on to something else, but seldom playing continuously for an entire movement.

> Blown hair is sweet, brown hair over the mouth blown,
> Lilac and brown hair;
> Distraction, music of the flute, stops and steps of the
>     mind over the third stair,
> Fading, fading; strength beyond hope and despair
> Climbing the third stair.*

There we cannot follow the thought because the utterance is not coherent. But elsewhere Eliot speaks continuously, and here we can hardly believe what he says:

> A woman drew her long black hair out tight
> And fiddled whisper music on those strings
> And bats with baby faces in the violet light
> Whistled, and beat their wings
> And crawled head downward down a blackened wall
> And upside down in air were towers
> Tolling reminiscent bells, that kept the hours
> And voices singing out of empty cisterns and exhausted
>     wells. †

These are coherent words, but illogical. They are descriptions of dreams, and suffering, and madness, translated into some-

---

* Eliot, *Ash-Wednesday* III
† Eliot, *The Waste Land* 377-84

thing beautiful. (You know, many people who like poetry and art are led to think that poets and artists ought to describe only beautiful things. They believe that a beautiful poem can *only* be a poem which describes some attractive experience, that a good picture can *only* be a picture of something which would be attractive to look at in real life. This is not true, and neither is the reverse true. There are some eminent artists — their leaders are the great tragedians — who have been able to make fine poetry, art, and music out of misery, squalor, and wretchedness. But sometimes it takes centuries before the public realizes this. I am certain that the early Christian artists would not have ventured to present to their public, as a work of art, a painting or a sculpture of the dead Jesus being lifted off the cross on which he had died; but at the highest points of medieval and Renaissance art, the Descent from the Cross was one of the noblest subjects that an artist could choose.)

So, then, Mr. Eliot's poetry is either incoherent or phantasmagorial; and it is an attempt to describe spiritual effort, and agony, and insanity. Is it unique therefore? or unique in our time? No, far from it. Apparently he is saying what other artists have been saying, often incoherently and fantastically, throughout his lifetime. You remember the pale, meager clowns and paupers of Picasso's 'blue period'; and the wildly distorted, yet powerfully memorable, human bodies and animals of his Civil War picture, *Guernica* (even one of the fragmentary heads in it is a classical profile, as it would be in a similar poem by Eliot). You recall the strange roughness of Prokofiev, his irregular rhythms and his moody wandering over the whole range of musical sound; his deliberate difficulty. You will perhaps think also of the mystical obscurity of Vaughan Williams's Sixth Symphony, and of the drifting harmonies of Benjamin Britten, shrill and faint, making, as Eliot himself says,

> Out of the sea of sound the life of music...*

---

* Chorus IX from 'The Rock'

You remember also how Pavel Tchelitchev in his paintings dissects a woman's head, so that you can still see the deep thoughtful eyes and the handsome profile and the curling hair, but also look through to the somber eternal skull within.

It is unfashionable to admire Salvador Dali, but he is a remarkable painter, and he is sensitive to spiritual currents. Some years ago he was terrified and overpowered by the conception of the atomic bomb. He saw it as the final dissolution of our material universe; and it drove him to meditate upon spiritual structures which are less easily dissolved. Therefore, for the last six or seven years he has been painting pictures which show human and divine figures rushing upward into the air and almost flying into pieces, surrounded by buildings, rocks, and other objects which are flying into pieces; or else floating in mid-air as though suspended by divine power in the moment of an atomic explosion. Perhaps the antithesis is crude: God and the atomic bomb; or more probably I have stated it crudely; but surely the conflict between fragmentation and incoherence on the one hand, and stability and poise on the other, is what we experience in Eliot's poems.

It is as part of that general movement of thought and emotion that Eliot wrote poems which began by being fragmentary and have very slowly become more complete and balanced, even though they are still cryptic. Evidently it is because he found that his world was broken into fragments — into separate meanings all disconnected or in conflict. He first had to state this spiritual disaster in some form which would be connected, even though it was only a collection of fragments, ruins propped up; then he had to think his way through to a new unity; and to state that new unity in poetry. His *Four Quartets* look like the record of the final achievement: that is why the last of them, 'Little Gidding,' contains a long episode closely resembling Dante, and ends with an image related to Dante's vision of God.

Now, is it worth penetrating any further? Is it worth asking what the explosion was? what was the initial disaster which blew Mr. Eliot's life into the fragments he has ever since been reassembling? Would it be an invasion of privacy to do so? No, surely not, provided we use only the poems, which Mr. Eliot himself has so often republished, and therefore wishes to be public knowledge. And yet, as soon as we look closely into the matter, we find ourselves embarrassed. The end is God. But the beginning is apparently sex, and some torments arising out of it. From the first part of Mr. Eliot's life, from his twenties, we have some well-organized little satiric poems about the contrast between Europe and New England, about the inadequacy of the middle-class soul. But then, in *The Waste Land*, and perhaps beginning a little earlier, we see a new experience: an experience of *guilt*, involving terrible weakness and inadequacy, blindness and powerlessness, and a life burned away into premature old age and lifelong repentance. So his poems seem to say. Some catastrophe, whose cause and course can be guessed, but only guessed . . .

We are not intended to know more. But we are meant to see the work of Eliot's mind gradually remaking itself: a negative and largely pagan soul building itself into a sincere and Christian and self-forgetting soul: a heap of ruins reconstructing itself into a shrine. Others in our lifetime have gone through this, or partly through it. It seems to have happened to Aldous Huxley and to Georges Rouault; we know that it happened to C. S. Lewis; outside Christianity, something like it happened to Paul Valéry and Thomas Mann; there are others, like Koestler and Orwell, who endured the initial disintegration and then were never able to reconstruct their fragments except on an improvised and unsatisfying plan.

If this is true, then we ought to think less of Eliot's poems and more of his plays. They are his largest coherent works. They are problems, which contain solutions. They are positive, solid creations. No doubt they are still oblique approaches to the question of guilt, sin, damnation, self-damnation; but they are more consistent and successful approaches: they present a world which is ultimately sane and manageable, even through martyrdom. So with John Donne; his poems are best understood as the prelude to the wisdom of his meditations and sermons. Mr. Eliot's poems, for all their beauty, are only the prelude to his plays, and to the wisdom of his later life. I hope that when his next volume appears it will establish him as a poetic, as a spiritual playwright: for writing plays — which must be filled with sympathy for many different characters — is one of the best ways for such a sufferer to recreate his world.

# The Magic-Maker

---

EVERYONE who enjoys modern poetry knows the name and something of the work of Edward Estlin Cummings. Many know his strong face, sensual but sensitive; many have heard him read his own poetry. Not so many are acquainted with his paintings, or the autobiographical prison record called *The Enormous Room* with which he first became famous; but those who are, find them impressive. Almost everyone who has ever been exposed to modern literature at all knows one thing about Cummings: namely, that he specializes in the freest of free verse — verse which has usually no rhyme, no regular stanza form, no regular danceable or singable rhythm, and which has, beyond that, skillfully distorted syntax, punctuation, and spelling — so that many of his poems make complex patterns on the first page, patterns which, being complex and at first sight obscure, still have a meaning, or rather a net of meanings, and are thus integral parts of the poems themselves.

Here, for instance, is a poem on fog. In a drifting mist, you can never tell whether a shape some distance ahead of you is a tree, or a person, or an effect of light, a visionary shadow; and a man who walks past you seems to change into a ghost as the cloud envelops him. In one of his poems Cummings describes that weird effect in a short lyrical paragraph which could, if necessary, be compressed into this statement:

> Slowliest, under fog's touchings, fingerings, whichs turn into whos, people become un

There are some pleasantly vivid and individual things in this. Cummings implies that fog is something like a sculptor and something like a hypnotist or a magician, since it changes things, very slowly, through its touching and fingering. Then there are two transformations, which are wittily opposed. 'Whichs turn into whos,' because, as you approach something in a fog, you first ask yourself, 'What thing is that?' and then, coming closer, you say, 'Now, who is that?' But, as you move away from them, 'people become un': they cease to be recognizable human beings at all, and become unpeople, without individuality or even humanity, shapes, mere things, vanishing. (The 'un' of the last disappearance is a subtle echo of the 'un' which is the first syllable of the poem.)

However, since fog moves very slothfully and gently, drifting and lapping more softly and smoothly than water, Cummings wants to convey that motion in the very arrangement of his poem. So he sets out his few words in minuscule lines, none longer than two syllables; in four tiny stanzas without punctuation or capital letters; and between them, so that you must read the poem with the same creepingly slow pace as the fog, he breaks up the key word 'slowliest.' The result is this:

> un
> der fog
> 's
> touch
>
> slo
>
> ings
> fin
> gering
> s

wli

whichs
turn
in
to whos

est

people
be
come
un

A charming little thing, isn't it? Even if you did not know that particular poem, you would, if you saw it, recognize that no one but E. E. Cummings could or would have composed it. Although he has written many poems in regular form — particularly sonnets, of which he is a distinguished master — he is best known for these capriciously printed free-verse lyrics; and for the strong, boldly self-defensive and self-assertive personality which lurks behind them, always clearly perceptible but never betraying itself. He is now one of our senior American writers. His poems are on the shelves of every good library. In 1952, he was honored by Harvard, which appointed him Charles Eliot Norton Professor of Poetry; and in his sixty-fifth year, 1958, he became the subject of a full-length biography, *The Magic-Maker: E. E. Cummings,* by Charles Norman (Macmillan). (It is good as far as it goes, but it is rather timid, evades some difficult issues with great suavity, and devotes, in my opinion, far too much time to Cummings's youth and too little to his most difficult period, the discouraging and discouraged middle years.)

He is a strongly built, energetic man, E. E. Cummings, with a great deal of zest for life, a great deal of originality, and a passionate love for art — for all the arts, from the most vulgar burlesque to the loftiest and most esoteric poetry. Yet he has never made a really solid impact on his world. Up to this time, for instance, he has not been awarded the Pulitzer Prize for poetry. He has been subjected to long and humiliating, or chilling, periods of neglect: in the late 1930's, he could not even find a publisher for his poems; and it is only in the last ten or fifteen years that he has once again gained some of the attention which he deserves but refuses to seek out.

There is one reason for this which is powerful, although it may not be obvious. Dylan Thomas, when he felt exuberant, used to say that he was the only British poet who was neither a homosexual nor a Communist; and, in the days when it was fashionable and helpful to be one or the other, or (preferably) both, E. E. Cummings was neither. He went to Russia during the 1930's; he disliked what he saw; he said so, in a curiously intricate and introverted book called *Eimi*. It was bitterly attacked; and some might conjecture that Cummings was put on the black list — although he had already attacked fascism even more violently and much more humorously than communism. Certainly he himself seems to think so; we, who are not concerned with black lists, must consider him not as a tool of politicians, nor as their victim, but as an artist and a man.

Here we come up against a difficulty. Cummings has produced a little shelf of boldly individual, highly original books. Nobody else could have written them. They are his work, in literature. Yet they are curiously ineffective. They are hampered, incomplete, almost evasive. In his first big prose book, *The Enormous Room*, Cummings told how he was thrown into a French concentration camp during the First World War. He filled the book with a marvelously living reality, slashed with humorous contempt for his French jailers and humorous affection for his fellow prisoners, even the vilest of them; he wrote it in violently non-traditional prose, so that it was rather like listening to the conversation of a brilliant man half drunk. Nevertheless, he did not make it what it might have been, one of the world's great prison books — partly because he scornfully ignored the crux of the problem of his own imprisonment, and partly because (even in spite of his sufferings) he could not take the whole thing seriously. The book was praised in Britain by T. E. Lawrence, and I read it soon after it was published there — about 1928, I think; but the essential part of it was an introduction, an adult and thoughtful introduction, by Cummings's father, explaining that Cummings had been arrested simply because, while he was serving with an American ambulance corps in France, one of his friends wrote a few letters home criticizing the French war effort; and if it had not been for that introduction, I should never have understood what the book was all about. Then consider Cummings's essays in prose, many of them written in the 1920's for two much regretted magazines, *The Dial* and *Vanity Fair*. They have recently been republished as *E. E. Cummings: A Miscellany* (Argophile Press, 1958). They are terribly witty, and brisk, but sometimes very silly, and surprisingly often they seem to avoid stating Cummings's true opinion on important facts — as though he were anxious simply to enjoy the cheap pleasure of shocking the booboisie; they sound like Mencken, with all Mencken's impishness, but without Mencken's clarity.

His plays I have read only in fragments, and cannot discuss. His poems are another puzzle. Individual they are; original; sometimes poignant; sometimes obscene; sometimes (in earlier days) loftily and Swinburnianly romantic; sometimes fantastically comic. But they are an odd collection, for a life work, or part of a life work. Taken all together, the collection looks much smaller than the man Cummings. It looks cute, and dainty, and finicky. Sometimes it resembles a group of Japanese netsukes, and sometimes a flea circus. You might say that this is a matter of form only. But no: if we look at the content closely, we shall see that Mr. Cummings's range is pretty narrow. It seems to me to be confined to three, or at most four, poetic subjects: critical or appreciative epigrams on people; poetic parodies; lyrical evocations of single aspects of nature in both city and country; and momentary experiences of sex, sometimes idealistic and sometimes grossly carnal.

Among the carnal poems are a fair number, written early in Cummings's career, about prostitutes. They are curious productions. Far more enthusiastic than the bitter paintings of

Rouault and Toulouse-Lautrec, they remind me of nothing so much as the underworld poems of François Villon — except for one thing. Villon belonged to the underworld. Cummings, born in Cambridge, Massachusetts, the son of a professor turned clergyman, was slumming, or at least rebelling.

To write poems about a lot of vulgar, diseased chippies, 'bestial Marj' and 'dorothy' drunk on the curbstone, and so forth, one must have a curious mixture of sensuality and fastidiousness — and those are qualities which one sees throughout Mr. Cummings's books. But in addition, one must be determinedly self-centered, regarding most people (even those with whom one has a close relation) as objects, rather than subjects. And here, perhaps, is one reason for the reticence of Cummings's work or for its inadequacy, or however we should put the difficulty. He is a monumental egoist. When he returned from Russia, he called his travel diary *Eimi,* which in Greek means 'I am.' (He was asserting his own existence, against a state machine.) When he gave his lectures at Harvard, he called them simply *i* — a small, lower-case i, which looks modest at first sight, but really emphasizes, by its difference from the normal, the individuality of Cummings. At the very opening of his lectures, he declared that he as a poet was egocentric, and then went on to justify this by saying that everyone was egocentric (implying that everyone was *equally* egocentric), including 'senators pickpockets scientists honest educators streetcleaners deafmutes murderers and mothers.' Yet in the same lectures he gave two vivid and noble character-sketches of his father and mother which proved that they at least were profoundly unselfish, devoted to helping other people whether known or unknown, and caught up in many causes far greater than their own individualities.

Another way of putting this is to say that he is still — even in his sixties — immature. It is wonderful that he should have such comical gusto and satirical snap and lyrical originality; but it is strange to see him still writing very much as he did when he was thirty. The contrast that springs to our mind is of course another poet born only a few years before Cummings, a man who has thought far more deeply and critically about religious and social problems without surrendering his own intense individuality: T. S. Eliot. Both Eliot and Cummings began publishing in the early 1920's, but Eliot has moved forward from that period, while in some way Cummings still belongs to it. That must have been an amusing time to be young and talented in; but some of those who were most deeply involved in it found that they had a hard job in growing up. Think of Hart Crane; think of poor Scott Fitzgerald; and think of a man who closely resembles E. E. Cummings in a few at least of his aesthetic quirks, Ezra Pound. Pound's immaturity, his belief that all originality meant rebellion, his egocentricity, and his disastrously limited education, finally corrupted his social sense and destroyed his mind; and, what was worse, they prevented him from ever writing the great poetic works which he had once planned. E. E. Cummings did not try so hard. He has remained sane, though eccentric; ambitious, yet diffuse; and although boldly original, a respecter of a few artistic traditions.

But the real truth about Mr. Cummings is that he takes very few things seriously. He is a joker. He thinks that most collective entities and many individuals are silly. This means that he has survived several difficult periods when everyone was conforming, to the right, to the left, and to the center; and he has maintained his own personality unblemished, although not unsuffering. He has mocked the conformists in a pleasant little poem of a dozen words:

> IN)
>     all those who got
>     athlete's mouth jumping
>     on&off bandwaggons
>                     (MEMORIAM

And in fact he mocks the whole world. Apart from some of the arts, and sex, and individual life, he thinks it is all ridiculously funny; and he is in poetry what the Swiss fantasist Paul

Klee is in painting. A *real* man or woman, he thinks, is like a real bird or a real blade of grass, or a tree, or a poem. Most people are distorted by the world; they are distorted and made comical; let us laugh at them, for a while, and then turn away to the few individual things which are truly real.

THOMAS

## *The  Wild  Welshman*

---

THERE is an old, old prophecy, made about the people of
Roman Britain fifteen centuries ago, when the invasions of the
pagan Germanic tribes from northern Europe began. Perhaps
a Druid conceived it. It says:

> Their tongue they shall keep,
> Their land they shall lose,
> Except wild Wales.

The prophecy was only partially fulfilled. The ancient Britons,
who were mainly Celts, managed to survive in Cornwall also,
in Ireland and in Scotland (still speaking Gaelic), and even
across the narrow seas in Brittany. Still, Wales was the strongest southern fortress of the ancient British culture which flour-
ished before the English arrived. To this day it is a land full
of antique customs and long-established habits of thought,
where it is not difficult to think oneself back two thousand
years or more into the past. Wales is both modern and ancient.
You can watch the miners coming up from a pit furnished
with modern equipment, and hear them swear at one another
in a tongue which was spoken before the Romans landed.

They are a peculiar people, the Welsh, and a difficult one: difficult to understand, even for themselves; difficult to live with, even for one another. Deeply emotional, but sternly self-controlled except on important occasions; distrustful of one another, hostile to strangers *; thrifty because of poverty, secretive because of pride, melancholy because joy is so dangerous, hard-working but without the Germanic complacency in labor for its own sake, sensuous but puritan, resisting the English conquerors and yet secretly admiring them, arrogant but polite, poor but superior, eloquent but shy, they are a folk with a great heart almost broken by an ancient grudge. Only half of them speak Welsh nowadays, although every Welshman knows some words of his old language. Still, they all think Welsh; they all feel Welsh; they are quite unlike the English and the other inhabitants of the British islands. It was Dylan Thomas, one of their own poets, who expressed their paradoxical heart in the simple words of a woman talking to her child: 'Oh, isn't life a terrible thing, thank God?' †

Dylan Thomas was born at Swansea in 1914, and died in New York in 1953. Although his tongue was English, and although he knew only the necessary few words (polite and impolite) of his country's language, his heart and his fancy were Welsh. Of his two names, one was the name of a Christian saint, the other that of a Celtic sea-god. He was so modern that he was often shocking, usually incomprehensible; yet some of the central difficulties of his poetry came from the age and obscurity of the ancient traditions which sustained it. In order to understand his poems, we must think of the Welsh and their remarkable character.

They are deeply religious. The lives of many of them are centered upon the chapel (usually Methodist) where they sing and pray and preach with an eloquence and fervor that astounds visitors from other lands where religion is taken more calmly. Even when they are not practicing Christians, they

---

* *Britannos hospitibus feros* Horace called them in his odes, 3.4.33
† Dylan Thomas, *Under Milk Wood*

tend to have a religious attitude to life: they are not logicians, not pragmatists, but mystics. Such was their greatest modern statesman Lloyd George. Such was Dylan Thomas in his poetry, where sexual love is a supernal experience like absorption in God, and where, though there is scarcely a trace of orthodox Christian thinking, the great images of Christianity constantly appear:

> This day's sun leapt up the sky out of her thighs
> Was miraculous virginity old as loaves and fishes,
> Though the moment of a miracle is unending lightning
> And the shipyards of Galilee's footprints hide a navy of doves.*

Then the Welsh love singing. Their choirs are famous throughout Britain; even those strict chapel-goers who think dancing is sinful will lift up their hearts in glorious hymns on the Sabbath; and one of the most moving crowd experiences possible in our time is to hear the entire Welsh contingent at an international football match drop its rowdy jokes and spiteful jibes and break into the rich slow harmonies of 'All Through the Night.' Therefore Dylan Thomas is a singing poet. His poems are all lyrics, with elaborately interlaced rhymes, and with their dancing lines arranged in a complex pattern like a choral dance or the parts of an intricate antiphonal chorus. Consider the first stanza of 'Over Sir John's hill.'

Over Sir John's hill,
The hawk on fire hangs still;
In a hoisted cloud, at drop of dusk, he pulls to his claws
And gallows, up the rays of his eyes the small birds of the bay
And the shrill child's play
Wars
Of the sparrows and such who swansing, dusk, in wrangling hedges.
And blithely they squawk
To fiery tyburn over the wrestle of elms until
The flash the noosed hawk
Crashes, and slowly the fishing holy stalking heron
In the river Towy below bows his tilted headstone.

---

* 'On the marriage of a virgin'

The subject is beautiful enough: a hawk in the sunset poised and pouncing over small birds, while a heron fishes sedately in the water. But look at the arrangement of the rhymes and half-rhymes: *hill still claws bay play wars squawk hawk heron headstone* woven together.* And look at the complex variety of the lines, one only a single syllable long, and another, next door to it, fifteen syllables in length. A single singer improvising might strike out such a stanza, once. Dylan Thomas went on to write four more stanzas in the same pattern, passing from the difficult to the almost impossible, like a singer outdoing his own echo.

Also, many of the finest of his phrases clearly came to him first of all as melodies, those unreasonable fragments of beauty which drift into the heads of most musicians and some poets. The planned and growing poems came later; but first the few words which were the song:

> All all and all the dry worlds lever †
>
> When I was a windy boy and a bit ‡
>
> Now as I was young and easy under the apple boughs **
>
> Twenty-four years remind the tears of my eyes ††

They almost sing themselves.

Even in the most exalted prose of the Welsh — for instance, in the prayers and sermons of their finest preachers — poetry is constantly breaking in. They have a word for the inspiration that overcomes one of their ministers when, after preaching for some time, he feels a new spirit of eloquence entering him and bearing him up and making him say things he has never meditated, so that he himself is astonished and his audience breaks into tears and cries of rapture. This in Welsh is called *hwyl,* the voyage, the course under sail. Dylan's poems are full

---

* The seventh and ninth lines have no corresponding rhymes.
† 'All all and all the dry worlds lever'
‡ 'Lament'
** 'Fern Hill'
†† 'Twenty-four years'

of that gale-force wind which makes his songs outrace ordinary reason. Even in ordinary life, the Welsh are inhabited by an electrical excitement which is quite unlike the clocklike regularity of the Saxon. They are more easily moved, they will break far more rapidly and loudly into argument, even their silences vibrate with suppressed feeling. Dylan Thomas's poems therefore are Welsh in that they are tryingtosayasmuchaspossibleallinonebreath. English and American poetry usually moves more slowly, spacing itself out as though in our flat wide plains it had more ease of movement. Wales is a country of spiky crags, and narrow twisting valleys, and angry little cataracts and seething brooks pushing their way through reluctant stones.

It is deeply moving to hear Dylan Thomas reading his own poems, as he does on a number of excellent phonograph records: moving, but perplexing and even disappointing. When he speaks a poem which is essentially dramatic — for instance, his address to his father, 'Do not go gentle into that good night' — then everything is clear, the rich voice enters our heart, the refrain hammers its way home through our blood. But when he reads a different type of poem, an irregular lyric packed with complicated and often conflicting images, then we can scarcely follow, we are bewildered even with the printed page open on our knee. Is Dylan reading wrongly, or are we looking for the wrong effect? Perhaps the answer to both questions is Yes. Dylan Thomas used to read his lyrics not as though they were poems full of song, but as though they were dramatic speeches straight out of a play which might have been a successor to *Hamlet*. Songs cannot be spoken in the level and only mildly varied tones of rhetoric; they should be sung and played, sung by different voices perhaps, and musicked by an orchestra. Or else, perhaps Dylan Thomas meant us to listen without fully understanding: to be like the devout Welsh congregations which would listen to their preachers creating, within a tiny tin-roofed chapel, a world which could be described only in terms beyond normal comprehension, like the vision of the Apocalypse.

In yet another way, his art is Celtic. One of the most marvellous books in the world is the Book of Kells. This is a Latin text of the Gospels, written and decorated by Irish scribes in the eighth century. Lovely as it is, it is bewildering to look at. Page after page is covered with rich patterns of scrollwork and cunning arrangements of tiny figures and fantastic designs partly geometrical and partly symbolical, swooping and swirling as intricately as water in a rocky streambed, tinted as variously as a flowering garden. It is astonishing to gaze at a page of the Book for ten minutes, picking out the quaint animals and the branch-and-leaf motives and the sunwheels or swastikas which survive from Celtic paganism, and the manifold curves and colors which must have taken months to plan and sketch and execute, and then to realize that the entire page is simply one large initial letter — C, or I, or Q — on which all the rest has been built up, like variegated coral and suave submarine plants settling upon a ship's anchor at the bottom of a shallow tropical sea. That particular type of art, devoted to tricky pattern-making, is very friendly to the Celtic temperament. Much early Irish and Welsh poetry is based on complex riddles. There are poems which have two or three meanings, and whose sense seems to change in every line. In Welsh at least there is another type of poem based on the magic of numbers, so that every theme is arranged and connected by threes, or by sevens. Welsh poetry, for all the subtlety and frailty of its emotions, was never a formless gush of excitement, 'a drift of mist and wind and sea-foam.' 'Its discipline is the strictest in the known world of literature, and it is beyond human ability to rave in an ecstasy while observing the requirements of a complicated alliterative system, with end rhymes and internal rhymes to find, and whilst paying due attention to stresses and the exact number of syllables.' * Dylan Thomas, though writing in English, works in that tradition. He writes poems which form a regular pattern on

---

* Gwyn Williams, *An Introduction to Welsh Poetry* (Faber, 1953), quoted and reviewed in *The Times Literary Supplement*, 20th February, 1953. The fine phrase 'a drift of mist and wind and sea-foam' is cited from this review.

the printed page, like a diamond or a pair of wings; * he plays magically with interwoven rhymes and assonances. He knows there is no such thing as 'free verse.' Part of his power comes from the competition between his wild emotions and his firm aesthetic control.

Dylan Thomas, then, is emphatically a Celtic poet. And he is better understood if he is put beside other poets of the Anglo-Celtic frontier. Like him, Robert Burns was a drinker and a womanizer, born and educated among a people whom some have called puritans and others hypocrites. Burns never learned much about his ancestry, but his father came from northern Scotland and was on the nationalist side in the 1745 rebellion, so that he was more Gael than Saxon. Although Burns's poems are far less subtle than Dylan Thomas's, they are more vigorous, and not less sincere; and they celebrate with comparable gusto the excitements of sexual love and the ravishments of nature.

Like Dylan again, Henry Vaughan was a Welsh mystic, who found in childhood the promise of eternal happiness:

> Happy those early days, when I
> Shined in my angel-infancy.†

He turned away from the world, looking toward God for that passionless tranquillity which alone could free him from the pains of this life. Thomas sought an earthly-heavenly joy in this world, in his own youth, his own body, and his own countryside; but he was very close to Vaughan when in boyhood he

> whispered the truth of his joy
> To the trees and the stones and the fish in the tide.
> And the mystery
> Sang alive
> Still in the water and singingbirds.‡

---

* Thomas, 'Vision and Prayer'
† Vaughan, 'The Retreat'
‡ Thomas, 'Poem in October'

## Death of a Poet

IN NOVEMBER 1953 at St. Vincent's Hospital in New York City, the brilliant Welsh poet Dylan Thomas, after lying for many hours in a coma, died. He had just passed his thirty-ninth birthday. The doctors said his death was due to alcoholic poisoning of the brain. On his deathbed he was surrounded by men and women who loved him dearly. They were grieved by the doom which had overtaken him; and yet nearly all of them knew it was inevitable. They had watched him killing himself for years.

One of them — a man who knew Dylan Thomas well and admired both his work and his essentially lovable character — wrote a book about those last years. It is *Dylan Thomas in America*, by John Malcolm Brinnin (Little, Brown, 1955). Well written, sympathetic, charmingly modest — when one considers that Mr. Brinnin was Thomas's agent on his American tours and helped him to make thousands of badly needed dollars, it is remarkable that he says comparatively little of the many, many headaches the job must have given him — charmingly modest, and infused throughout with a sense of bitter sorrow for the loss of a difficult but charming friend and a difficult and marvelous poet, this is a book which is very hard to forget. It is full of stories which are almost unbelievable to anyone who did not know Dylan Thomas personally. He was not merely a terrific drinker; he was a rioter. He loved shocking people, the grander and more learned the better — he himself used to call it the Provincial Push, or the Up-Rimbaud-and-At-'Em attack. And in his cups he used to make passes publicly at beautiful women, making his intentions perfectly clear by word and act. Some of the stories in this book sound as though they were imaginary, and yet there is reason to believe that they are true. They were invented by that perennial naughty boy with the wild and whirling imagination, Dylan Thomas himself; he not only invented these fantastic escapades, but in person performed them.

It must have been a difficult book to write. It must have been a painful book to write. Not only Dylan Thomas appears in it — in circumstances so degrading as to provoke acute embarrassment even in the minds of readers who never saw him close-to; but also several of his mistresses; and his beautiful and strange wife, whose last appearance is in a strait jacket, departing for a 'rest home.' Both Thomas's life and his death were agony for her. The agony is apparently not yet over. At her request, the author and publisher of the book inserted a statement over her signature saying that, although she was 'not quarrelling with Brinnin's presentation of Dylan,' she still considered that it was 'onesided' and did not 'do justice to the circumference of the subject.' That is probably true; but after all, Mr. Brinnin did not set out to write a complete life of Thomas, which would be an enormously complicated and absorbing task, half a life-work; he made his book center on the poet's visits to the United States on reading tours, adding only a few reminiscences of his own trips to see Thomas in Wales and in London. Dylan Thomas's entire life would be far richer, but it would also be even more painful.

As we read this book, and realize that it is the story of a man who was, in spite of his remarkable talents, busily and almost incessantly engaged in killing himself with drink, we have to ask, *Why?* Mr. Brinnin himself acknowledges that he can scarcely answer the question. That part of Thomas's life he could share only with an effort, and could only partially understand. Women who knew Thomas even better also found him a mystery if they attempted to penetrate his mind — a mind whose difficulty and complexity were only partially reflected in his enigmatic poems. Those who found him easiest to be with were apparently able to accept him merely as a jolly, talkative, amorous, wildly imaginative, outrageously violent tosspot, and to ask no questions of, or about, the inner man. But if one loves poetry, and his poetry in particular, one will be shocked and saddened by this book about him, and compelled to ask, again and again, *Why?*

The obvious reasons which have driven other artists to drink and drugs were scarcely operative in his case. Baudelaire's troubles began with his upright but hard stepfather, and continued with his absurd desire to live like a rich nobleman and an extravagant dandy. De Quincey started opium eating because of severe neuralgia. Poe was rootless and poor and friendless. Dylan Thomas was physically very sound, seems to have been fond of both his parents, had a handsome wife and children, and earned a lot of money; although he had perpetual financial troubles, they were rather a symptom than a cause of his central difficulty.

Perhaps it was not one difficulty but a combination of factors — each of them powerful, all of them together almost insuperable.

The first of them was that very physical strength. He had too much energy, and he did not use it up sanely. When he met Katherine Anne Porter, he suddenly lifted her in both his strong arms until her head was an inch from the ceiling, and kept her there. He could stay up drinking for hours and hours, when most men would simply have fallen asleep, or passed out. There have been other writers like this, notably Byron, who blazed with vitality; but Byron had the good sense to work it off in physical exercise — he boxed, he fenced, he went for long gallops on horseback, he swam for hours through dangerous seas, and in spite of many bouts of fever he remained fundamentally healthy until his last illness. It is one of the problems which every creative writer has to face and solve: what to do with himself between the rare moments in which literature comes into his mind. Thomas Wolfe, who was a regular giant, could not solve it either. Dylan Thomas's great readings of the best British poetry were one way, and a very fine way, of taxing his physical strength and restoring some sort of balance; but it would have been well for him if he had found other ways of pouring out his energy, if only by walking over the earth or swimming in the sea. As he said of himself,

> The force that drives the water through the rocks
> Drives my red blood.*

In trying to understand his friend, Mr. Brinnin speaks several times of Dylan Thomas's 'load of guilt,' but he never makes it quite clear what kind of guilt. Certainly it was not a profound sense of sin. Something of it was the sense that, although a husband and a father, he was not providing regularly for his family, and that he could not undertake, he could not even endure without rebellion, the repeated effort to write something salable and to earn money by working on schedule.

More important than his guilt was his insecurity. He came from a respectable, middle-class Welsh family, but he himself called certain types of people 'the grand'; sometimes he would say anything to shock them; sometimes, with a big cigar and a lordly manner, he would try to persuade himself that he was one of them. Also, the United States, with all its wealth and power, is terribly impressive to most European visitors — whether they will admit it or not. (Most of them feel this impressiveness, but try by hostility or constant carping to defend themselves against it.) There is a rather touching story about Mrs. Thomas on her first day in America. She was given a drink in an ordinary mid-town hotel in New York. The first thing she said was 'Is this a posh bar?' — 'posh,' in non-U English slang, means 'extremely smart.' And Mr. Brinnin himself says that Thomas at first thought of himself as 'a mendicant poet come to America in a fear that he might lose everything, including his identity.' That would explain the peculiar

---

* Thomas, 'The force that through the green fuse drives the flower'

fact that he had to steal some shirts from Mr. Francis Biddle's house; compulsive and unnecessary stealing is always a sign of profound envy. Then again, although Thomas wrote beautifully both in prose and in poetry and was widely read in English and American literature at least, he was not a trained critic, was embarrassed by professors and people who asked him technical questions about the aesthetic side of literature, was never at home with the jargon of the little magazines, and was apt to reply to any such question with a vague remark, a Welsh evasion, glum silence, or a dirty epigram. And, worst of all, he suffered from the insecurity that besets nearly every creative artist: the feeling that he had already done all he could, that he had written himself out by the mid-thirties, and that even his previous success was a fraud and he himself an impostor. That is a bitter agony to every artist. There are ways, through discipline and long preparation and thoughtful application, to overcome it, but he never seems to have discovered them or been able to use them.

One further aspect of his insecurity — whether it was a cause or a symptom we cannot tell — was his wife trouble. His wife Caitlin was handsome, and he loved her as much as he could love anyone except himself, but they had terrible rows in private and in public, accompanied by physical violence. Mr. Brinnin speaks of one evening party which was broken up by a fight between them, 'rooms littered with smashed glasses, overturned tables and broken *objets d'art.*' They fought like Cait and Dog.

Quite apart from all that, there was another cause for his love of the bottle; and this is one which might not occur to most people. It is that he was a Welsh visionary. In Wales, poets and preachers have long been respected for their ability to enter another world, to be rapt away into a state of wild excitement in which they see sights no ordinary mortal can see, and describe them in a frenzy of eloquence, pouring out words which are almost incomprehensible and yet convey, in their very richness and rapidity and fantastic strangeness, something of the ecstasy of inhabiting a dream. The Welsh call this rapture the *hwyl*. Mr. Brinnin once at least saw Thomas — in the company of the musician John Cage — spend a long time, quite sober, talking incessantly and ecstatically, in a state of wild and fanciful and uninhibited gaiety. Yet all the time he was perfectly sober. It was in such a mood of sober excitement that he conceived his poems and worked some of them out. Only, we may suspect that, like drug-addicts, when the *hwyl* did not visit him of its own accord, he would try to summon it through drink; and he usually failed.

Stronger than his hope of the *hwyl,* much stronger than his social and intellectual insecurity, was one other impulse in him, perhaps the most central of all. It was recognized by many of those who knew him. Mr. Brinnin again and again — although he is speaking of a man in his late thirties — uses phrases such as 'babyish,' 'boyish,' 'unhappy child,' and even 'pouting.' Thomas felt that his thirty-ninth birthday, which he passed in New York, was an occasion not for rejoicing and congratulation, but for gloom. It was a sort of death for him. He wrote most of his poetry about childhood and adolescence, and, if he could, he would have remained a child all his life. My guess is that his realization of the loss of childhood hit him hardest in his early thirties. At thirty, he recalled his youth with happiness but also with tears, as we see from his exquisite 'Poem in October.' This is only a guess, but I venture to make it because the same trouble overtook at least two other British poets at that same age. Wordsworth and Coleridge, both visionaries, traversed a crisis of great gloom in 1802. They both felt that there had 'past away a glory from the earth': that custom, routine, encroaching age, lay upon them 'with a weight heavy as frost and deep almost as life.' * They realized that they had been poets, and had seen nature with visionary eyes, because they had still been children; but now they had left childhood behind for ever. They saw ahead of them that which Dylan Thomas tried constantly to escape: the world of prosaic regularity and of repetitive, inevitable responsibility.

---

* Wordsworth, 'Intimations of Immortality' II and VIII

Coleridge tried to take refuge from his realization in two narcotics, opium and German philosophy. Wordsworth faced his, and, in his magnificent ode, 'Intimations of Immortality,' accepted it. Dylan Thomas would never accept it; and the central reason why he drank was that he wished to defy

> time, the quiet gentleman
> Whose beard wags in Egyptian wind.*

He was determined to

> rage, rage against the dying of the light.†

Both his chief intoxications, poetry and liquor, were assertions of the impossible. They were the search for eternal youth, the simple paradise of playing ball with the other boys in a park. (For more than twenty years he kept in his wallet a newspaper photograph of himself at the age of twelve, taken just after he had won a race in the school sports; a very thin, small, frightened boy, he was the essential Dylan Thomas.) In fact he refused to grow up. He killed himself rather than grow old, and, in the words of one of his finest lyrics,

> Time held him green and dying
> Though he sang in his chains like the sea.‡

---

* Thomas, 'Should lanterns shine'
† Thomas, 'Do not go gentle into that good night'
‡ Thomas, 'Fern Hill'

# Poems

*Kicking His Mother*

KICKING his mother. What does this mean? Who has been doing anything so barbarous and unfeeling, so indescribably repulsive, as brutalizing his own devoted female parent? Kicking his mother! Who could do such a thing and still be respectable, and even admirable? Only one kind of human being in the world: a baby.

'Kicking his mother' is the opening phrase of a delightful lyric by one of the most inventive and amusing of modern poets, W. H. Auden. It is a poem about a newly born baby, apparently addressed to its parents. Although it sounds, when read without due attention to rhythm, like epigrammatic prose, it is in carefully written verse, seven eight-line stanzas made up of two couplets and one quatrain each.

> Kicking his mother until she let go of his soul
> Has given him a healthy appetite: clearly, her rôle
>   In the New Order must be
> To supply and deliver his raw materials free;
>   Should there be any shortage,
> She will be held responsible; she also promises
> To show him all such attentions as befit his age.
>   Having dictated peace,

With one fist clenched behind his head, heel drawn up to thigh,
The cocky little ogre dozes off, ready,
    Though, to take on the rest
Of the world at the drop of a hat or the mildest
    Nudge of the impossible,
Resolved, cost what it may, to seize supreme power and
Sworn to resist tyranny to the death with all
    Forces at his command.

A pantheist not a solipsist, he co-operates
With a universe of large and noisy feeling-states
    Without troubling to place
Them anywhere special, for, to his eyes, Funnyface
    Or Elephant as yet
Mean nothing. His distinction between Me and Us
Is a matter of taste; his seasons are Dry and Wet:
    He thinks as his mouth does.

Still his loud iniquity is still what only the
Greatest of saints become — someone who does not lie:
    He because he cannot
Stop the vivid present to think, they by having got
    Past reflection into
A passionate obedience in time. We have our Boy-
Meets-Girl era of mirrors and muddle to work through,
    Without rest, without joy.

Therefore we love him because his judgments are so
Frankly subjective that his abuse carries no
    Personal sting. We should
Never dare offer our helplessness as a good
    Bargain; without at least
Promising to overcome a misfortune we blame
History or Banks or the Weather for: but this beast
    Dares to exist without shame.

Let him praise our Creator with the top of his voice,
Then, and the motions of his bowels; let us rejoice
    That he lets us hope, for
He may never become a fashionable or
    Important personage:
However bad he may be, he has not yet gone mad;

Whoever we are now, we were no worse at his age;
   So of course we ought to be glad

When he bawls the house down. Has he not a perfect right
To remind us at every moment how we quite
   Rightly expect each other
To go upstairs or for a walk if we must cry over
   Spilt milk, such as our wish
That, since, apparently, we shall never be above
Either or both, we had never learned to distinguish
   Between hunger and love?

A cheerful little poem: as all poems about new babies ought to be. When awake, babies are so intensely full of vitality; even when they are asleep you can feel them throbbing and sizzling and pumping out energy like little dynamos; it would be a shame to write of them in solemn regular elegiac tones. They are funny, also, with their hideous red faces and their eyes which do not focus, and the hole in their skull where the brain is too big for the brainpan, and their astonishing ability to grip tightly, to bite like wild beasts, to yell the place down, and to survive hardships that would kill you and me. Astonishing creatures: it is always a delightful experience to visit a house containing a new baby, and to see how, although blind, largely deaf, and speechless, the little creature still contrives to dominate the entire family.

This is the point from which Auden begins his exploration of the child's personality. His entire poem is a description of the different aspects of an infant's character — at the period before it has any *individual* character: when it is not yet Joe or Joan, but simply The Baby. He begins with the most striking fact about an infant, that it is a dictator. It has just been fed and put to sleep, but already it has established — like some dictators of the recent past — a New Order. It calls for Raw Materials. It even looks like a dictator, with its clenched fist upraised and its energetically bent knee. The first phrase of the poem is meant to shock us, in the same way as a new baby shocks its parents both before and after its birth. 'Kicking his mother until she let go of his soul': you know how an unborn baby kicks and jumps with fantastic energy, as though it wanted to get moving, to be born, and start its separate life: that separate life is what Auden means by saying that his mother had to 'let go of his soul.' This is the baby as a tyrant.

Next, the poet turns to another important fact about the baby: its attitude to the world it has entered. A newly born infant cannot see or hear properly. It cannot play with toys, for it cannot recognize a golliwog or an elephant. It cannot sharply distinguish its own body from its parents and the food they give it, except that the parents and the food smell and taste a little differently from itself. And it knows nothing of late and early, day and night, spring and fall: sometimes it is drinking, sometimes it is digesting, sometimes it is eliminating — and so, like a tropical country, it has only two seasons, the Dry Season and the Wet Season. More confusing still, it cannot sort out the mass of experience which pours in upon it: apparently it is unable even to differentiate the rumbling and gushing noises within itself from the squeaks and roars of the outside world. In spite of all this, says Auden, the baby is not a solipsist, believing that it alone exists while the rest is illusionary and unreal; it is a pantheist, wholly united with its universe. This stanza strikes me as one of the most intelligent and touching pieces of verse written in this century, and reminds me of the marvellous chapter in which Jules Romains describes the birth of a baby from the point of view of the baby itself.* After the baby as a tyrant, we have seen the baby as a philosopher.

Third, Auden recalls another fact about babies, which is that they are incapable of doing wrong. This has not always been the view of Christians. At the very beginning of his *Confessions* St. Augustine speaks sadly of the concept that none is pure from sin before God, not even an infant of one day; and he recalls with horror how he has seen a baby, too young

---

* *Les Hommes de bonne volonté* 9 (*Montée des périls*) c.8

even to speak, committing the sin of envy by glaring bitterly at another baby which was competing with it for milk.* But most of us would scarcely agree with this. We should rather say, as Auden does, that babies have no vices — yet. They have no double thoughts and concealments, as we have. They always tell the truth, as saints do — although for a different reason: the saint thinks of eternity, the baby thinks only of this immediate moment. Therefore, even when the baby screams in fright or yells with anger and desire, we cannot call it bad.

> Still his loud iniquity is still what only the
> Greatest of saints become — someone who does not lie:
>    He because he cannot
> Stop the vivid present to think, they by having got
>    Past reflection into
> A passionate obedience in time. We have our Boy-
> Meets-Girl era of mirrors and muddle to work through,
>    Without rest, without joy.
>
> Therefore we love him because his judgments are so
> Frankly subjective that his abuse carries no
>    Personal sting. We should
> Never dare offer our helplessness as a good
>    Bargain; without at least
> Promising to overcome a misfortune we blame
> History or Banks or the Weather for: but this beast
>    Dares to exist without shame.

Last of all, Auden envies and admires the baby because it is purely human. He is an anxious man, himself. He writes a good deal about the trouble of existing. He finds human life pretty unsatisfactory. So he ends the poem by telling the baby's parents that it is now better and happier than all grownups can claim to be. Our minds are divided; its mind is simple. Our passions are conflicting; its emotions are unified and clear. We are split personalities; the baby, though small, is solid.

---

* *Confessions* 1.7

Let him praise our Creator with the top of his voice,
Then, and the motions of his bowels; let us rejoice
    That he lets us hope, for
He may never become a fashionable or
    Important personage:
However bad he may be, he has not yet gone mad;
Whoever we are now, we were no worse at his age;
    So of course we ought to be glad

When he bawls the house down. Has he not a perfect right
To remind us at every moment how we quite
    Rightly expect each other
To go upstairs or for a walk if we must cry over
    Spilt milk, such as our wish
That, since, apparently, we shall never be above
Either or both, we had never learned to distinguish
    Between hunger and love?

The title? I had almost forgotten the title, just as many
friends of the parents forget the new baby's name. It is called
*Mundus et Infans*, which means *Pure and Speechless*, and also
*Pure and Infant*, and also, by a peculiar twist of the Latin
language, *The Universe and a Baby*. Auden is a knowledge-
able fellow; he no doubt intended that. The poem is full of
double and triple meanings, because a baby is full of double
and triple meanings: for instance, 'His distinction between Me
and Us is a matter of *taste*.' And it has a good deal of psychology in it: so, the baby inhabits 'a universe of large and
noisy feeling-states.' Even the sad, final remark that grownups
wish they had never learned to distinguish between hunger
and love, between gross appetite and ideal admiration ... that
comes from a mind which has thought deeply about the psychology of sex.

The atmosphere of the poem will strike many baby-lovers
as wrong, but it is right. It is not tender. It is not full of hushed
prayers and soft breathings. Instead, it has fists clenched, and
loud mouths, and eager appetites, and plain straightforward
deafening yells. This is correct. Very few poems about new
babies convey the real facts about them — their enormous greed

for life, their uncompromising self-assertion, their lack of delicacy in all situations, their fundamental strength. They are terrible creatures. If only they were six feet high, instead of being about one foot high, they would rule the world. As it is, they can dominate and terrify several adults: mold a father, and crush a mother.

There is one thing sad, and perhaps bad, about the poem. It is that Auden admires the baby with a sort of regret. He says it is superior to us because it does not think and make decisions. This is true in one way, but in another it is false and wrong. Auden's weakness has often seemed to his critics to be that he wishes to return to school, to childhood, to the cradle — that he shrinks from life. They have said that life is a series of challenges which the poet should accept, not a collection of traps which he ought to evade. This may be true. It may be one of his weaknesses, but every poet, and every human being, has his weaknesses. It is the task of the poet to translate his individual frailty into a new understanding of humanity. Auden has not always managed to do this, but here, and in certain other poems, he has solved the problem with wry effectiveness — with something between lyric and satire. His dislike for women, his skeptical attitude toward religion, his humorous cynicism, his deeply concealed optimism — they all appear in this poem on the new baby, and they are all expressed in the first phrase, a phrase as disgusting and vital as the appearance and movements of a child one minute old, which has until then been 'kicking his mother until she let go of his soul.' We all did that. Only poets remember it.

*A Drinking Song*

---

A GOOD idea, in poetry, or prose fiction, or art or philosophy, lasts for centuries. It can be used by many different creators, and will inspire each of them differently. It is one of the greatest pleasures of literature, to recognize a cadence from one good writer in the work of another — not a theft, but an echo, or a tribute.

There is one beautiful little echo which has traveled over sixteen centuries, first sounding in Greek and then coming down through French to English. It is a drinking song, which turns at last into a love song.

Nobody knows who wrote it originally, and nobody can do much more than guess when. It is in a cheerful little dancing meter:

> Ἡ γῆ μέλαινα πίνει,
> πίνει δὲ δένδρε' αὖ γῆν,
> πίνει θάλασσα δ' αὔρας,
> ὁ δ' ἥλιος θάλασσαν,
> τὸν δ' ἥλιον σελήνη.
> Τί μοι μάχεσθ', ἑταῖροι,
> καὐτῷ θέλοντι πίνειν;

*(Anacreontea* 21)

Now here it is translated into English:

> The black earth drinks and drinks again,
> The trees in turn drink in the earth,
> The sea drinks up the breezy air,
> The sun in heaven drinks up the sea,
> The moon drinks up the glowing sun.
> Tell me, friends, why do you think
> That I myself ought not to drink?

It is a simple little poem, based on a good idea. For a long time, people used to believe it was written by the famous Greek poet Anacreon, who loved parties, and pretty girls, and drinking, and wrote fine poems about them all. It is in the meter which was one of his favorites. But the experts now believe it was not by him but by one of his many imitators. This particular poem can scarcely be placed more accurately than by saying it must have been written fairly late in Greek history; for it is based on a rather advanced philosophical idea — the idea that the whole universe is a unity, which is kept going by a constant process of interaction . . . the sun causing evaporation from the sea, the moon getting reflected light from the sun, and so forth. When the poet says

> The sea drinks up the breezy air

he is thinking of the rain clouds that feed the sea; we should think of rivers, but there are very few big rivers in Greece, and they do not flow steadily and voluminously like ours. A German scholar proposed that the poem was actually written by a fairly distinguished Jewish author called Aristobulus, who lived in the second century before Christ and was one of the first men to apply Greek philosophical ideas to the Old Testament; there are thoughts rather like this, although less frivolous, in his authentic writings; but then some other German scholar blew the idea up, and put the poem among the works of the versatile and copious author Anon.

During the Dark Ages after the fall of the western Roman empire, Greek was forgotten in western Europe. For centuries

Anacreon was only a name. Generations passed. In the late Middle Ages Greek began to come slowly back to the West, and scholars and poets began to enjoy for themselves the Greek poetry which they had for so long known only indirectly, through imitations and allusions in the Roman writers. Connoisseurs, like the Medici, began to send agents to the Near East to buy up manuscripts of Greek books; and, one by one, the great writers of Greek literature emerged from the long darkness. It was an age of delighted discovery. Men greeted the appearance of a new classic with the same rapture as that with which they admired a famous piece of sculpture disinterred after a thousand years of burial in the earth, with the same excitement as that felt a few years ago, in our own lifetime, by the Greek fishermen who found something in their nets, and drew up a magnificent statue of Zeus, made for and revered by their distant ancestors.

The poems of Anacreon were first printed in Paris by Henri Estienne in 1554. This little drinking song was among them, for it was believed to be by Anacreon himself. The young French poets were delighted with the new discovery; for after all what could be more sympathetic to the French than poems about good wine and poems about *Amour*? A graceful French translation of them was published very soon, by Remi Belleau; and even before that the leading poet of all France, Pierre de Ronsard, inserted an imitation of this very poem in his monumental collection of Odes. He added one line, to make two neat four-line stanzas:

> La terre les eaux va boivant,
>   L'arbre la boit par sa racine,
>   La mer salée boit le vent,
>   Et le Soleil boit la marine;
>
> Le Soleil est beu par la Lune;
>   Tout boit, soit en haut ou en bas:
>   Suivant ceste reigle commune
>   Pourquoy donc ne boirons-nous pas?
>     (*Quatrième livre des odes, xxxi*)

Here is a translation of Ronsard's echo of Anacreon:

> Earth drinks the waters as they run,
>   The earth is drunk up by the trees,
>   The briny ocean drinks the breeze,
> The sea is drunk, too, by the sun;
>
> The moon drinks down the sunbeam's light;
>   The whole world drinks, above, below;
>   It is a general rule, and so
> Why should we not drink tonight?

This is pretty straightforward: just a little fancier in vocabulary than the original Greek; arranged in rhyming stanzas, not in blank verse; but it has one addition. Ronsard is rather careful to explain that, as he puts it,

> The whole world drinks, above, below;
> It is a general rule . . .

Yet that is just a little less subtle. The Greek poet, whoever he was, gave five lines to describing the interlinked phenomena, and then let his listeners draw their own conclusion; a great deal of the best Greek literature is built on implication; but Ronsard was a little more obvious, and just a little more prosy.

Another hundred years passed, and the idea was imported into England. This time it was taken up by a brilliant poet, who had been a child prodigy, publishing a remarkable book of poems while he was still at school. He was Abraham Cowley, born in 1618. He is not much read now; we think of his age as the age of Milton and Dryden; but he was immensely ambitious. One of his ambitions was to rival the great lyric poets of Greece and Rome, and so in 1656 he published his own adaptation of some of the poems attributed to Anacreon. Here is what he made of the drinking song:

> The thirsty Earth soaks up the Rain,
> And drinks, and gapes for drink again.
> The Plants suck in the earth, and are
> With constant drinking fresh and faire.

The Sea itself, which one would think
Should have but little need of Drink,
Drinks ten thousand Rivers up,
So fill'd that they o'rflow the Cup.
The busy Sun (and one would guess
By's drunken firy face no less)
Drinks up the Sea, and when h'as done
The Moon and Stars drink up the Sun.
They drink and dance by their own light,
They drink and revel all the night.
Nothing in Nature's sober found
But an eternal health goes round.
Fill up the Bowl, then, fill it high,
Fill all the Glasses there, for why
Should every Creature drink but I,
Why, Men of Morals, tell me why?

It is delightful, isn't it? But see what remarkable changes
Cowley has brought in. The original in Greek was seven lines
long — just long enough for a toast, as it were. Cowley's version
is twenty lines long. The original had Greek economy. This
has baroque amplitude. You imagine the Greek singer with a
head of short curly hair and a little wreath of flowers on it;
but Cowley appears with a long periwig covering both his
shoulders, and a huge lace collar.

Then Cowley has made the whole thing much funnier than
the original. As Dr. Johnson said (in that well-known clumpy
style of his), 'His power seems to have been greatest in the
familiar and the festive,' and this proves it. It is quite a good
joke to say that the sun must be something of a drunkard because of his jolly red face; and it is rather fine humorous
imaginative poetry to make the moon and the stars dance by
their own light. The Greek would never have said, 'Nothing
in Nature's sober found,' for that would have seemed impossible, perhaps blasphemous, to him. Nature is what is; and
the word cosmos means 'order.' But, having said 'Nothing in
Nature's sober found,' Cowley redeems it by a handsome and
original metaphor, 'An eternal health goes round.'

There is one small mistranslation, or deliberate change. The Greek spoke of the sea drinking the air, that is, the clouds and mists; Cowley, with true baroque richness, makes the sea drink 'ten thousand rivers.'

And there is a great deal of detail, which reminds us of the description of Creation in the poem which came out eleven years later, Milton's *Paradise Lost*. The Greek said only, 'The trees in turn drink in the earth.' Cowley puts in a more vivid word, and adds a little joke:

> The Plants *suck* in the earth, and are
> With constant drinking fresh and faire.

And finally, perhaps we can trace the difference between paganism and Christianity, or at least Puritanism, in the different endings of the two poems. The Greek had friends who were telling him to take it easy; but Cowley in the seventeenth century had censors, to whom he cried, 'Why, Men of Morals, tell me why?'

About a hundred and fifty years passed. The Greek poem was read by a young English poet of twenty-seven, living in Italy — an eccentric and passionate young man who, although he is often called a romantic, was a devoted student of the classics. This was Shelley, who, if he had not been murdered before he was thirty years old, would have given our literature something to be put on the same bookshelf as the plays of Shakespeare. He knew Greek very well, and he knew this poem as an Anacreontic, a poem about drink. Only he did not care for drinking: he was always intoxicated, simply with pure water and his own wild, whirling imagination. He was like the poet whom Coleridge described in 'Kubla Khan': 'he on honey-dew had fed, and drunk the milk of Paradise.' On the other hand, he was very susceptible to beautiful girls; he had had two wives and several fancies. Beauty was a stimulus to Shelley. So he changed the old drinking song into a love song, and called it 'Love's Philosophy.'

> The fountains mingle with the river,
>   And the rivers with the Ocean,
> The winds of Heaven mix for ever
>   With a sweet emotion;
> Nothing in the world is single;
>   All things by a law divine
> In one spirit meet and mingle.
>   Why not I with thine? —
>
> See the mountains kiss high Heaven
>   And the waves clasp one another;
> No sister-flower would be forgiven
>   If it disdained its brother;
> And the sunlight clasps the earth
>   And the moonbeams kiss the sea:
> What is all this sweet work worth
>   If thou kiss not me?

Now, for the first time, the little poem became something like a masterpiece. Shelley was a far better writer than the Greek follower of Anacreon; than the French Ronsard, despite all his talents; than the baroque decorator Cowley. And he was more passionate: so he took an idea of the second grade of intensity, and made it strong, and individual, and urgent. We should hardly believe it was based on the Greek original, if he himself had not underlined the connection by calling it 'An Anacreontic.'

It is a splendid little poem, 'Love's Philosophy.' Of course we cannot tell exactly who inspired it; but we know that Shelley wrote a copy of it in his own hand and presented it to Miss Sophia Stacey; and there is another poem, written in the same year, called 'To Sophia,' which speaks of soft limbs and beautiful deep eyes: that particular poem was not published by Shelley's wife, as so many of his others were; and so, perhaps . . .

Anyhow, it is a masterpiece. Again the poet has altered the original theme and treatment. The follower of Anacreon simply said, 'All things drink, why shouldn't I?' Shelley changed it into love; and then he analyzed love into two different aspects, putting each in a single stanza. Love is the delight of two spirits in one another, and so Shelley says,

> Nothing in the world is single
> All things by a law divine
> In one *spirit* meet and mingle.
> Why not I with thine?

But love is also the delight of two people in each other's bodies, the strength of the man, the beauty of the woman: so Shelley finishes his poem with the image of an embrace:

> The sunlight *clasps* the earth
> And the moonbeams *kiss* the sea:
> What is all this sweet work worth
> If thou kiss not me?

He has drawn two images out of one, the old original image of the interlocking unity of all nature.

Being Shelley, he has abolished the slight monotony of the original poem, which spoke rather naively of drink, drink, drink; instead, he gives us (or gives his sweetheart) mingle, mix, meet, kiss, and clasp. And he has done the same kind of thing seriously which Cowley carried out humorously: he has brought in pantheism. In Cowley's version, Nature is drunk, and an eternal health goes round. In Shelley's version, Nature is ruled by God, and is happy:

> The winds of Heaven mix for ever
> With a sweet emotion

(exquisite phrase, containing both movement and passion)

> Nothing in the world is single;
> All things by a law divine
> In one spirit meet and mingle....

It is astonishing to see a little seven-line poem written by an unknown Greek in imitation of a famous Greek, surviving for something like two thousand years, changing first into a Renaissance ode, then into a lavish baroque witticism, and finally into a romantic love poem aimed at converting one girl to admiring the beauties of nature. As the morality becomes more difficult and limited, the poetry positively improves; or is it that we think drinking far less important than making love? And *were* the Greeks better balanced?

*Seventeen  Syllables*

---

IN SOME WAYS, the Japanese are an exquisitely civilized people. In some ways...

A splendid exhibition of their art was displayed in the chief cities of the United States in 1953. It was impossible to look at the best of the Japanese pictures in it without feeling a deep sympathy, almost an affection, for the artists who produced them. They loved nature. They loved nature dearly. Portraying human beings, they were usually conventional and trivial; in most of their religious pictures, they were remote and even surrealist; but they could paint a pine branch covered with thick, fluffy snow, or a tall, lonely heron in a pool, or a group of bright-eyed ducks among the reeds, with a tender grace and certainty which came only from love.

Their technique was masterly. Within their limitations (particularly those of perspective) they could depict practically anything they wanted. And they had the rare art of omission. Sometimes, in a large composition containing trees and crags and weather, they would leave one quarter of the area blank — except for a faint cloud or a few snowflakes. But far above their technique was their deep understanding and passionless love of nature. As Auden says in *The Age of Anxiety*,

> one knows from them what
> A leaf must feel.

We think of most Oriental art as detailed, and intricate, and rather too closely finished; in fact, some of the pieces in the exhibition were clearly the work of laborious years. Yet there were others which, although finished pictures, seemed to be scarcely more than sketches. A trunk of a tree would be rendered with three or four rapid strokes of the brush dwindling away into thin streaks of ink or color, making no effort to sustain the illusion that the tree was real. The Japanese like that. They enjoy it as we enjoy our Impressionist painters. They admire the quality of play, almost of magic, in it: the little miracle by which an artist, with a few blobs of color or a few dashes of black, conjures up a pool of water or a clump of bamboos, and then — simply by not *trying* to be complete and literal — reminds us that art is not reproduction but vision, and induces us to complete the picture by our own imagination.

There is one kind of Japanese poetry in which the same principles seem to be applied: incompleteness, feathery delicacy of touch, sympathetic love of nature mingled with humor and tenderness, noble subjects indirectly approached, tact, suppleness, an apparent absence of effort.

Have you ever looked out over the roofs of a large city, in the early morning or the evening after rain, when the light is falling aslant, making some windows bright and others dark? At such a time, gazing into the cloudy sky, you sometimes see a sudden curving glint in mid-air, a silver-gray flash which is really reflected but which seems, for a second or so, to shine by its own light. It vanishes again; but if you keep watching, a little lower down you will see a flock of pigeons in flight. A few moments before they were startled by something; they rose above the housetops, invisible because they were gray against gray clouds; then all in one movement they swooped round, to fly over and settle elsewhere; and, as they turned, the light caught their wings.

A particular type of Japanese poetry is like that sudden glint on the wings of flying birds. Other writers would make a complete poem out of the incident: sudden noise, fluttering birds, beating hearts, soaring flight, gradual reassurance, and the returning calm as the flock comes to rest in some safer spot. But *this* kind of poetry mentions only the rapid curving glitter in the sky; the reader must do all the rest.

The Japanese call it a *haiku,* or *hokku,* which means something like 'a beginning,' and so carries the meaning of deliberate incompleteness, or a creative activity shared between poet and reader. Surely it is one of the shortest poetic forms ever invented. It has seventeen syllables: no more, no less. They are arranged in three lines, of five, seven, and five syllables each. (Here we might see a parallel to the Japanese system of flower arrangement, where the standard pattern is a triad, with a strong central unit flanked by two weaker units in a harmonious but asymmetrical balance.) There is no rhyme, and no fixed meter: merely the brief outline, three groups of syllables, seventeen in all. The subjects of these poems are unlimited, but usually they contain some reference to the seasons or the time of day. Practically every Japanese knows some of the famous *haiku* off by heart, and thousands of new ones are composed every year.

Let us look at a few of these little things — to see how an effective poem can possibly be written within the compass of seventeen syllables. Like the originals, our translations will be brief, ending almost as soon as they begin; but they will not keep the triadic Japanese form, and their grammar will be a little clearer than the abrupt, almost telegraphic language of the Japanese poets.

First is a single sentence by Hyakuchi:

> I enjoyed the evening coolness
> with one who does not say all he thinks.

That is all. But you see how much is in it, and how much more is implied. There are: the season of the year (it is summer, hot summer, because the poet has been longing for the evening); the sounds of the world (after the noisy day, it is becoming quiet, so that even speech would be an intrusion); the light (growing dimmer into the restful darkness); the situation (two men sitting together, far from noisy parties); the mood (rest and meditation); and the thought behind the whole (that there is greater understanding, of nature and of friends, in almost silent companionship — not in complete silence, but in those brief words which are more eloquent than long speeches or busy conversation). Chopin might have translated that into music, as one of the Preludes.

Here is another *haiku*, by the most famous of all Japanese writers in this style: Basho, who was born just over three hundred years ago, gave up the life of a nobleman and courtier, and became an ascetic, a nature-loving pilgrim, a student of Zen Buddhism (most imaginative of all Buddhist sects), and a superb poet, teacher of poets: he says —

> The cry of the grasshoppers
> does not show how soon they are to die.

All life is brief — the life of the man as well as the life of the insect. But the vivid energy of the grasshoppers' perpetual shrill chorus makes them the masters of the summertime; they are wise; they live their lives without worrying about death, and enjoy life so intensely that they drown out the very thought of death with their song. Or do they know, and therefore sing all the more eagerly?

Next, a delightful springtime poem by a modern poet, Sho-u:

> The birds, singing among the flowers,
> laugh at men who have no leisure.

Observe how every one of these poems at once suggests a picture: usually a picture containing some contrast. In this, the contrast of bird song and glum human activity, of carefree creatures enjoying the beauty of the spring and harried men worrying about their work and their families and their property, is clear enough. But it would not surprise me to learn that the poet also had in his mind a painting in which the sparkling eyes of a bird on a flower-laden branch and the delicate lines of his head and his feathers were contrasted with the stodgy, thick face and heavy, drooping clothes of a man passing beneath, with his head bent by his anxieties, his short-sighted anxieties, which are making him as ugly as he is unhappy.

Here is a very early *haiku*, which within its three lines contains as much as an entire short story, or one chapter of a novel. It is by Kigin, and is called 'Love Unconfessed':

> 'Oh, my thinness is caused by summer heat,'
> I answered, and burst into tears.

It is a little drama. The speaker is evidently a girl: she is in love, so much in love that she is growing thin and pale, letting concealment, like a worm i' the bud, feed on her damask cheek. And it is the young man she loves who, knowing nothing of her sufferings, asks her why she is so thin (and by implication, ugly); and then — the unkindest cut of all — suggests that she must be in love with someone and pining away. If he is as blind as that, he could never love her: so she has just enough strength left to lie once again:

> 'Oh, my thinness is caused by summer heat,'
> I answered, and burst into tears.

A sad little poem. Two cheerful *haiku* to take the bitter taste away: one by Kikaku:

> Blessed is the beggar,
> wearing heaven and earth for summer clothes.

And another word-painting by Soseki:

> In this crystal-clear spring
> the stones at the bottom seem to move.

And one more, a sublime and rapid thought by the eighteenth-century poet Ryota:

> Moonlight. May I be reborn
> as a pine tree on a mountain peak!

Yet the oddest thing about these exquisite poems and the equally exquisite paintings is that they should have been produced by a nation which is also capable of beastly treachery, violence, and cruelty. Invasion, corruption, torture, cold-blooded medieval savagery of the vilest kind — how can they even exist in the same world as such works of art? The delicate sensibilities of *The Tale of Genji,* the tea ceremony, and the flower arrangers — how can they possibly belong to people who would blindfold a captured soldier, make him kneel, behead him over his own grave, and photograph this filthy crime while it was being committed?

I believe the answer is to be found in another of these poems. Some time before the outbreak of the Second World War, when the Japanese were pressing forward into China and were about to threaten the whole Pacific and Asian world, the emperor announced that the subject for the annual *haiku* competition would be Peace; and he himself wrote a model poem:

> Peaceful is morning in the shrine garden:
> if the whole world were filled with such peace!

At the time, some Western observers interpreted this as absurd hypocrisy; but they misunderstood the Japanese, and did not know the art of *haiku,* which depends on suggestion and implication. By choosing that subject and expressing that wish in his own poem, the emperor stated his own policy, and indicated that he had been unwillingly overruled by the army. He was lining up the artists, the thinkers, the sensitive people on his side. He was in fact declaring that Japan was — like many civilized peoples — not one nation but two. Japan has two souls: one, that of the soldier and the businessman; the other, that of the poet and the sage. Occasionally they coincide; sometimes they conflict; sometimes they have little or nothing to do with one another. To understand any nation fully is to understand *both* aspects of its character. But although we may admit the courage of the *samurai* and the energy of the Japanese industrialist, they are scarcely likable, and often repulsive. As human beings we admire more whole-heartedly those others, the men who transferred to paper the rustle of rain-lashed reeds, who could build a snow-loaded mountain with a few lines and dots of an agile brush, and who could put into seventeen syllables the whole beauty of a valley lying white under the harvest moon.

## Scorn Not the Sonnet

---

Do YOU ever wonder why so much bad poetry is written now-adays? Not merely mediocre, but bad: painful; atrocious. There are a number of different reasons — social, intellectual, spiritual; but one reason is that most people who try to write poetry have never learned how to use poetic forms. Most bad poetry published at present is either in simple lyric meter or else in free verse. Both these mediums are difficult to use. It is harder to write a good poem in free verse than to write a good poem in heroic couplets or Spenserian stanzas — just as it is harder to produce good music by improvising and inventing one's own form than by writing a sonata, a dance-suite, or a fugue. For a young poet to begin by writing free verse is like trying to compete with Frank Lloyd Wright before one has learned how to design a six-roomed house.

Very few people realize how many different things a good poetic pattern can do: how many different types of feeling it can carry. I remember that I was taught by the avant-garde critics of my youth to despise 'traditional forms.' It took me quite a long time to realize that a traditional form can be very useful for carrying novel and startling meanings; and that almost any poetic pattern, however old-established, can be reshaped and vitalized until it looks as new as when it was invented.

One of the most flexible forms in all modern western literatures is the sonnet. The best living sonnet-writer is W. H. Auden; and he has used the sonnet to say things that would have astonished all his predecessors. As you look at his sonnets, and then glance back over the best sonnets of earlier generations, you feel tremendous respect for the inspiration latent in a single apparently arbitrary and artificial poetic pattern.

The sonnet is one of the most illustrious international poetic forms. There are splendid sonnets in English, French, German, Italian, Spanish, Portuguese, and doubtless other languages too. It is a neat, but not a rigid pattern. Essentially it is a lyric poem: that is, it is derived from singing and implies the movement of a dance. (Many of the best sonnets could easily be set to music and sung.) But it is a meditative lyric: its music is slow, rich, and complex.

It is fourteen lines long. Its meter is nearly always the five-beat iambic line (although a few eccentric sonnets are in longer or shorter lines); and it always contains a system of rhymes, which interconnect and punctuate the sonnet.

The fourteen lines are arranged in sections, each shaped by the system of rhymes. They are never set out in the most obvious pattern for fourteen lines: in two stanzas of seven lines each. Why? Because that would not be a complete pattern. If there are two equal stanzas of seven lines, there is no reason why there should not be a third and a fourth and a fifth stanza. Instead, in order to make the sonnet a form complete in itself, its fourteen lines are arranged asymmetrically.

Sometimes they are set up in three four-line verses, followed by a couplet. This was the pattern which Shakespeare generally used in his youthful sequence of sonnets.

> My mistress' eyes are nothing like the sun;
>   Coral is far more red than her lips' red:
> If snow be white, why then her breasts are dun;
>   If hairs be wires, black wires grow on her head.

I have seen roses damask'd, red and white,
But no such roses see I in her cheeks;
And in some perfumes is there more delight
Than in the breath that from my mistress reeks.

I love to hear her speak, yet well I know
That music hath a far more pleasing sound:
I grant I never saw a goddess go, —
My mistress, when she walks, treads on the ground:

And yet, by heaven, I think my love as rare
As any she belied with false compare.*

Three four-line stanzas, with three sets of alternate rhymes: ABAB, CDCD, EFEF; closed with a couplet GG. Three assertions, all saying the same kind of thing; closed by an explanation and an affirmation. The entire sonnet is an expansion of a good anti-romantic notion: 'Most poets say their girls have eyes brighter than the sun, and other supernatural beauties; I cannot say that for my girl, but I love her as much as any extravagantly overpraised mistress.'

There are some good sonnets in this particular pattern, but not many. Most poets turn away from it. They feel that the three four-line stanzas are monotonous, because they look like the beginning of a long series of ballad verses rather than the body of a poem complete in itself; unmelodious if they contain (as this sonnet does) three different sets of rhymes; and almost impossibly difficult if they are built on two single interlacing rhymes. Also, the final couplet usually seems too neat, too pat, too mechanical. Therefore poets usually split the sonnet into one block of eight lines and another block of six lines, each held together by internal groups of rhymes. Within the eight and the six, subtler interconnections are made by arranging the rhymes in pairs, triplets, or quartets.

Imagine yourself a poet starting with a short lyrical thought, which might go well into the peculiar form of the sonnet: a

---

* Sonnet 130

fourteen-line poem divided into unequal segments of eight and six. At once, this shape will suggest several shapes for your idea. Eight lines, followed by six lines. It might be a question followed by an answer, or a doubt followed by a reassurance, or a statement followed by a justification, or a complaint followed by a consolation, or a boast followed by its own self-criticism. There is one of the essential powers of the sonnet. It moves. It develops. It does not — like a simple lyric — merely state a feeling. It grows and expands. It is something like a fugue; and indeed the best short fugues are parallel to some of the best sonnets, because they say something simple, and then elaborate on it, using both intellect and emotion.

William Wordsworth, writing at the opening of the rich nineteenth century, saw nothing around him but people devoted to money, heaping up riches far more than they would ever need, or feverishly searching for a quick profit. He said they thought of nothing else; they could not even see that the world around them was beautiful. Then he thought of the ancient Greeks, who liked money too, but at least enjoyed the loveliness of nature, and, although called 'pagans,' were not computing machines. Better, he said, to be a pagan, and to think that the trees and the waters were inhabited by kindly spirits, than to have nothing in one's mind but profit margins and expense accounts. This contrast shaped itself into one of his greatest sonnets.

> The world is too much with us; late and soon,
>   Getting and spending, we lay waste our powers:
>   Little we see in Nature that is ours;
> We have given our hearts away, a sordid boon! *
>
> This Sea that bares her bosom to the moon;
>   The winds that will be howling at all hours,
>   And are up-gathered now like sleeping flowers;
> For this, for everything, we are out of tune.

---

* Not a good phrase, but the idea is sound: he means 'We have given our hearts away' to the Bank and the Exchange, and they were not worth much even as a gift.

So far, the statement. It is made in two four-line sections: first, the importance of Money, second, the neglect of Nature. Now, after four words of transition, the comment, and the contrast.

> It moves us not. — Great God! I'd rather be
>  A Pagan suckled in a creed outworn;
> So might I, standing on this pleasant lea,
>  Have glimpses that would make me less forlorn;
> Have sight of Proteus rising from the sea;
>  Or hear old Triton blow his wreathed horn.*

This fine sonnet, with some memorable phrases, and a excellent theme, is tied closely together into a unity by the careful rhyming: only two sets of rhymes in the eight-line block, the 'octave,' and two more in the six-line block, the 'sestet.'

With a looser scheme of rhymes, but with the same basic pattern of contrast, W. H. Auden has composed a sonnet which is somehow complementary to this poem of Wordsworth. Money, said Wordsworth, has replaced the old gods. The gods and monsters have been killed, says Auden, but they still live within our souls. (Probably he is thinking of Jung's doctrine that all the gods of each section and era of the world are projections of the emotions, fears, and hopes of mankind: so that, when rationalist criticism destroys them, they return as psychological forces within our individual and collective being.)

> And the age ended, and the last deliverer died
>  In bed, grown idle and unhappy; they were safe:
>  The sudden shadow of the giant's enormous calf
> Would fall no more at dusk across the lawn outside.
>
> They slept in peace: in marshes here and there no doubt
>  A sterile dragon lingered to a natural death,
>  But in a year the spoor had vanished from the heath;
> The kobold's knocking in the mountain petered out.

All dead, the supernatural beings, killed by knights and neglect and disbelief. Artists, and those who dealt with the occult,

---

* 'The World Is Too Much with Us'

regretted their death. But the supernatural beings were alive, deathless, dangerous, all the more because human beings misunderstood or denied their real nature and power.

> Only the sculptors and the poets were half sad,
>     And the pert retinue from the magician's house
> Grumbled and went elsewhere. The vanquished powers were glad
>     To be invisible and free: without remorse
>     Struck down the sons who strayed into their course,
> And ravished the daughters, and drove the fathers mad.*

Contrast, yes; but the sonnet need not move through contrast alone. It may say one thing in its octave, and then, in its sestet, intensify what it has already said. It may at first be calm, and then, towards the end, become airborne. Such is one of the first famous sonnets in English. It was written by a medical student of twenty who loved poetry. He had been pretty well educated: he had learnt Latin and read a lot of Latin verse, and he had heard of the marvellous epics of the Greek Homer, but he had never seen Homer in any form. The son of his schoolmaster lent him a magnificent English verse translation of Homer, and the youngster sat up all night long reading it. Then he wrote a poem about his experience, 'On First Looking into Chapman's Homer.'

In the octave he says that he has already visited many regions of poetry as an admiring traveler:

> Much have I travelled in the realms of gold,
>     And many goodly states and kingdoms seen;
>     Round many western islands have I been
> Which bards in fealty to Apollo hold.

And he has heard of Homer's poetry, but has never entered it until Chapman's translation revealed it to him:

> Oft of one wide expanse had I been told
>     That deep-browed Homer rulcd as his demesne;
>     Yet did I never breathe its pure serene
> Till I heard Chapman speak out loud and bold.

---

* Auden, *In Time of War*, Sonnet XII

Then, suddenly, he was not like a tourist, but like an explorer, discovering a new ocean on this earth, or a new planet in heaven.

> Then felt I like some watcher of the skies
> When a new planet swims into his ken;
> Or like stout Cortez when with eagle eyes
> He stared at the Pacific — and all his men
> Looked at each other with a wild surmise —
> Silent, upon a peak in Darien.

At such a point, the sonnet, one of the smallest and neatest of poetic forms, touches one of the largest and greatest, the epic. Versatile, thoughtful; difficult but not too difficult; memorable; recalling tradition and yet welcoming novelty; smooth in rhythm, suave in rhyme; challenging and accommodating; favored by Milton and Shakespeare and Keats, Ronsard and Verlaine and Heredia, Rilke and Petrarch and many more, it is one of the channels through which much great poetry has flowed. As Wordsworth himself said, in one of those poems where his prosaic mind fought with his creative imagination, 'Scorn not the sonnet!'

## *Propaganda and Poetry*

---

IN A CERTAIN sense, everything which is written to be read (if it is not pure fact like a railroad timetable) is propaganda, because it attempts to present a point of view, and to convince the reader that it should be accepted. Never was there a greater fallacy (or falsehood) than the dogma that an author is interested only in 'art for art's sake,' that he is producing simply patterns of words without meaning, that he wishes to make no impact on the intellect and emotions of his readers, that he does not wish to *change* them. Still, one of the problems of writing is that it is hard to convey propaganda without becoming obvious, and thereby evoking disbelief or contempt. The whole subject is full of questions which have not yet been thoroughly analyzed. For instance, would you say it was easier to write effective propaganda in prose, or in poetry? Allowing for the fact that, nowadays at least, it is easier to write prose of any kind than it is to write poetry of any kind, it is actually more difficult to convey a propaganda message in prose than it is in poetry. This is because poetry (like music) makes a more immediate appeal to the emotions, while prose asks to be meditated and criticized. Prose makes us think; poetry sets our hearts beating faster and more strongly. It was a wise man who said that he believed if a man were permitted to make all the ballads, he need not care who should make the laws of a nation.

One strikingly effective dose of propaganda in poetry has been well known to me ever since I was a schoolboy; but it is only in the last few years that I have realized how strong the dose is, how carefully it was devised, and how skillfully it was mixed in with the poetry. It worked on me in two different ways, and, I think, I really believe, it changed my whole life — and changed it unconsciously, as propaganda is designed to do. I think it may have changed the lives of quite a large number of people, and although its efficiency is now diminished to the vanishing point, it worked very well for several generations.

It is a short book containing only four poems, published in Britain in 1842. Its title is *Lays of Ancient Rome*. Its author was a brilliant intellectual who turned into a wise and far-sighted statesman: Thomas Macaulay. It is unusual nowadays for politicians to publish volumes of poetry, but that was an age of many talents. One of Macaulay's contemporaries continued to write novels even after he became Prime Minister of Britain.

Some people have called the *Lays of Ancient Rome* tinsel and sham. I cannot agree. On their own level they are good, sound poetry; it is the same level, roughly, as Sibelius's *Finlandia* or Tchaikovsky's *1812 Overture*. The style in which they are written is now out of fashion, but in appreciating poetry one must try to ignore fashion. They are ballads, written in the same vigorous, cantering meter as the original English and Scottish ballads, and obviously inspired also by the romantic poetry of Sir Walter Scott. They are retellings of boldly exciting episodes in the very early history of ancient Rome.

The most famous, 'Horatius,' tells the splendid story of the invasion of Rome by the Etruscans from the north, which was stopped by a single warrior: Horatius himself, who, with two comrades, held the bridge across the river Tiber until it was cut down behind him, and then (though wounded and wearing full armor) jumped in and swam back to safety. The most pathetic, 'Virginia,' shows us a Roman father stabbing his daughter to death in the city street, to save her from being enslaved and dishonored by a brutal nobleman. The broadest and deepest, 'The Battle of the Lake Regillus,' describes another invasion of Rome by the Etruscans, who are determined to break the young republic and put Etruscan kings back on the throne; but, with divine assistance, the Romans smash them in a tremendous conflict. The duels between individual champions in this ballad still stir my blood. I do not know, and scarcely even care, who the heroes are and what place they have in history. It is enough to know that they are brave and to watch them fight.

> Mamilius spied Herminius,
> And dashed across the way.
> 'Herminius! I have sought thee
> Through many a bloody day.
> One of us two, Herminius,
> Shall never more go home.
> I will lay on for Tusculum,
> And lay thou on for Rome!'

The last and most mystical of these poems, 'The Prophecy of Capys,' takes us right back before the foundation of the city, shows us the twins, Romulus and Remus, asserting their rights, and gives us a forecast of the future prowess and warlike mastery of the Romans yet to be. Tough people, the Romans, their toughness symbolized in the she-wolf which suckled the twins when they were cast out, and kept them alive for their future vengeance.

> The ox toils through the furrow,
> Obedient to the goad;
> The patient ass, up flinty paths,
> Plods with his weary load;

With whine and bound the spaniel
  His master's whistle hears;
And the sheep yields her patiently
  To the loud clashing shears.

But thy nurse will bear no master,
  Thy nurse will bear no load;
And woe to them that shear her,
  And woe to them that goad!
When all the pack, loud baying,
  Her bloody lair surrounds,
She dies in silence, biting hard,
  Among the dying hounds.

No, no; I am convinced that, though bright, this is not tinsel nor silver foil; this is true steel. Here is a Roman soldier volunteering to hold the bridge while his comrades hack it to pieces behind him.

Then out spake brave Horatius,
  The Captain of the Gate:
'To every man upon this earth
  Death cometh soon or late.
And how can man die better
  Than facing fearful odds,
For the ashes of his fathers
  And the temples of his Gods?'

Not only is that good poetry of its kind, but I am certain that it is true. I believe that is how men feel in those simple, primitive times when right is right and wrong is wrong, and liberty is far more important than life. I believe that is how the Romans felt in those days; and, for all their terrible barbarities and weaknesses, they gave an example of patriotism to all later history. And it is bound to move any citizen of a free republic to watch the overthrow of a brutal despotism and the assertion of democracy and freedom. The Tarquins, the dynasty of Etruscans who ruled Rome as kings until their expulsion, are the villains of two of these fine ballads. You remember the infamous crime which actually caused the

Romans to rebel against them: the rape of the Roman lady Lucretia, who killed herself after being outraged by the Tarquin prince Sextus. Macaulay never tells this story, but it is always in the background, everyone knows it, and it is deeply, passionately felt. The evil prince appears in the Etruscan army as it moves toward the bridge.

> But when the face of Sextus
>     Was seen among the foes,
> A yell that rent the firmament
>     From all the town arose.
> On the house-tops was no woman
>     But spat towards him and hissed,
> No child but screamed out curses,
>     And shook its little fist.

In the second battle, at Lake Regillus, Sextus is the first to retreat, but he is not quick enough.

> And in the back false Sextus
>     Felt the good Roman steel,
> And wriggling in the dust he died
>     Like a worm beneath the wheel.

I am not ashamed to admit that I got the same kind of pleasure out of these poems at the age of ten or eleven as boys nowadays get out of motion pictures of Western adventure; and frankly, I still find the walkdown, with hero and villain shooting it out in the empty street, less thrilling than a hand-to-hand duel with cold steel.

> Then, whirling up his broadsword
>     With both hands to the height,
> He rushed against Horatius
>     And smote with all his might.
> With shield and blade Horatius
>     Right deftly turned the blow.
> The blow, though turned, came yet too nigh:
> It missed his helm, but gashed his thigh;
> The Tuscans raised a joyful cry
>     To see the red blood flow.

> He reeled, and on Herminius
>  He leaned one breathing-space;
> Then, like a wild cat mad with wounds,
>  Sprang right at Astur's face.
> Through teeth, and skull, and helmet,
>  So fierce a thrust he sped
> The good sword stood a handbreadth out
>  Behind the Tuscan's head.

Macaulay's first aim in writing these poems was historical reconstruction. He was doing the same sort of thing (on a smaller scale) as Shakespeare in writing *Macbeth* or Vergil in writing the *Aeneid*: giving a picture of a vanished age. He obviously liked thinking about the Romans when they were still uncorrupted; he admired their energy and their heroism.

But he had a second motive, a very peculiar one. He was by vocation a historian. Therefore he had to keep thinking about the sources for the history of the past. Now, we have several histories (in Greek and Latin) of the early days of Rome; but they were written many generations after the events they describe. Therefore the question is: on what were they based? Were there written records of those far distant days which the historians could use? And if so, what were the records like? Were they like the Bible, mainly a prose narrative? Or were they more like the *Iliad*, a vivid but incomplete group of poetic scenes? A German historian called Niebuhr, one of the founders of modern historiography, proposed that the early history of Rome as it has come down to us was based not on any continuous record, but rather on ballads describing single adventures, like that of Horatius at the bridge: poems which did not attempt to analyze economic forces or strategic problems, which admitted and enjoyed phenomenal adventures and miraculous interventions, and which blended much imagination and emotion with a smaller proportion of hard fact. None of these poems has survived; we hear of them only remotely and vaguely; but it is far from improbable that they existed. In the *Lays of Ancient Rome* Macaulay is trying to show what they would look like; and, allowing for the change from Italic to Anglo-Saxon styles, he succeeded very handsomely.

But, where does the propaganda come in? I never noticed it when I read these poems as a schoolboy. I simply enjoyed them — as I enjoyed reading the authentic ballads of 'Edward' or 'Sir Patrick Spens.' Still, looking back, I am absolutely certain that these poems were among the most potent initial forces which made me give up my life to the study of the classics. Beginning a strange pair of ancient languages at the age of eleven, studying nouns and verbs and trying to translate simple sentences, I felt merely curiosity about their peculiar structure, but I could not feel much emotional interest in the people who spoke them — until I read the *Lays of Ancient Rome,* and saw that the Romans were real, that they had character, that they were in fact more exciting than the drab city dwellers I saw all around me and perhaps more like my Covenanting Scottish ancestors.

These poems were therefore propaganda for the classics. But they contained a more subtle dose of propaganda than this. As you read them (at least when you are young and malleable) you are convinced that kings are cruel despots; that monarchy means tyranny; that hereditary aristocracy is a cloak for privilege and vice and crime; and that the worthiest way to live is as a citizen of a free republic, such as Rome was when it threw off the monarchy of the Tarquins. Now, Macaulay was a 100% Liberal. His father had been one of the most powerful propagandists for the abolition of slavery, and Macaulay himself was a Whig member of the first Reform Parliament. In the year 1842, when the *Lays* were published, the young Queen Victoria had been on the throne for only four years; she was still unpopular, and three attempts had been made to assassinate her. It would therefore have been possible for a man like Macaulay to say openly that the monarchy ought to be abolished and that Great Britain would be happier and more stable as a republic. It would have been possible, but it would have been indiscreet and injudicious. It would have

been rabble-rousing rather than constructive political thinking, at that time. What Macaulay could do was to present the
Whig point of view both emotionally — through these poems
and others — and intellectually — through the superb *History
of England* which he was then preparing to write, and which
is in fact a history of the overthrow of the royal house of
Stuart. In another poem, less well known than the *Lays*, he
shows us the triumph of Cromwell over King Charles I, and
describes Charles in a phrase of unforgettable bitterness:

The Man of Blood was there, with his long essencèd hair.

These words have the same fiery conviction behind them that
makes us, in the *Lays of Ancient Rome*, side with Horatius
and the free Romans against the Tarquins and false Sextus.
And it was that conviction, subtly instilled into me while I
was still a schoolboy and though I was enjoying poetry, not
reading propaganda, that prepared my mind to approve democracy, with all its risks and dangers, rather than the powers
and privileges of hereditary aristocracy, and to prefer a republic to a monarchy. This is an important choice. It was not
an easy choice to make. When I made it, the step was taken
with full intellectual understanding of its meaning. But the
emotional preparation for the step, without which it would
surely have been far more difficult, was made when I was still a
little boy, and read and reread the *Lays of Ancient Rome*.

# POEMS ON INSECTS

*Diminuendo*

———————————

SOME TIME ago I was ill for a couple of weeks. I went into the country to recover, and stayed in a pleasant house among trees and flowers. One afternoon I slept for an hour or so after lunch. When I woke, I lay for a while, relaxed and thoughtless, gazing at the ceiling. Three or four flies had got into the room, and were playing around the ceiling lamp. I watched them idly, wishing I had the energy to get up and swat them. Then suddenly, instead of hating them, I began to enjoy their company. They were not harming me. Instead, they seemed to be playing a complicated game, or dancing an intricate three-dimensional dance. Back and forward, round and round in interlacing spirals, up and down and catercornered they flew, never touching one another and yet passing so close that their wings almost brushed. When I tried to pick out one particular little dancer and watch him, I found it was absolutely impossible: in ten seconds he was lost in the maze. Occasionally one of them, as if tired, would land on the lamp-shade; and I found it delightful to watch the grace and ease with which he alighted (upside down) and stood there (upside down) regarding the others, until (as though caught by the continuing excitement of their aerial ballet) he dived out again into mid-air and joined them. Normally I hate flies. Like all insects they look not only revolting but terrifying when seen in a magnified photograph; and the housefly in particular is a foul color (that dirty black), has an ugly crouching stance and lives in filth. Yet on that sunlit afternoon, watching the four little dancers high in the air, I felt something more than tolerance for them — something oddly like affection.

Was this the effect of illness, I asked myself? Or had anyone else ever felt the same? At once a line of poetry flashed into my mind:

> Busy, curious, thirsty fly...

and I remembered that at least one poet had written a poem expressing kindness and hospitality to a housefly. With a slight effort I got out of bed and looked for it. Yes, there it was: *To a Fly Drinking Out of His Cup,* by the strange old English antiquarian William Oldys, who died in 1761.

> Busy, curious, thirsty fly!
> Drink with me, and drink as I!
> Freely welcome to my cup,
> Couldst thou sip and sip it up:
> Make the most of life you may;
> Life is short and wears away.
>
> Both alike are mine and thine,
> Hastening quick to their decline!
> Thine's a summer, mine no more
> Though repeated to three score.
> Three score summers when they're gone
> Will appear as short as one.

A charming thing: a lyric poem in the Anacreontic style — technically an ode; light in form, light in subject, humorous in tone, and yet with a basis of melancholy in its comparison of the short life of the fly to the short life of human beings.

Short life, inevitable death...suddenly I recalled another poem on a fly, this one almost as brief, almost as light in tone, but far more somber in meaning. It was a meditative lyric, sixteen lines long, by the Amherst poet Emily Dickinson, acute-angled and diamond-hard.

> I heard a fly buzz when I died;
> The stillness in the room
> Was like the stillness in the air
> Between the heaves of storm.
>
> The eyes around had wrung them dry,
> And breaths were gathering firm
> For that last onset, when the king
> Be witnessed in the room.
>
> I willed my keepsakes, signed away
> What portion of me be
> Assignable — and then it was
> There interposed a fly
>
> With blue, uncertain, stumbling buzz
> Between the light and me;
> And then the windows failed, and then
> I could not see to see.*

Emily Dickinson saw the fly as an emblem of death. Oldys saw it as a symbol of the brevity of life. Nowadays we are all so conscious of the dangers of infectious disease that we can scarcely look at a fly without seeing it as a carrier of sickness: those agile little feet are coated with typhoid bacilli, that busy, curious, thirsty proboscis may transport the virus of polio-myelitis. It needed a considerable effort for me to look at the flies in my bedroom merely as ballet dancers of the air. The normal attitude of modern people to flies has been put excel-lently well by Karl Shapiro, in a fine poem on the grotesque and poisonous aspects of the little beasts. Its opening stanza will show its quality.

---

* 'Dying'

> O hideous little bat, the size of snot,
> With polyhedral eye and shabby clothes,
> To populate the stinking cat you walk
> The promontory of the dead man's nose,
> Climb with the fine leg of a Duncan-Phyfe
> > The smoking mountains of my food
> > > And in a comic mood
> > > In mid-air take to bed a wife.*

Revolting, isn't it? And yet admirable poetry: a curious conversion of ugliness into something like grace — just as a mere prehistoric fly, stuck in the resin coming from a prehistoric pine tree, changes, when the resin hardens into amber, into something like a jewel.

Now, the average man would say that it was quite impossible to write poetry about anything so ignoble as a fly; and that, even if it were possible, it would be a waste of time. And yet there we have seen good poets exercising their art on flies, and saying something impressive too. In fact, anything which is part of this astonishing world we live in can provide the material for poetry — anything, provided that the poet feels some concern for it, some active relationship between it and him, be it wonder or sympathy or even hatred. Flowers, birds, trees, animals are obvious subjects for poetic meditation; but the more fantastic inhabitants of the planet can also become poetry — fish in their shining armor, the reptiles who gaze at us out of eyes that are infinitely old, and the small, ruthless, elaborate world of insects.

A fairly large volume could be made out of nothing but European and American poems on insects. The butterfly with its brilliant colors and its drunken flight, the bees with their strongly moral habits, their diligence and their unique power of producing sweetness and light — these are obvious subjects. Even those dreary and sometimes terrifying socialists, the ants, and those deft assassins, the spiders, have had good poems written about them.

---

* Karl Shapiro, 'The Fly'

If you read the *Metamorphoses* of Ovid, you will soon find the beautiful myth of Arachne, the girl who prided herself on her fabulous weaving and competed with the goddess Athene, and, after the contest, hanged herself and was changed into a spider: that is why she is always hanging, and always, with superb skill and infinite diligence, weaving. Or, if you look at the Bible, you will find in the Book of Proverbs a handsome couplet praising the same animal for her wisdom and resolution:

> The spider taketh hold with her hands,
>    and is in kings' palaces.*

As for the ants, the contemporary poet William Empson has a characteristically clever sonnet about them; while the fastidious cavalier with the delightful name, Sir Richard Lovelace, once wrote a poem reversing the advice of the Book of Proverbs, and telling the ant to take it easy for a while, to relax and listen to music.

> Forbear, thou great good husband, † little ant;
>    A little respite from thy flood of sweat;
> Thou, thine own horse and cart, under this plant,
>    Thy spacious tent, fan thy prodigious heat;
> Down with thy double load of that one grain;
> It is a granary for all thy train.
>
> Cease large example of wise thrift a while
>    (For thy example is become our law)
> And teach thy frowns a seasonable smile:
>    So Cato sometimes the nak'd Florals saw.
> And thou almighty foe, lay by thy sting,
> Whilst thy unpaid musicians, crickets, sing.‡

Even that delicate little pest, the mosquito, has inspired good poets with good poems. The exquisite Greek epigrammatist Meleager begged a mosquito to fly away from his bed to his sweetheart's, and to sound its little trumpet in her ear,

---

* Proverbs xxx 28
† husbandman, farmer
‡ Lovelace, 'The Ant'

so that she might wake, and rise, and come to him. In Latin there is a large and occasionally amusing poem about the death of a mosquito which stung a sleeping shepherd and woke him; he slapped it and killed it, and then noticed a poisonous snake which had been about to attack him if his sleep had not been broken. That night he was visited by the reproachful ghost of the mosquito, who described the world of the dead to him in tones so terrifying that, in the morning, he erected a monument to the insect and added an epigram in pure Latin verse.*

Even verminous insects can be converted into poetry. The French poet Ronsard reflected that a flea could become more intimate with his sweetheart than he himself could; and he wrote a poem ending with the wish that, for one evening, he himself might become a flea, with such privileges:

> Que pleust à Dieu que je pusse
> Pour un soir devenir puce! †

This was imitated by the Scottish poet Drummond of Hawthornden in a slightly naughty but highly imaginative poem, 'The Happiness of a Flea':

> How happier is that flea
> Which in thy breast doth play
> Than that pied butterfly
> Which courts the flame, and in the same doth die!
>
> That hath a light delight
> (Poor fool) contented only with a sight;
> When this doth sport and swell with dearest food,
> And, if he die, he knight-like dies in blood.

But it has been reserved for a native American poet to write a poem on an insect so small that it is practically invisible — no

---

* This complicated joke was believed for many centuries to be a schoolboy poem written by the greatest of Latin poets, Vergil; and the question is not quite settled even today.
† Ronsard, 'Gayeté,' Pléiade edition 2.760

more than a tiny black dot on a sheet of paper. The poet is in the much beloved Robert Frost (who also has good poems on an ant, a spider, and a white-tailed hornet); the poem is *A Considerable Speck.*

A speck that would have been beneath my sight
On any but a paper sheet so white
Set off across what I had written there.
And I had idly poised my pen in air
To stop it with a period of ink
When something strange about it made me think.
This was no dust speck by my breathing blown,
But unmistakably a living mite
With inclinations it could call its own.
It paused as with suspicion of my pen,
And then came racing wildly on again
To where my manuscript was not yet dry;
Then paused again and either drank or smelt —
With loathing, for again it turned to fly.
Plainly with an intelligence I dealt.
It seemed too tiny to have room for feet,
Yet must have had a set of them complete
To express how much it didn't want to die.
It ran with terror and with cunning crept.
It faltered; I could see it hesitate;
Then in the middle of the open sheet
Cower down in desperation to accept
Whatever I accorded it of fate.

I have none of the tenderer-than-thou
Collectivistic regimenting love
With which the modern world is being swept.
But this poor microscopic item now!
Since it was nothing I knew evil of
I let it lie there till I hope it slept.

I have a mind myself and recognize
Mind when I meet with it in any guise.
No one can know how glad I am to find
On any sheet the least display of mind.

## Could It Be Verse?

---

'WHEN I hear the word *culture* I reach for my revolver,' said the late Marshal Goering. We all agree he was a barbarian; but, confidentially, when you hear the word *poetry* do you reach for a mystery story? Quite a lot of people do: or at least, they turn their mental receiver off, and begin to think about something more interesting. And yet, you know, if they see a new poem by Ogden Nash in a magazine, they read it with pleasure, and cut it out, and carry it around in their wallet, and show it to people. It is not that they really dislike poetry. No: they have simply been told that the word *poetry* means only serious verse, deeply tragical like the work of Robinson Jeffers or mystical and hard to understand like Eliot's *Four Quartets*; and they feel disinclined to make the effort of understanding such poetry — or, quite often, they feel temperamentally unsympathetic to it. It is the same with music. Many a couple would never think of claiming to be music-lovers, and have never entered a concert-hall to hear a symphony orchestra; but they never miss a new musical show on Broadway — they saw *The King and I* four times — and they have a large collection of pop records.

The truth is that both poetry and music have been too narrowly restricted to serious poetry and solemn music. I think I first noticed this several years ago, when I got hold of two anthologies of poems which were all intended to be amusing. One is *The Oxford Book of Light Verse,* edited by W. H. Auden, who has a high reputation as a difficult and serious poet. The other is *What Cheer,* edited by David McCord, himself a considerable craftsman in light-verse-making. After they had been on my bedside table for some weeks and I knew most of their contents, I began to wonder why many of the poems collected in them had not appeared in other anthologies, too. In particular, I wondered why there should be an *Oxford Book of English Verse,* nearly all serious, and an *Oxford Book of Light Verse,* nearly all funny.

Then the parallel with music struck me. Both Richard Rodgers and Samuel Barber are American musicians. One is not necessarily inferior to the other because one is gay and romantic while the other is mainly serious: they are to be judged as craftsmen on their techniques, and as artists on the completeness and richness of their views of life. There have been some famous musicians most of whose work was non-serious. Joseph Haydn was happiest when he was having fun. Richard Strauss's finest work is full of deliberate joking, usually very successful. A sense of humor is as necessary a part of a complete vision of the world as a sense of pity and terror.

And in fact many of the most famous poets of the past and the present have written both serious and light verse. Think of Eliot's cat poems; of Pound's numerous jokes and ploys, of the sly humor of Robert Frost. Robert Browning made English verse play tricks which astounded his more austere contemporaries; and there was both a tragic hero and a harlequin in George Gordon, Lord Byron.

So, when we talk of modern poetry, we ought not to assume that it is all gloomy and most of it unintelligible. We ought, as well as admiring the poetic technique of Robert Lowell and Marianne Moore, to enjoy the skill of other American contemporaries who are able and conscientious craftsmen, equally sincere if differently appealing. These are not hacks, but real poets who compose because they have something to say; they have a genuine feeling for language; and they are, each in his way, creative. The most famous American light versifier is Ogden Nash, who has succeeded in one of the things all poets long to achieve — he has created an original style, recognized and loved everywhere as his very own. Almost equally well-known is Phyllis McGinley, whose *Love Letters of Phyllis McGinley* became a best-seller in the fall of 1954. Then there is an ingenious Harvard poet called David McCord, whose poems combine the delights of poetry with those of Scrabble. And there is a brilliant Cornell professor, Morris Bishop, who has been scintillating with wit for over twenty years. His latest is called *A Bowl of Bishop* and is dedicated 'To my Public, wherever she is.'

All these poets, just like the writers of serious verse, are interested in exploring the resources of language and of poetic technique; and sometimes they use skills which their serious contemporaries neglect.

To begin with, they all know that poetry involves delight in the actual *sounds* of language — just as one of the prime qualities of good painting is delight in color for its own sake. Most of the important serious poets, having practically abandoned rhyme and apparently despising the illogical melodious aspect of speech, fail to give us that particular delight. The most prestidigitatious manipulator of sound effects is surely McCord. Here is his description of the Chinese section of a museum — regal, precious, and yet not quite dead:

> Then the glance slants
> To the jade blade
> With the gilt hilt
> In the shade made
> By the chance stance
> Of the Ming King
> In the tomb gloom
> Of the Sing Wing.*

Dame Edith Sitwell might not be ashamed of that.

---

* 'Nightmare in a Museum'

Now consider Morris Bishop describing an intellectual who has been reading some contemporary books of higher criticism and can stand it no longer:

> Weary of evaluating basic criteria,
> Weary of implementing orientation,
> Of visualizing motivational factors wearier
> He bade a vindictive farewell to civilization.
>
> The jungle apes sought he out; and upon them spying,
> He gained of the simian language a smattering.
> 'His gesture is a challenge!' the pleased primates were crying.
> 'It is indeed a dynamic concept!' he heard them chattering.*

Mr. Bishop prefers European railway carriages to American coaches, because in Europe the passengers sit facing one another: there might be a lovely girl with whom one could exchange glances. But that is impossible on American railroads:

> How, to one's vis-à-vis, hint at a date at eight?
> Where is no vis-à-vis, there is no tête-à-tête.†

And, like many of us, Mr. McCord has been infuriated by people who come back from Mexico and insist on speaking Espanish with a new especial acthent. So he has produced a poem called 'A Hex on the Mexican X':

> Returned from Mehiko he'll grab,
> If he has luck, a tahikab.
> And shouting to the driver: 'Son,'
> He'll shout, 'make haste to Lehington
> And Sihy-first.' And now he's there,
> Ehaling fresh monohide air.
> Manhattan leaps from plinth of stone;
> His soul sings like a sahophone.

This is conjuring. It has its place not only in poetry but in all art. In the visual arts of today it is most like the pictures of

---

* 'Lines prompted no doubt by an escape-mechanism'
† 'Railroad-coach seating-arrangement, I cannot but deplore you'

Saul Steinberg and certain pen-and-ink drawings of Salvador Dali, in which the black line on the white paper takes wings and flies over the whole surface, in curves as intricate and spontaneous as those of a skater or a flying swallow.

Poetry uses not only the sounds of vowels and consonants but the *rhythms* which they make in each particular language. Rhythm is one of the hardest problems of the modern poet, now that poetry has almost lost its connection with music and dancing. The light poets solve this problem by making their rhythms new, unexpected, and amusing by their eccentricity. Ogden Nash is the master of this. Much of his poetry appears to be prose until you suddenly reach the end of a couplet and see that it must be verse. Here is the close of a splendid satiric poem he wrote on Mother's Day, attacking the contemptible misuse of motherhood as an advertising gimmick to help merchants to sell more quick-fading flowers and more junky gifts. He spells out M O T H E R as though in neon lights:

> M is for the preliminary million-dollar advertising appropriation,
>
> O means that she is always white-haired, bespectacled, and at least eighty-five years old,
>
> T is for Telegraph message number 31B which contains a tastefully blended expression of sentiment and congratulation,
>
> H is for the coast-to-coast questionnaire which proved conclusively that seven-and-one-half citizens out of every ten with incomes of $5000 a year or better would rather have their mother than gold.
>
> E is for the Elephants which everybody is very glad didn't sit down on their mothers,
>
> R is for Rosemary which is for Remembrance of the fact that a mother is one thing that you will never have more than one of,
>
> Put them all together and before you can say H. St. C. Wellington Carruthers, they spell the second of two things that everybody who loves their mother only

once a year and then only at the instigation of the
Chamber of Commerce is a son of.*

Does this kind of thing correspond to anything in the other
arts? Yes, surely it does. It is syncopation. What Nash does
with language and with the unexpected twists of verbal
rhythm, Gershwin and others do with melodies based on the
off-center beat. Whenever I read one of Nash's long bravura
passages, wandering away off into the stratosphere and then
reverting to the rhyme which everything but my subconscious
ear has forgotten, I think of the conversion of a straightforward melody into wild arabesques under the flying fingers of
Errol Garner or Art Tatum.

We should not forget the fact that two recent and successful
innovations in poetic form have both been in the field of
rhythm and have both been light and gay. One is the limerick,
first popularized by Edward Lear. The other is the clerihew,
invented by Edward Clerihew Bentley (who wrote *Trent's
Last Case*) and named after his middle name: a four-line stanza
dealing flippantly with a distinguished figure, and deliberately
jolty in rhythm, like this:

> George the Third
> Ought never to have occurred.
> One can only wonder
> At so grotesque a blunder.

Or this, which can still be practiced by busy men who want to
take the evening off:

> Sir Christopher Wren
> Said 'I am going to dine with some men.
> If anybody calls
> Say I am designing St. Paul's.'

---

* 'Epilogue to Mother's Day, which is to be published on any day but
Mother's Day'

There is one other kind of rhythmically playful poetry which simply cannot be talked about. It must be read. This is the kind of verse which plays with the appearance of words on the printed page. E. E. Cummings is the master of this: it is surprising to see how many of his apparently complex poems are really simple little lyrics in more or less free verse which have been given an extra dimension of meaning by novel typographical arrangement. Among the light versifiers, Morris Bishop follows him closely: he has one poem on dialect, printed partly in our own letters and partly in the International Phonetic Alphabet, which must be seen to be appreciated.

But all this is subordinate to the main point, which is the feeling and the thought. If poets do not think and feel, they are little more than interior decorators. And the unexpected thing is that many light poets think and feel quite as deeply as the self-confessed serious poets. When you look through *The Oxford Book of Light Verse*, you are constantly arrested by a quip or amused by a trick, and then made to reflect by the underlying idea. The light poets of today not only feel deeply, but sometimes write gravely: not too often, but often enough to make us realize that they are much more than jugglers. Like the Greek epigrammatists, they choose to conceal most of their deeper thoughts in order to make those which they reveal more truly impressive. Here is a single four-line poem by Phyllis McGinley, called 'The Old Philanthropist':

> His millions make museums bright;
>    Harvard anticipates his will;
> While his young typist weeps at night
>    Over a druggist's bill.

Some writers would have expanded that into an entire short story, and made it less effective. And here is the quatrain with which Ogden Nash closes his book *Family Reunion* — an admirable poem on an unpoetic subject, middle age:

When I remember bygone days
I think how evening follows morn:
So many I loved were not yet dead,
So many I love were not yet born.*

No, the difference between these poets and their serious colleagues is not simply that they are light and the others are heavy. All original poets, all careful craftsmen of words, are serious writers. There are other differences, more genuine.

One difference is that Ogden Nash and those like him address the public directly, while Eliot and Pound and the others have a partly private utterance, which we are permitted to overhear and, if we can, to interpret. Another important distinction is that the light poets are optimists, although they are occasionally serious and even sad, while the others are mostly pessimists, viewing life as a bitter struggle, or at best a tragic farce. And, further, the light poets actually enjoy the patterns made by sounds; they use them not only for emphasis, but for delight; they know that one of the roots of our pleasure in art is the instinct for *play*; and so, as Haydn played with musical notes and rhythms, and as Rubens played with colors and curves (and what colors! what curves!), they play with the sounds and even the appearances of words — while their serious colleagues either neglect such patterns, or else use them to make their own subject-matter still stranger and more complex.

But these are not differences between good artists and bad artists, between important and trashy writers. They are simply differences of technique and purpose between several craftsmen, all, it may well be, equally valuable, and, I am sure, all equally conscientious. You can see this most clearly in perspective. When I am trying to understand the literature of the Renaissance, I read the uproarious and indecent Rabelais as well as the serious and anxious Montaigne. Italian poetry begins with a hymn by St. Francis and a vision by Dante, but the

---

* 'The Middle'

first masterpiece of Italian prose is the naughty *Decameron* of Boccaccio. And in one of the finest of Plato's dialogues, the *Symposium*, after an evening in which Socrates and his friends have discussed the inmost and the highest meanings of love, the scene closes with Socrates sitting between the host, the tragic poet Agathon, and the famous comedian Aristophanes: he is attempting to persuade them that the best writer of tragedy must also be the best writer of comedy. It is well after midnight; and, anyhow, no one could argue with Socrates; at last they both pass out; and, symbolically, Socrates covers them up and leaves them, snoring gently together — the tragic poet dreaming of the inexplicable gods and the pitilessness of fate, and the comic poet dreaming of the inexplicable race of mankind and the laughable absurdities of human life.

# HORACE

## *A Little Latin Lyric*

———————

USUALLY we think that a lyric poem ought to be simple and straightforward, charging right into its subject with reckless abandon, caring nothing about structure or logic, singing out directly and avoiding all subtleties, all implications. The young cowboy advances and begins, 'Oh, what a beautiful morning!' The young lover cries, 'O my luve's like a red, red rose.' The opponent of slavery raises her hymn, 'Mine eyes have seen the glory of the coming of the Lord.' All clear, plain, passionate statements, conveying their simple emotions simply.

Yes, but it need not be so, and it has not always been so. There are some poets who, even though they feel the surge of the emotion that makes a lyric poem, are unable or unwilling to put it into direct words. They prefer to wait; to catch the surge after it has reached its peak and is sinking back; to express only part of their excitement, and possibly not the most important part; to speak in phrases which are almost riddles, so that the hearer or reader has to guess at some of their meaning. This is not, usually, the cult of obscurity. Some poets, like some artists, prefer to give an impression rather than a detailed photograph, a sketch rather than a finished painting. There are some emotions which are better appreciated if they are expressed indirectly. Most Japanese short lyrics are indirect and deliberately incomplete. A number of Eliot's and Dylan Thomas's lyric poems are tangential to their subject. And, although we usually think of Latin as a bold, strong, heavy, punch-straight-through language, there is one Latin lyric poet who prefers to bend its strong iron into unexpected curves, to eschew its unexampled power of direct statement for a more subtle technique of implication.

This is Horace. He lived and wrote under the emperor Augustus. In the year 23 B.C. he published a collection of eighty-eight lyric poems which he called *Songs*, and which we now miscall *Odes*. They are quite short, most of them; several are only eight lines long; but they made him a reputation which has lasted for two thousand years. One of them in particular has long been a favorite because it handles a delightful but rather difficult subject so obliquely and so deftly. It is only sixteen lines in length, but it contains at least as much material as the average short story.

Horace was about forty (probably) when he wrote it. He addressed it to a girl with whom he had been in love not long before. Her name is Pyrrha, which means simply Blonde. There is nothing whatever in the poem that needs explanations or footnotes — except for one allusion at the end. You ought to know that, just as modern Italian sailors call upon the saints when they feel they are in danger of shipwreck, and sometimes even make vows to dedicate something to their patron saint if they survive, so in ancient Italy they prayed to the god of the sea, and, if they were saved, they would put up a tablet in his temple recording their escape (sometimes adding a picture of the shipwreck), and hang their clothes beside it as an offering and a proof of his power.

The poet begins by imagining the beautiful blonde Pyrrha sitting beside one of her newest lovers, cool in a grotto, surrounded with flowers.

What slim elegant youth, drenched in effusive scent,
now sits close to your side, Pyrrha, in some recess
      rich with many a rosebloom?
Who loves smoothing your yellow hair,
chic yet daintily plain? How many gods profaned,
what indelible vows he will lament, and oh,
      what dark hurricane-lashed seas
he will watch with a pallid cheek!
Poor fool, golden he thinks you will for ever be,
heart-free always, he hopes, always adorable —
      yet knows not the deceitful
offshore squalls. To a novice, you
shine too temptingly bright. Here on the temple wall
one small tablet of mine, offering up my clothes
      (all I saved from a shipwreck)
says Thank God, that I just escaped.

The translation is my own. The meter is as close a corre-
spondence to the original as I can manage: it is a subtle variation on a slow waltz rhythm: Poor fool, golden-he-thinks you-
will-for-ever be. . . .

Now, there is a good deal in this little poem, but it is expressed indirectly, off beat, by implication. First, the poet implies but never directly utters the chief contrast which fills his
mind: *Pyrrha, you are beautiful but you are dangerous, fickle
and dangerous.* It might have taken him a single quatrain to
say this. Instead, he moves aslant. He asks, 'Who is making
love to you now, Pyrrha? — poor fool, what he will have to go
through! *I* ought to know!'

Then — and I must say that this seems to me to be extraordi-
narily skillful — there is a leading image which is implied, and
which grows more powerful as the little poem draws toward its
end, but which is never stated directly. It appears first in the
sentence

      what dark hurricane-lashed seas
he will watch with a pallid cheek!

It is hinted at in

      golden he thinks you will for ever be.

and again in

> knows not the deceitful
> offshore squalls.

The beautiful sentence

> To a novice, you
> shine too temptingly bright

is both literally true — of a lovely blonde with smooth yellow hair knotted low on the nape of the neck, and doubtless those heavenly blue eyes — and at the same time part of the image. And in the last stanza, where Horace reflects, with a rueful smile,

> Here on the temple wall
> one small tablet of mine, offering up my clothes
> (all I saved from a shipwreck)
> says Thank God, that I just escaped . . .

— in that stanza the image is almost fully developed. It is a metaphor which is perhaps a little difficult for us if we have seen only the Atlantic and Pacific Oceans, and perhaps the Great Lakes; but we can grasp it. The girl, Pyrrha, gold and blue and lovely, is like a summer sea; but on that sea a dangerous squall can swoop down in a matter of minutes, lashing its surface into a black rage, overturning the little ships which, a few moments earlier, were sailing blithely and too trustfully over the dancing, laughing waves. That kind of sudden storm is particularly common in the Mediterranean. Shelley and the yacht he was sailing in were lost in a squall that lasted for no more than twenty minutes; and although some think he was murdered, his boat might possibly have been capsized by a violent blast. I remember once setting out from Naples to sail to Capri (which is seventeen miles away) in bright sunshine, under a dazzling blue sky; before we had gone seven miles, the rain was lashing down on us, the ship was pitching and rolling like a canoe in the rapids, groans and cries surrounded us and spilled Chianti reddened the decks — yet as we reached Capri, the skies were clearing, and the sun beamed on us like the radiant laughter of a fickle coquette.

We learn a great deal about Pyrrha from these short four verses. Indirectly but clearly, Horace tells us that she is as beautiful as a summer sea, but as dangerous. He tells us also that she is not quite a natural beauty. Her blonde hair is artfully arranged to look naive: *simplex munditiis,* says Horace, which Milton translated (wrongly, I am afraid, because he missed the sophisticated flavor of *munditiis*) 'plain in thy neatness,' but which could be better put as 'elegantly simple' — there must be some phrase which could cover it in the vocabulary of *Vogue.* Her new love scene is set in a grotto, with roses climbing up the walls and hanging in clusters from the roof. That kind of grotto the Romans often built, or adapted, as an annex to a summer place. The recent discovery of some fragmentary sculptures which may have belonged to the emperor Tiberius, in a western Italian village called simply Grotto, Sperlonga, shows us how luxurious, and at the same time how artificial, they were. Even Pyrrha's new lover will be a little overdone, drenched with flowing perfume. We can almost smell it, and see it ready to drip off those black glossy curls. A new lover ... yes, of course, Horace adds that Pyrrha is the sort of girl who will always have some new lover hanging on her lips. His name scarcely matters, provided that he has enough money and is enough of a simpleton to believe her and worship her.

About Horace himself, his poem tells us something too. It tells us that, at the age of forty, he is still amorous enough to have made a fool of himself quite recently over a beautiful heartless girl; but it implies that he is gradually growing more cautious, more mature. He is not looking forward to his next conquest. He is looking backward on his narrow escape. On the other hand, a man who is entering his years of discretion, or aging, cannot fully enjoy it. Youth is too wonderful to be wasted on the young; but in practice it almost always is. Therefore Horace, without much sympathy, and with more than a touch of jealousy, wonders about the slender youth who has succeeded him as the lover of Pyrrha. Here there is an almost too subtle piece of indirectness: for the new adorer is specifically described as being *gracilis puer*, 'a slender youth,' whereas Horace was now no longer a youth, nor — as we know from his own poems and the jokes of his friends — slender; in fact, he was short and tubby. He looked like a tankard. Other poets have written poems about the agonies of growing up. Some have written poems about the painful spiritual problems of losing youthful idealism. Horace is one of the few who have been able to make poetry out of the process of reaching middle age.

One further charm in this little poem — a charm which has not often been pointed out, although it has often been felt by readers (other than professors). This is that it is essentially witty; it is gay. Some of its humor can never be conveyed even by the most skillful translation into English, simply because English is a less pliable language than Latin. Horace was one of the revolutionary poets who took what had been a hard, sober, often inflexible speech, and made it supple, light, intricate. The first question in the poem is

> What slim elegant youth, drenched in effusive scent,
> now sits close to your side, Pyrrha, in some recess
> rich with many a rosebloom?

But in Latin the words are so arranged that they make a picture of the scene. The question begins:

> Quis multa gracilis *te* puer in rosa...?

which, to the Romans, meant

> What many slender you boy among a rose...?

The girl (addressed as 'you') is in the center. The slender boy has his arms around her, and the bower of roses is draped on each side of the couple ('what many slender you boy among a rose...?'). This is not conventional Latin. When it came out, it made its first readers stare and gasp, as T. S. Eliot did when he published *The Waste Land*. But it is very effective, in that (if you know Latin decently enough to appreciate the structure of a poem) you never forget such a witty arrangement of words, and you are astonished, every time you recall it, by the skill of Horace in displacement and postponement and cantilever construction. Sometimes it makes you think of the art of the impressionist painters. If Horace himself had not arranged his sentences so tightly and planned his dancing meter so deftly, one would be tempted to translate the poem into impressionist terms, in the Ezra Pound manner:

> roses
> youth around you slender
> many roses

But that would be to ignore, to abolish one of Horace's most carefully devised effects, which is to combine perfect organization and control with apparently improvisatory freedom of fancy.

Still, apart from the extreme skill of wording and phrasing, there is a great deal of wit in the handling of the themes of the poem. In some ways, sex is funny. Yet a perfectly beautiful woman is not usually funny — at least not to men, certainly not to men who can be stirred by her loveliness and find it almost irresistible. Death is not funny, either, still less death in a storm at sea. 'Fear death by water,' says T. S. Eliot, and who does not? Now, imagine writing a poem in which a beautiful girl is compared to the sea, which looks enticing and then, in a sudden storm, seizes and drowns helpless sailors. Not a comic theme, you would say? But yet it might be — if you yourself have escaped, although destitute and bankrupt and suffering from exposure and shock, bringing nothing out of the sudden disaster but your own dripping and ruined clothes, which you will gladly, so gladly, strip off and offer to the sea spirit who saved your life when you thought you were dead; and if your successor in the arms of the pretty blonde, poor fool, is to be involved in another storm of the same kind, terrified, wrecked, perhaps utterly destroyed. . . .

## *Memories of Heaven*

ONE of the most painful experiences anyone can have is to lose faith in himself and in the work of his life. To wonder why you got married and raised a family; why you spent twenty or thirty years in a business which will apparently never do more than just barely support you; why you ever settled in a place which you detest and tried to make a circle of friends who turn out to be selfish and vulgar oafs — that is a spiritual agony in which it is difficult to be courageous. Fortunate are those of us who have never felt it: may it never come to them! Among those who have to endure it, perhaps the most bitterly tormented are the men and women who once hoped to be creative artists. To be trained as a musician, to have a promising debut, and then to find that one cannot compose anything new and original; to publish several novels or books of poetry, and then to run dry — that is not only a cruel disappointment, but, because it implies the loss of a sensitivity which one formerly enjoyed, a permanent grief. It was partly to escape this loss and to comfort this grief that Dylan Thomas drank so furiously hard; possibly Jackson Pollock suffered from the same despair in the last years of his life; it was this black shadow which fell over Hugo Wolf and Robert Schumann.

Strange as the idea seems, this sorrow can be conquered; or, if not conquered, at least used. It is a strong passion; and any strong passion can be converted into a moving force, sometimes in daily life, often in the arts. What caused the profound suicidal gloom of Rachmaninoff's music is not clearly known; but it is evident that he used his own bitter misery as a motive, and, by converting it into symphonic music, made it easier for himself to bear. One of the most famous and noble poems in our language was created by a man who had passed through the same agony, was sorely scarred by it, knew he would never return to his earlier happiness, and yet was determined to live and to translate his anguish into beauty. This is an ode by William Wordsworth, called by the rather clumsy and obscure title *Intimations of Immortality from Recollections of Early Childhood*. He published it in 1807, when he was thirty-seven years old; but he had worked on it for several years, and it was the outcome of a period of pain and pessimism through which he had passed at the age (always crucial for men) of thirty-two.

Wordsworth was a fine poet, with an original and sincere view of life and a charmingly naïve style which, although apparently childlike in its simplicity, could rise to astonishing heights of pathos and rapture. Together with his friend Samuel Coleridge, when they were both in their twenties, he published a collection of *Lyrical Ballads* which helped to change and purify the entire current of English poetry. At first this volume was sneered at and parodied and dismissed with contumely. But it was right; and its two young authors, Coleridge and Wordsworth, knew that it was right. It would last; it has endured. Apparently they both had fine careers before them. They would write much more that would live. But then a dark cloud fell upon them. They could write no more. They could not even feel what (as young poets) they once had felt with such fervor that it was easy to turn it into musical words and vivid images. Their spiritual lives had come to an end in darkness and despair — or so it seemed.

There were several different reasons for this. Coleridge had become a drug addict, although he was scarcely thirty; he was finding it more and more difficult to think and write normally because he was apt to be either dreamily incoherent or else miserably depressed. Politically, they were both saddened by the failure of the French Revolution. They had been optimistic young revolutionaries in the early days when (as Wordsworth put it)

> Bliss was it in that dawn to be alive,
> But to be young was very Heaven! *

However, they saw it following what we, today, recognize as the customary path of revolutions, but what was for them a bitterly disappointing process of degeneration: the first upsurge of liberalism had passed into a blood bath of terror, with mob trials and mob executions and indiscriminate destruction, and then the revolt had been taken over, with a whiff of grapeshot, by an intelligent, ruthless, conscienceless, ambitious dictator. Neither Coleridge nor Wordsworth was ever very explicit about sex; but sexually also they were ceasing to be young. Coleridge's little son was nearly six years old. Wordsworth had an illegitimate daughter who was now ten, born of a French girl whom he had loved in his early, idealistic period; and he was torn between regret for that romantic past and his plans to marry a quiet English girl from his own milieu. To have a growing child is to cease to be young.

The two young poets talked their trouble over, again and again; but they could find no explicit solution, no remedy. They had lost so much. They no longer felt their accustomed joy in the scenery of wild nature — although they lived in one of the most beautiful and unspoiled regions of England, the county of Cumberland, with its lakes and mountains and lonely little farms. They had lost their empathy with wild and naïve life: the movements of animals, the voices of children and birds, the dance of winds and clouds, the happiness of trees and flowers. They knew that they could now no longer expect the special ecstatic pleasure of youth, that sense of novelty with which young people confront each experience, and almost

---

* *The Prelude* 11.108-9

every dawning day. Now the poets felt that even their emotions were dying. Instead of the excitement, the joy or pain, the energy and rapidity of sensation with which they had once watched the world and lived their own lives, they were dull, neutral, apathetic. They had nothing to look forward to except adult life with its routine and repetitiousness, and then old age, that preparation for death.

There was no escape which they could see. Yet they had one consolation. Perhaps they could never again write poetry on their old themes in their former youthful manner; but at least they could read poetry, understand poetry, and love poetry. They talked, therefore, of what they had read in the previous months before their meeting; and they escaped a little from their despondency. A good book, for a poet, is a stimulus almost as powerful as a mountain landscape or a love affair. They knew this, and besides Coleridge loved to talk, and Wordsworth was content to listen; and on these terms they discussed the fine odes written nearly three hundred years earlier (on Greek and Latin models) by rare old Ben Jonson. A few days later, they read Jonson's lyrics; and after an interval for incubation, they started once more to write poetry.

Coleridge produced an ode called, simply, *Dejection*. It is not a very good poem: too many repetitions and clichés, and too much vague phraseology which covers, instead of exploring, the emotions he felt. Yet now and then it does express the despair which had afflicted him.

> Those thin clouds above, in flakes and bars,
> That give away their motion to the stars;
> Those stars, that glide behind them or between,
> Now sparkling, now bedimmed, but always seen:
> Yon crescent Moon, as fixed as if it grew
> In its own cloudless, starless lake of blue;
> I see them all so excellently fair,
> I see, not feel, how beautiful they are!

But Wordsworth wrote a masterpiece, the Ode, *Intimations of Immortality*. It is one of the favorite English lyrics, because we all use phrases from it without even recognizing them. Two or three of the eleven sections which make it up are poetry of the absolutely first rank: with a noble and difficult meaning expressed in clear, brilliant, but perfectly natural phrases and symbols; and the poem as a whole is a triumphant success in one of the most complex of lyrical forms, the Pindaric ode.

Its meaning is hard to elucidate, because it is an attempt to answer a hard question; the question posed to Wordsworth by the decay of his youth, the loss of his fresh sensibility, the numbing of his poetic gift. Both the meaning of the poem and its essential beauty can be seen in one single, one immortal paragraph: twenty lines which should not be read or heard in a few moments, but learned, and recollected, and remembered, and treasured.

> Our birth is but a sleep and a forgetting:
> The Soul that rises with us, our life's Star,
>   Hath had elsewhere its setting,
>     And cometh from afar:
>   Not in entire forgetfulness,
>   And not in utter nakedness,
> But trailing clouds of glory do we come
>     From God, who is our home:
> Heaven lies about us in our infancy!
> Shades of the prison-house begin to close
>     Upon the growing Boy,
> But He beholds the light, and whence it flows,
>     He sees it in his joy;
> The Youth, who daily farther from the east
>     Must travel, still is Nature's Priest,
>     And by the vision splendid
>     Is on his way attended;
> At length the Man perceives it die away,
> And fade into the light of common day.

Behind this wonderful piece of lyrical poetry lies a wonderful mystical concept: the answer to the question 'Why do we become sad and dull as we grow up?' Wordsworth (like

Thomas Traherne) replies 'Because children have memories of heaven. Before we were born, our souls were actually alive in heaven, where there is nothing ugly or mean, nothing colorless or somber. There it is divine rapture simply to look, and to listen. So, for the child on this earth who is still young, it is exquisitely delightful to gaze at a field of fresh grass or a green tree: the commonest things of earth are illuminated for him by the light which he knew in heaven; he still has some of the sharp, ecstatic perceptions which are those of the soul undulled by the body. Some years later, as a growing boy, he retains something of the keen sensibility that irradiated all the life of the child; but less, and always less. At last as a grown man, he sees that radiance die away, and fade into the light of common day.'

Unexpectedly at this point, in the middle of the poem, there is a charming eccentricity: two stanzas of rueful humor. Wordsworth turns away from his visions of heaven and his heaven-inspired children, and sees something quite unlike the cherub trailing clouds of glory: a real little boy, of five going on for six, who is so anxious to grow up that he spends all day imitating adults and their solemn social activities,

> A wedding or a festival,
> A mourning or a funeral,

and other parts of 'the dream of human life.' This was Hartley Coleridge, the son of his friend Samuel Coleridge, a child who in fact did grow up too early, was prodigiously clever, and had a wasted life. Wordsworth in the poem looks back from his own reluctantly attained maturity and asks the 'six years' Darling,' the 'little Actor,' why he is so eager to shed his immortality and plunge into the routine of life. Soon, he says, too soon that young soul will be laden down heavily.

> And custom lie upon thee with a weight,
> Heavy as frost, and deep almost as life!

But the little philosopher will not listen, cannot understand. To us, looking back on Hartley Coleridge's unhappiness and his charm and his failure, it is another proof that the Ode is a great and far-seeing poem.

The central theme of the poem is very strange: the idea that we were living souls in heaven before we were born. Many of us hope for heaven after we have lived on this earth, and died; but before birth? This is not a regular Christian idea; but also it is not the fancy of a single poet. Ultimately, it comes from Plato. Plato makes his master Socrates say that, since all human beings can understand certain concepts which are universal (such as good and bad, equal and unequal) and since these concepts do not appear in their pure form anywhere in this world, we must have learned them before entering human life. Therefore we learned them in heaven, the perfect world above this world, the world of the Ideas, the Ideals, the 'Forms.' In this life, when we seem to ourselves to be 'learning' such things as mathematical relationships, we are really working back to what we have always known. In spite of the difficulties put in our way by age, and the body, and the imperfect senses, we are *remembering* the truth. For Plato, this is one of the main proofs that the soul is immortal. From Plato the neo-Platonist philosophers of later Greece, and their followers in modern Europe, and in particular certain mystical English poets, took it over. From them Wordsworth learned it. But in his poem he altered it.

Wordsworth did not much care about mathematics, and would have found it hard to follow Plato in his argument that because an ignorant slave could, under careful evocative questioning, work out a geometrical theorem, the slave's soul must have known the truth in its prenatal life. Instead, he based his poem on the clear fact that the world is wonderful and that only children really enjoy its wonder. That fact saved Wordsworth from despair, and was the central motive of his great poem. The body grows old, and frail, and obtuse, and then dies. The soul may also lose its sensitivity and creative powers, and so be preparing, through a long period of aging and anaesthesia, to die. But, by watching the happiness of the young, by becoming a sympathetic spectator of the rapture of spring (even although he could no longer share that rapture), and by *remembering* the heavenly ecstasy which, as a child and a young boy, he had once enjoyed, he could find reassurance. The soul, which had lived before its birth into the body, so intensely that its happiness had been felt for years in this world, was truly immortal. What he had now to do was what all human beings must do: to endure the loss of childish happiness, to remember heaven, and to accustom himself to hear

> The still, sad music of humanity.

Of that still, sad music, although his own gayer and more rapturous melodies were silenced for ever, he became, from time to time, a noble voice.

*The Poet and the Urn*

———————

Do YOU ever think it is a cruel and unnecessary business to analyze a great poem? Does it ever seem to you like the dissection of a living thing — an act which sacrifices the essentials of vitality and unity in order to produce knowledge of minor details? Do you object to it because you feel it will be bound to ruin your enjoyment of that poem, and perhaps of all similar poems, forever in the future? If so, you have the majority on your side. Most people who like poetry distrust and hate anyone who tries to analyze poetry; and they are right for at least one reason — which is that the final criterion for any poem is not the beauty or vividness of any one of its details, but the cumulative effect of the total work. At first, and at last, every poem should be judged and prized as a whole.

And yet it is necessary to analyze any poem which has claims to greatness. If it is sympathetically done, it is always helpful. First of all, analysis dispels the vagueness of our own minds. After we read a fine poem, we are apt to be a little bit numbed: overwhelmed by the intensity of the poet's speech, haunted by his melodies and rhythms, bewildered by the richness of his imagery. That is a blissful state; yet when we emerge from it we may find that we have missed some of the essentials of the poet's thought. And, furthermore, if we analyze the poem we may find that it is not (as we had thought) a simple statement, but two, or three, or even more, conflicting utterances, that the poet is saying several different things at once, and describing not a unified experience, but a dispute, a spiritual battle which the poem can report but can scarcely reconcile.

One notable example is a poem which almost everybody knows, and yet not everybody fully understands. I read it first when I was fifteen, and loved it, but I did not understand it for twenty or thirty years, because I never tried to analyze it. It is the *Ode on a Grecian Urn*, written in May, 1819, by John Keats, at the age of 23. Its last couplet is famous, and deservedly famous:

> 'Beauty is truth, truth beauty,' — that is all
> Ye know on earth and all ye need to know.

Although the poem is quite short, five stanzas, fifty lines in all, there are many exquisite pictures in it, and several immortal phrases:

> Heard melodies are sweet, but those unheard
> Are sweeter.

> What little town by river or sea shore,
> Or mountain-built with peaceful citadel,
> Is emptied of its folk, this pious morn?

— and the beautiful line on the lovers immobilized and immortalized in art:

> For ever wilt thou love, and she be fair!

The subject of the poem need give no one any trouble or cause any puzzlement. On the contrary, it seems both clear and imaginative. An *Ode on a Grecian Urn* is surely an address, in poetry, to a Greek vase. The poem evokes the carvings on the vase, and describes them indirectly but eloquently. Its essential thought is that beauty is permanent, one of the few permanent things we know on this earth — as is shown by the fact that, although the artist who created the vase, and his subjects, the men and women whom he depicted, and their beliefs and their emotions, all have vanished from this earth, they can still live on so strongly as to move a poet of this far later world. That is an important thought; but it is not obscure in any way.

True. But as soon as we read the poem analytically we begin to find difficulties, and when we look more deeply into it we find still more.

The most obvious difficulty is this. Keats is apparently describing not one Greek vase, but two; and the two are quite different from each other.

There are five stanzas in the poem. Four of them describe a scene of wild excitement; apparently a frenzied dance of young men and girls, or perhaps of ardent young gods and mortal maidens. Keats speaks of a 'mad pursuit' and a 'struggle to escape,' and in one fine couplet he images a girl and her lover:

> For ever warm and still to be enjoyed,
> For ever panting, and for ever young.

This scene takes place in wild woodlands far from human habitation, 'in Tempe or the dales of Arcady.'

But one stanza of the poem pictures a scene which is wholly unlike an ecstatic dance and revel. 'Who are these coming to the sacrifice?' asks the poet, and goes on:

> To what green altar, O mysterious priest,
> Lead'st thou that heifer lowing at the skies,
> And all her silken flanks with garlands drest?

In the following lines he speaks of a procession of worshipers, ordinary citizens of some 'little town by river or sea shore,' who have left the streets silent and deserted to attend the ceremony. He does not describe them, but it is clear from the words he uses ('peaceful' and 'pious') that they are engaged in a calm and decorous ritual. This scene, a priest leading a gentle animal wreathed with flowers toward a rustic altar, followed by a group of his fellow citizens and fellow worshipers, has apparently nothing to do with the wild dance described in the other four stanzas. One is a bacchanalian rite far in the wilds; the other is a reverent and controlled ceremony of communal worship near a town.

Now, Greek artists in classical times never mixed up two different scenes with disparate emotional tones. The sculptor or painter who decorated a vase would not think of mingling half-naked bacchantes with decently dressed churchgoers, any more than we should put voodoo drums into a Bach choral prelude and fugue. It must be Keats who has mixed them up. Why did he do it?

Another problem is that no one has been able to find any single thing very closely like the Grecian urn Keats had in mind. His other inspirations we know well. Chapman's Homer is still in print; the Elgin marbles still repose in the British Museum; the nightingale still sings. Keats did not travel widely; it ought to be possible to identify the Greek vase which inspired him. And the identification ought to be made easier by the fact that the 'urn' was not one of the ordinary vases made of pottery and decorated in black or red paint. It was (he says himself) 'with brede [i.e. embroidery or decoration] of marble men and maidens overwrought,' which means that it was a marble vase with carvings on it in low relief. There are such urns, but they are much more rare than the painted pottery vases, and it should be easy to find a particular one which has been carefully described by an eminent poet. But no one has done so.

A number of different marble urns have been suggested; but either they are not very like the two poetic descriptions in Keats's ode, or else it is difficult to prove that Keats had any opportunity of seeing them. Still, we do know that one of his favorite places for rest and inspiration was the British Museum, where he would spend hours in rapt wonder, gazing at the

Greek sculptures. Now, in the British Museum there is a magnificent marble vase, part of the Townley collection, which
does show a bacchic revel. Exquisitely carved youths and girls,
naked or in thin dresses, move across the foreground, the girls
dancing, the men striding dramatically forward, amid every
element of wild excitement combined with beauty and grace.
Although it is a minor work, it shows the inimitable Greek
genius for making stone behave as though it were thin cloth
flying in the air, or flesh pulsating with life. The pose of every
figure is delightfully individual, and the composition of the
whole, in spite of its unbridled energy, marvelously harmonious. There is no musician; but as we see the rhythm of the
dancers we can almost hear the music; there are no trees, but
there is a leopard or a lynx couchant, which shows that the
revel is among the wild woods; and near the center there is
a pair of lovers, the youth bending toward the girl for a kiss
and 'winning near the goal.' The whole scene is carved on a
huge marble urn which was meant to be used as a mixing
bowl for the wine served at a large and luxurious party. This
Grecian urn Keats could indeed have seen; and, to judge from
other descriptions of bacchanalian dances in his poetry (e.g.,
*Endymion* 4.193-267), he had seen and admired several such
works of art.

But then there is the other picture (or rather the other piece
of sculpture): the calm religious procession. We know of no
Grecian urn which shows such a subject. Of course Keats might
have imagined one. He was perfectly capable of imagining far
stranger and more fanciful scenes. Yet we know that he loved
Greek sculpture deeply, and that he would sit for hours gazing
at its masterpieces before translating them into poetic descriptions. And he speaks of this particular scene not as though he
were inventing it, but rather as though he had witnessed it and
were trying to understand it more deeply, endeavoring to see
through it, into its past and its inner meanings.

Now, there is one calm and dignified religious procession in
Greek art which Keats did know and admire. It is not carved
upon an urn. It is spread flat upon a wall. And yet that makes

no significant difference, for even on the vases a procession is still a procession. What Keats knew well was the procession of the people of Athens, to the festival of Athene, on the frieze of the Parthenon: part of the Elgin marbles.

You might object that Keats knew perfectly well what that procession was, and that he would not, as he does in the ode, ask what it was and where it came from. Yes, but he also knew perfectly well what a bacchanalian revel was, for he described such revels elsewhere in his poems; yet he asks what the dance is, as he asks what the religious procession is — because he wants to make the ode out of questions and answers. The questions are 'What is this mad riot?' and 'What is the meaning of this grave ceremony?' The single answer, given by Keats under the inspiration of his knowledge of Greece, is 'Beauty, expressed in revel and reverence.'

Now, if the two scenes on Keats's urn came from two quite different sources, one from a bacchanal on a wine bowl, the other from a procession on a temple wall, and if they have quite different spiritual climates, why did the poet think of combining them?

There are two answers to this. The first is superficial; the second is deeply revealing.

In fact, Keats did know of one Grecian urn which, quite against the rules of Greek good taste, did combine elements of a bacchic dance with elements of a religious rite. He had never seen the urn, which is now in the Louvre in Paris; but he did know a reproduction of it, which came out in a big series of reproductions of classical art published in Paris.* Not only that; he actually traced the reproduction with his own hand, which means that he admired the piece greatly enough to want to keep it and to meditate on it. It is a big marble mixing bowl. It shows eight figures lined up on both sides of an altar.

---

* A handled mixing bowl signed by Sosibios, made probably in the first century B.C., certainly in Athens, and stolen by Napoleon's forces from the collection of the Villa Borghese in Rome. The reproduction was in the *Musée Napoléon,* published in 1804.

But modern scholars who have gone into the theory of Greek art point out that the figures do not blend and cannot blend into a single harmonious composition, and that the sculptor was merely a skillful hack who copied them individually from earlier models and then arranged them in a perfectly meaningless pattern. There are four bacchic figures — three dancing maenads and a satyr, plus the quiet, clever god Hermes and the calm, wise goddess Athene, plus one of the Muses and a naked soldier doing a war dance. The whole thing is as artificial as a set of figures cut out by children from magazines. Keats could not possibly know that, but he did see the strange combination of revel and ritual, and his ode, with its repeated questions, is an effort to find some meaning in it. (This once more illustrates the peculiar rule that a second-rate stimulus often produces first-rate art.)

But there is a deeper reason why the young poet made his evocation of ancient Greece contain two pictures and not one — although Keats himself perhaps could not have formulated it in so many words, and although the classical scholars of his day would certainly not have believed it. It is a fact which was first pointed out by the philosopher Nietzsche (who began his astonishing career as a professor of classics). The Greeks, said Nietzsche, were not cool, calm, quietly harmonious men and women devoted to the life of pure reason and ignoring all else. They did not inhabit a world of pure white temples and lofty, passionless, intellectual discourses, and live with a self-restraint so long practiced that it had become habitual and easy. No, the civilization of the Greeks was a difficult tension, an almost irreconcilable conflict. The conflict was a struggle between the life of reason, for which they were uniquely gifted, and the dark forces of the passions, to which they were terribly sensitive. When they put all their energies into pure thought and the self-control and self-abnegation which it demands, they were in danger of starving their emotions and getting out of touch with the world. When they yielded to their passions, they could be swept away. Therefore their life, and most of their best art, were a continuous battle between the power which they personified as Bacchus or Dionysus — the deity who drives men and women into the wilds, whose servants are savage animals, whose rituals are close to madness — and the power they called Apollo, the god of reason, vision, and healing. It is (said Nietzsche) this tension that produced Greek tragedy, in which the forces of Dionysus and Apollo meet and are reconciled through art. It is through that tension that Greek artists were enabled to do what few other artists have done; to show even sensuality as something holy and beautiful, and to make purity and restraint visible in forms both dignified and lovable. Such a conflict need not exist in the soul of all artists and poets, but it will in all those who are deeply sensitive to Greek art and literature. So then, if our analysis is correct, it has shown that Keats put two different and conflicting scenes onto the same visionary Grecian urn, first, because he was puzzled by the work of a skillful but conscienceless late Greek artist who did just that, for purely decorative purposes; and second, because with his marvelous insight he realized that in the soul of Greece there were both a priest and a reveler, both an outrageous satyr and a wise, tranquil god.

*Penetrating a Book*

---

THERE are two kinds of reading. One is the attentive assimilation with which you take in a new and interesting book saying things you have thought of but never expected to see in print, describing characters and situations which are almost unknown to you and yet deeply sympathetic. The other is the strange combination of familiarity and novelty with which, for the third or the thirtieth time, you reread a novel, a collection of essays, or a poem which you know well and have read before, but are still exploring. Most people do not know this second pleasure of reading, which is rereading. We are too apt to think that, if we read a book we have already gone through once, we shall merely be repeating an experience — like going to the same play once in the afternoon and again in the evening. And this is true of most books. Most books, frankly, are not worth reading twice. Many are not worth reading once; but let us not even speak of those. The books that matter are worth reading again and again throughout a lifetime. (And a large number of unusual books, which cannot claim to be great but which are interesting for special reasons, are worth reinvestigating several times at fairly long intervals. They deserve the same kind of attention that we give to eccentric but talented artists such as Hieronymus Bosch and Paul Klee and Scarlatti and Scriabin, who seem to produce something new and unexpected whenever we return to them.)

I am still learning to read many books which once I thought I knew well. Let me set down one example of this process of slow understanding, taken from my own intellectual and aesthetic life. I do so not from vanity, but because it is a case history I know from experience.

One of the great books of the world is an epic poem in Latin by the poet Vergil. It is called the *Aeneid*, which means 'The Story of Aeneas.' It tells how Aeneas, a prince of Troy, after fighting the invading Greeks for ten years, saw his city captured by treachery. Through the flames and the looting and the carnage he escaped, carrying his old father on his back and dragging his little son by the hand; his wife fell behind and was lost. With some hundreds of Trojan survivors, he built a fleet of ships and set out to find some country where they could settle, make a new city, and begin to live again. After many adventures — including a passionate love affair with the Semitic queen Dido of Carthage, who killed herself when he left her — Aeneas landed with the best of his followers in Italy, at the mouth of the river Tiber. The old king Latinus who ruled there gave him some territory on which to build and betrothed his daughter Lavinia to him. At last Aeneas had reached his new home and could reconstruct his shattered life and found a family. But a devilish deity, a sort of feminine Satan, stirred up the girl's mother and her former suitor against Aeneas: there was a bitter and unnecessary war, in which (after finding some allies elsewhere in Italy) the Trojans imposed their will by force. In a final decisive duel, Aeneas fought and killed his young rival Turnus. The poem ends as his hard, sharp, remorseless sword plunges home.

This is one of the books which I am learning to understand. For years, for many years, I hated it — although it is supposed to be a masterpiece which, as a classical scholar, I am expected to enjoy. To study Greek and Latin and not to like the *Aeneid*?

That would be like a musician's hating *The Mastersingers*, or a lover of architecture loathing the Cathedral of Notre Dame. But I abhorred the poem for years. And now . . .

I cannot possibly tell how many times I have read the *Aeneid*. I read much of it first in school. Then I neither liked nor disliked it, because I was so busy grappling with the language. Latin is a pretty difficult language anyhow, and Vergil made it far more difficult than it was by nature. The Romans themselves found the *Aeneid* hard to understand. In college, when I could read more fluently, I went over the poem line by line with considerable care and interest. But at that time I was an aesthete, trying to be one of the avant-garde. In painting I cared only about cunning techniques and startling subjects, in music I adored delicious dissonances and cross rhythms, and so in the *Aeneid* I paid attention only to its bizarre and rather perverse tricks of style and its exquisite, almost hypersensitive sound effects.

At the next stage, when I went to Oxford, they made me read the poem with more penetration. Now I really began to loathe it. Why? Because its theme and its structure are imitated fairly closely from the Greek epics which we know under the name of Homer. Its first half, about the wanderings of the Trojan DP's, parallels the *Odyssey;* its second half, about the war and triumph of Aeneas in Italy, the *Iliad*. Aeneas himself is a character who occurs in the *Iliad*. Incident after incident is copied from Homer. The plan of the entire poem, twelve neatly symmetrical books alternating between heaven and earth, energy and relaxation, debate and action, is clearly a 'classical' plan intended to imitate the *Iliad* and the *Odyssey* and to improve upon them. Unoriginal. What more final condemnation is there in the mind of a young man?

But worse, when my teachers made me examine the plot of the poem, I found it repellent because it was so uniformly somber. Nobody has any fun in it. Nobody laughs.* Aeneas

---

* There are two forced laughs in Book Five, where an old man is nearly drowned and a young man falls and gets himself covered with blood and dung.

himself, when we first meet him, although he is the hero, is weeping and longing for death; when we last see him, he is gloomily killing an unarmed and helpless man. Throughout the poem we see little but a long succession of disasters: epidemics break out; people welcome the refugees and then turn savagely against them; their women go mad and set fire to their precious ships; they are pursued by a female devil, haunted by a curse, racked by self-doubt and despair. Almost the only period of serenity in the entire poem is out of this troubled world altogether, in the remote eternal abode of the dead and the unborn, where Aeneas' dead father, now immortal, shows him the majestic phantoms of his descendants, the mighty Romans of the future who are waiting to be born.

This, in my twenties, repelled me. I was too naïve to think that it might perhaps be a gloomy job to find a new land and make history, as the Jews did when they entered Canaan and the Pilgrims settling in Massachusetts; and that the life of DP's looking for a home was perhaps unlikely to provide much material for light romance and comedy. Further, I underestimated the characters. Aeneas, the pious Aeneas (as he is usually called), seemed to me only a stiff, unsympathetic lay figure, because — although in fact he goes to bold extremes of passion, contemplates suicide, seduces a beautiful woman and deserts her, and commits at least one murder for equivocal reasons — he maintains a hard Roman dignity throughout; and because (although Vergil actually made his character develop from initial weakness to final strength — strength, I now believe, in excess) the poet prefers not to take us inside his hero's mind, and leaves us to do what I was then unfitted to do, to reconstruct in imagination that grand process, the growth of a hero.

Anyone who knows the *Aeneid* and understands poetry will see at once the huge treasure of art and psychology and historical understanding which I was ignoring, all the inventiveness and unobtrusive originality to which I was deaf and blind. Of course the form of the *Aeneid* is the traditional form of the epic poem — just as a play on the stage, to be most effective and lasting, takes the traditional form of two or three acts, seldom more than five, lasting for about two hours. And of course the characters are drawn from tradition and partly modeled on those of Homer, because Vergil's purpose was to link his own country and its civilization with the earlier civilization of Troy and Greece, and to show the world that the Romans were the inheritors, maintainers, and transmitters of the most venerable Mediterranean culture, instead of being (as their detractors said) half savages from the backwoods who had attained world power by a combination of treachery, greed, and brute force.

It was only after twenty years or so of reading and rereading that I began to comprehend this purpose. I must have taught the poem very badly, very often, because of my failure. But now I think I see it a little better. Vergil meant the *Aeneid* to be for his people something like the Bible for the Jews and the Christians. The epics of Homer are wonderful poems, they contain subtle character drawing (far superior to that of Vergil), magnificent drama, superb language, drastic narrative; but they are curiously temporary, they have no meaning except an individual meaning. One tells the story of a temporary strategic failure, and the other of a personal success. The *Aeneid* tells the story of the founding of a nation. The Greek epics are like *Beowulf* or the *Song of the Nibelungs*; the *Aeneid* is meant to do the same work as the early books of the Old Testament, to tell how, under divine guidance, a nation was transplanted through trial and danger so that it might have a magnificent future.

Having realized this, and having determined the purpose of the poem which I now knew was great, I was still worried by its emotional tone. Why was the *Aeneid* so unhappy? It told the tale of a noble mission, in which a people was guided by God out of miserable defeat and exile to found a state which should last for eternity and help to civilize the known world. Surely this is a happy theme? Surely it should be bathed in the sunrise beams of the approaching triumph? But it is not. The *Aeneid* is a profoundly sad poem. As it opens, a female fiend is calling up a hurricane to wreck the exhausted ships of the Trojans on the dangerous coast of North Africa. As it closes, the hero is wondering whether to kill a helpless wounded man or not: the sword remains poised in air for a hideous instant, and then plunges home. There the poem ends. There is no happy festival of peacemaking, no marriage and coronation, no thanksgiving banquet. The last page is full of blood, and groans, and wounds, and death. Only in the center of the poem, where Aeneas visits the world of the dead and unborn, is he truly happy. When he leaves it, he leaves through the gate of false dreams, because this world is a false dream. Time is unreal. Only eternity exists, and in this world it is difficult to live out of time.

For many years, I thought that this was Vergil's mistake. I really believed that he had intended to write a glorious, optimistic poem about the entry of the Trojans into Italy, the event which was to lead to the foundation of Rome, and to prefigure the extension of Roman civilization throughout the Western world; that he had meant it to be the story of a crusade with a happy ending; and that he had simply bungled it. But — remember that when you reread a great book, you do not necessarily ever solve all the questions which it poses — but I still do not surely know what Vergil meant. All I know is that he was not simply doing political propaganda for the Roman Empire and for the first Roman Emperor, Augustus. Did he mean that all political activity on a large scale was necessary and could be noble, but involved enormous suffering both for statesmen and for their subjects? *Tantae molis erat,* he says on the first page of his poem in a line whose slow, effortful rhythm images the laborious upbuilding of the Roman state, *tantae molis erat Romanam condere gentem.* In the same way, perhaps some of us might think that it would have been happier if the great old thirteen colonies could have remained just as they were originally founded, undisturbed by foreigners, unchallenged by the urges which called them, first, to conquer a continent, and then to drive America onward to world leadership. Yet we might realize that we now *must* shoulder this enormous and painful burden, and shoulder it with a sigh. I think that Vergil did not mean that the Roman Empire, and higher civilization generally, were fundamentally wicked, and that the placid anarchic Golden Age was better; but did he wish us to understand that all human life is a dream, and a bad dream, full of avoidable lust and necessary cruelty, while the existence which we shall have after death (if we have earned it), in eternity, is alone peaceful and pure and calm and happy? I do not know. I must read the *Aeneid* once again.

*Olympian Spring*

In the year 1919, the Nobel Prize for literature went to a Swiss poet who was even then very little known, and is now all but forgotten. His name was Carl Spitteler. He himself never expected to gain immediate and widespread popularity; but once, talking of his own work, he said 'Ein gutes Buch frisst sich doch endlich durch' ('A good book manages to eat its way through in the end'), and it looks as though his forecast would prove to be right. His complete works have recently been reissued in a special commemorative edition by one of the most distinguished publishing firms in Switzerland (Artemis, Zurich). Although they have not been translated into English, it would be an attractive job, rather like the recent translation of Kazantzakis's *Odyssey* from modern Greek into English.

We think of the Swiss as practical people, optimistic on the whole, and full of simple Christian piety. Carl Spitteler was impractical, a mystic, a convinced pessimist, and (although religiously minded) not a regular Christian in any sense. Nevertheless, his work seems to breathe the inmost spirit of Switzerland: not that of the prosperous little watchmaking cities, nor the cozy villa-colonies round the lakes, full of bankers and coupon-cutters, but the country as it appears from the air. To the eyes of the train-traveler or the walker, Switzerland is beautiful; but from the air it appears, as it is, a hard rough country. Much of it is cruel, inhospitable mountain ranges, much of the rest is cold, half-barren highland territory. Its greatest beauties are peaks, the Matterhorn and the Jungfrau and the Eiger, on which no human life can survive unaided for more than a few hours; and the winter season, deep in snow, is fabulously lovely, but its loveliness is close to death. That is the aspect of Switzerland which Carl Spitteler knew and presented in his poetry.

His greatest work was an epic poem, *Olympian Spring*. Hardly anyone in any western language has succeeded in writing epic poetry, for at least a century. But Spitteler paid no attention to contemporary fashions in literature. He belonged to no school. He had no disciples. He created a classic which stands by itself, and is virtually ageless.

*Olympian Spring* means 'The Youth of the Olympians.' It is a poem about the birth and adventures of the gods. They are, at least in name, the deities whom we know from Greece: Zeus the ruler, Apollo the spirit of light and poetry, Aphrodite the embodiment of beauty and love, Hephaestus the misshapen craftsman, and so forth. That sounds conventional: something like Keats's youthful fragment *Hyperion*. But if it had been conventional, it would probably never have won the Nobel Prize, and certainly would not have been worth reading or rereading. At best, it might have been like those imposing and shallow paintings by classicizing artists of the eighteenth century — 'Council of the Gods,' 'Apotheosis of Hercules.' Far from it. Spitteler's Olympians have the names of Homer's gods, and some of their attributes; but they do not all have the same characters as their prototypes, and their adventures are quite original. Even their relationship to heaven, to fate, to the human world, and to one another is notably different. Since all myths contain symbolic meanings, the result of Spitteler's remolding of the Olympian pantheon is that his gods, although Greek, carry and embody his own personal vision of life.

Before studying its inner meanings, let us look at the outward form of the poem. It is a very ambitious work. An epic on such a theme must be large, rich, and spacious. It fills over six hundred pages, some twenty thousand lines, divided into five main sections and each of these again into three or four or more shorter episodes. It is in rhyming couplets, but instead of the usual five-beat measure, Spitteler has chosen a strong swinging six-beat pattern which allows him more scope for his powerful rhetoric and for the big compound words into which he packs so much imagery.

The language is Swiss German. Not pure German, because it contains many dialect words and ejaculations, used for effects of simplicity and gaiety: for instance, the happy craftsman Hyphaistos cries out:

Juchhe! How rich the world can be! Juchheissaheiss!

Not only Swiss dialect words, but many German slang words and phrases (usually with a strong working-class flavor) are introduced in lighter descriptions or in conversations: for instance, the angry gods tell Ares not to interfere in an argument but to 'keep his own nose clean,' and the noise of a big banquet is summed up as 'tiddlediddledum and brouhaha.' These are not isolated examples. Sometimes long passages of satire (comparable to Milton's description of Limbo or the naughtier parts of Ariosto) are filled with words and cries and turns of phrase which are not only coarse but downright vulgar. This will strike some readers as being one of the most serious faults in the poem. Often the gods do not sound like gods at all, not even like noble men and beautiful women, but like drunken farmers and quarreling fishwives. When a god curses or a goddess storms, even their anger should be noble.

On the other hand, there are many passages of purely poetic description which are broken by no such error of taste. Spitteler was Swiss and lived most of his life in Switzerland. His imagery, therefore, has the bright and super-childlike clarity of Alpine landscapes, and often shares the grandeur of the Alps. His figures cannot be called heavy or clumsy. Often they sound as interesting as the new chords used by Debussy or Strauss, and especially when two or three come together they make his imagery and his atmosphere brilliantly clear. Thus he can describe a thick and violent thunderstorm in the two words 'stormclouds heavenhightowering,' or speak of dancing water as 'fountaineddywhirls,' a word full of delicate liquid consonants.

Another essential of poetry is at his command — rhetorical variety. The difficulty of writing any long book, but particularly a long poem in the epic manner, is that one tends to fall into unconscious repetitions of sentence-structure, to build all one's paragraphs along similar lines, to succeed one bald statement with another bald statement and another bald statement, to find favorite rhythms which will jog along comfortably to the end, and thus to betray something like an ineradicable poverty of thought. Spitteler avoids this with ease. He is an eloquent poet. What he is going to say at the foot of any page, although it follows logically and imaginatively, cannot be guessed from what he says at the top of the same page. He shifts his point of view, carrying the reader with him: sometimes to stand beside the gods and watch their conflicts, feel their angry gestures and hear their violent words, sometimes far above until we hear the little clouds talking to one another in the sky. He is careful to avoid the monotonous succession of sentences describing simple actions, which lulls the reader to sleep. Instead, he varies action with conversation, he describes objectively or he asks the reader for comment, he laughs with surprise or shouts with horror as the story develops. Within a single page he will put two sentences and an ejaculation into one line, and run a single sentence down through four big couplets. It is this gift of eloquence which again and again reassures us, when we are bewildered by the strangeness of Spitteler's myths or half-shocked, half-bedazzled by the cruelty of his mysticism, that he is not a woolly eccentric but a

man who has thought long, seriously, and in the end successfully about the highest problems.

For his thought is very strange. Even the story he tells is
strange. No one who knows the Greek myths could bear to
read six hundred pages which merely told them all over again.
What Spitteler does is to take the outline of one of the major
myths — the tale that Zeus and the other gods displaced the
older dynasty of Kronos and ruled the world from Mount
Olympus, not without frequent rivalries and even quarrels —
and to rewrite it with radically altered emphases, with many
new adventures and motivations, and with a strangely enlarged
view of the universe as background. We do not meet the Olympians first as divine children. Zeus is not born on Crete, or
concealed from his cannibal father by cymbal-clashing priests.
Pallas does not spring fully-armed from his head after he becomes king. Aphrodite is not born of the foam. No, they are
immortals, and so they are never born. We first see them lying
in the underworld, sleeping a sleep which seems to have had
no beginning. Like veins of gold a thousand miles deep in the
earth, they could slumber unseen in the dark forever. But their
time has come. The prince of the underworld awakens them,
sets them free, guides them out of the rain-soaked gloom of
hell, and sends them on their way up to Mount Olympus. It is
only slowly that they begin to talk to one another; and at first
they have no names or personalities, they are scarcely even
male and female, but embryos, bewildered and frightened and
weak.

As they climb, subdued, anxious, almost fearful, they meet a
majestic procession moving downward. This is the dynasty of
gods which has been ruling mankind until then, and has now,
by the inexorable decree of fate, been deposed. It is returning
to the dark underworld, to be once more absorbed into impo-
tence and endless sleep. Its leader, Kronos, looks with contempt
at the miserable beings who are to succeed him. With a roar of
defiant protest he reins back his horse and attempts to turn
and ride upward once again, to resume his power. But not even

gods can resist fate. As Kronos turns, the very earth quivers under him, the mountain heaves and casts him downward, there is a long shuddering rush, and at last, like the reverberation of some mighty tree precipitated down a steep cliff, the 'belated echo' of his fall is heard from far below. After his glimpse of what will after many years be their own fate, the young Olympians struggle up again toward the summit. Soon they have risen high above the clouds; they are surrounded by the rich sunshine of the high Alpine peaks; they are welcomed (with a cheerful yodel) by Hebe, the goddess of youth, who gives them shelter and food and drink; and at last they move higher yet, to their own realm, Olympus. Now they have their names and their personalities. They are the gods.

Yet, it seems, they are not the only gods. There are other divinities, whom we meet as the poem grows. There is Uranos, the god of Heaven, who rules calmly and happily all day, with his seven lovely daughters, in a castle high in the clouds; but who disappears below in the darkness each night, to fight the strong, cruel, and stupid monsters of the underworld which are constantly threatening to destroy the peace of Heaven. And other deities and spirits inhabit earth and sky. The realm of the newcomers is apparently to be the world of mankind as we know it, with the mountain-and-cloud palace of Olympus above it as their stronghold. But they were called into life, and their actions are constantly watched, by a much higher god. He is, it seems, eternally dominant. His powers are questioned and sometimes attacked, but never overthrown. He is loved by none, and feared by all, and obeyed. He is Ananké, Necessity. Spitteler calls him 'the ruler who is ruled' or 'the force that is forced,' *der gezwungene Zwang,* for none can escape Necessity, not even himself. And he is cruel. He watches the gods and men to discover and punish the least transgression of the eternal order; he enjoys breaking up a festival where men and gods revel together and for a moment try to forget duty and mortality; his 'yellow tiger-eyes' pierce into every secret, and his servant is cruel Moira, Fate. Once, even, a young hero roused mankind to revolt against Ananké, stormed his castle, and made him take flight; but he escaped into the gigantic Machine which moves on forever in the secret places of the universe, against whose iron breast and fiery armor all rebellion is useless. The revolt was broken, and the Machine rolled on forever over the tiny wormlike bodies of mankind. In one of the finest passages of the poem, towards the end, Zeus gazes out upon the stars, from the balcony of his palace one night. And a sudden gust of wind blows the stars aside like a curtain. Behind them, in the heart of the universe, he sees what their glitter usually conceals: he sees the 'mill of the worlds' moving relentlessly round and round, trodden by 'Ananké's angry giant-feet,' pouring out suns which clash and destroy one another, with now and then a frail fragment of life after which Ananké savagely hounds his attendant, Death. Then the pretty curtain of stars closes once again.

Under Ananké, then, the Olympians are given the world to rule. It seems to have a ruler already. Hera, the Amazon queen (not a goddess as in Homer, but a proud and bitter mortal woman), reigns over mankind with her warrior-maidens. She will give herself only to the god who proves best in competing for her hand and for the mastership of the earth. And here again the story is changed, it is given deeper meanings. Apollo, Hermes, Poseidon, and other deities, who have now learned to use their own names and are beginning to realize their powers, vie with each other in feats of strength and displays of wisdom. Zeus, after one defeat, plays little part in them. But, as he walks alone in meditation through the forest outside Hera's palace, he meets a spirit stronger than himself. It is Gorgo, who like her master Ananké is both savage and powerful. Loathsome as she is, Zeus becomes her lover, and she shows him how to enter Hera's castle and seize the monarchy. The other gods protest bitterly, and even threaten revolt, but it is useless:

> The ruler's first of virtues is to hold the rule.

Apollo, the bright spirit of wisdom and beauty, ought to have become master of the world; but fate prefers to give power to someone more cruel and treacherous, and Hera, who is cruel and treacherous herself because she is a woman, kneels to Zeus, accepting him as lord and master.

After this conflict, there is peace for a time. The gods now know who they are, and what they can do. Through the wide world they wander, each on a quest of his own for adventure and fulfillment. Their journeys are told in the third section of the epic, *The High Time*. Each episode is independent. Some, like Poseidon's endeavor to do the impossible, are broadly comic; others, like Apollo's conquest of the outer air, are loftily heroic. But there is gay humor throughout this section. This may sound surprising, for most epics are portentously solemn, and we have already called Spitteler a pessimist. Yet many pessimists can laugh, if the laugh contains a bitter note of satire; and some pessimists (such as Nietzsche) have believed that laughter (with music) made almost the only consolation available to man in an otherwise intolerable life. And in fact, although Spitteler had no direct models, one of the poets he admired most was the brilliant Italian Ariosto, whose epic *Orlando Furioso* is surely the most amusing long poem ever written. *Olympian Spring* is the only epic I know which contains satire on both gods and men.

Aphrodite, the goddess of love and beauty — you can imagine what a French author would have done with her adventures! Not so Carl Spitteler. He thinks most people are blind to beauty and distrust love; so the lovely divinity is driven back to heaven almost before she has time to be any more than mildly naughty. One night she slips out of the palace of heaven and makes her way downward among mankind. In the dawn, she reaches a little town. The people are just about to wake and go to work. In the town square Aphrodite notices a handsome fountain, its jets playing merrily in the early sunshine, surrounded by statues of beautiful naked water nymphs. On an impulse she hides her clothes in a corner and steps up among the nymphs, equally naked and far more beautiful. She stands perfectly still, still and perfect. One passer-by notices her, and then another; and then a little crowd gathers. Why, they say, there's a new statue; never saw that one before; wonder if the artist had the idea of adding it to the fountain group? And they go on to criticize it. Ah, that's a terrible piece of modernistic art, says one: look at the coarse heavy modeling and the crude distortions of the muscles. Yes, it's an outrage, says another, a real outrage to put up such a piece of cheap hackwork in our square; it's one of the ugliest statues I ever saw in my life; you can see where the fellow's chisel slipped while he was working; and then look here, this limb is utterly unlifelike, it's hopelessly out of proportion; no living body ever looked like that, or *could* look like that; it's not a matter of beauty, it's a matter of plain simple reality — and with a contemptuous finger he prods the beautiful goddess on a vulnerable spot. She can resist no longer; she breaks into peals of laughter, higher and more melodious than the water of the fountain. At once the citizens stagger back in astonishment, and then they start forward in fury. It's an outrage, they shout, shameless hussy, vile degenerate — and in a moment the poor goddess is running for her skin up a sidestreet, pursued by an angry mob and as naked as a jaybird. She could, of course, have turned and struck them all blind and impotent; but Aphrodite has a kind heart, and anyhow she could scarcely have made them much more blind than they were. With a burst of superhuman speed, she escapes and goes back to heaven, laughing with inextinguishable laughter.

But the adventures of the gods become too gay, too careless. The divinities have too much fun. Also, just as slowly and imperceptibly as (in the beginning) the new deities came to knowledge of themselves and their identities, so the needs of mankind loom larger and larger. At first, while the gods cut their capers, men merely watch with admiration. Then they begin to protest. They are humiliated by the exploits of some gods, and scandalized by the escapades of others — notably the beautiful Aphrodite.

The Power above the gods also hates happiness. Ananké therefore calls a halt. When Zeus proposes to hold a great festival at which Aphrodite, returned from earth in triumph, is to be the star, Ananké drowns it out in torrents of rain. (As a lover of the mountains, Spitteler loathes clouds and moisture. His underworld is not smoky and fiery, but cold and clouded with ever-drifting rain.) The deluge almost abolishes mankind, and cools the spirits of the gods.

Now Zeus regains a sense of his responsibilities. He thinks of the human race. He sees their sorrows. He almost loves them. Yet he is disgusted with their lives and insincerity. He offers them a giant ape under the name of Zeus, and see, they worship it. At this he is furious — all the more when he himself, on a journey through the earth, is arrested, imprisoned, and threatened with death for failing to worship the false god. He determines then to obliterate mankind, and directs the Furies to load the high mountains with lightning and the seeds of thunder, which will at last explode and bury the lying race under avalanches of rock. The gods intercede. He refuses to listen. The catastrophe is ready, when Gorgo, the fateful spirit who gave him the rule of the earth, reappears, forces him to his knees, threatens to depose him utterly if he does not prove worthy of his kingship, and breaks his will. At last he has learned some wisdom. Yet he was not wholly wrong. Mankind still lies and cheats. To enable him to learn the truth, and to teach mortals themselves the truth, he creates the heroic mortal Heracles, and (in spite of Hera's ill will) sends him down to save the race of man.

So the poem ends, in a reversal of its opening. At first the new gods made their way up from beneath to the heights of Olympus. Now a new hero sent by the king of gods makes his way down from Olympus toward the earth. At first the gods thought only of play and the exercise of their own powers. Now they and their apostle think of the hard work of helping humanity. Nothing else has changed. Ananké is still the cruel tyrant of the universe. Death is still one of his favored helpers. Men are still weak and foolish. But the gods have grown up, and a redeemer has sprung from their new wisdom.

Like all good allegories, *Olympian Spring* has many meanings. It would scarcely be worth reading, despite its power, if it merely explained a single theory of the world through the gestures of a set of personifications. But the rise of the gods can be taken to symbolize many processes which we know, and it will help us to understand them better. It is like the growth of the human spirit, from helpless speechless childhood through energetic and careless youth, and then, through conflict, suffering, and the grudging acceptance of necessity, into maturity. Or again, it is like the appearance in history of a nation or a creed, starting from nothing except the darkness in which primitive forces lie asleep, then spreading out into a hundred manifestations of strength and beauty until at last it settles down — sometimes into cruel selfishness, sometimes, with better guidance, into self-forgetfulness and work for the redemption of others. It is an allegory of the progress of reason, or of the growth of civilization, or of the course of history; these, and many other things. It is a wise poem.

The artist who stands closest to Spitteler is probably Richard Strauss. There are some remarkable coincidences between their works. Strauss's *Alpine Symphony* sounds like the music for the first section of Spitteler's epic; his *Hero's Life* is closely paralleled in the bitter episode where the Flatfootfolk create, out of sewer-gas, a rival Sun to displace the sun of Apollo from heaven; *Thus Spake Zarathustra* and *Death and Transfiguration* have much of Spitteler's lofty mysticism; the humor and variety of the High Time reappear in *Tyl Ulenspiegel's Merry Pranks* and in *Don Quixote;* the fiendish cruelty of *Salome* and *Electra* would not be strange to the creator of Moira and Gorgo. Even in their faults they are similar, for the vulgarity of Strauss's *Domestic Symphony* can be paralleled from some passages in *Olympian Spring,* for instance, the humiliation of Aphrodite. And in their technique it is easy to see resemblances: both love strange-sounding compounds, new chords, echoes of the myriad sounds of nature (Strauss makes clarinets bleat like sheep, Spitteler makes words croak like frogs and scream like eagles), and unexpected changes of rhythm. The Swiss are fond of comparing Spitteler to the mystical artist Böcklin, and indeed some of his grand evocations of the spirits of wild nature do resemble Böcklin's pictures in their majestic breadth of vision. But he moves much more, his thought is more active, his characters do not rest, but struggle and suffer with superhuman energy. Böcklin takes us into a world of contemplation, Spitteler into a world of action. Even in the first words of each new episode, the sensitive reader can hear the pulse of a forthright courage recalling the opening themes of Strauss's *Don Juan* and *Hero's Life*.

His thought would seem completely individual, if it were not strangely paralleled by another writer who was an exact contemporary of his. This was Friedrich Nietzsche. The two men worked quite independently, and did not study each other's books. Once Spitteler wrote a review of Nietzsche, and Nietzsche retorted with a typical snarl; but they never met, and did not mold each other's ideas. Yet both preached a pessimism derived from Greece, and used comparable symbols to make it clear (for instance, Apollo struggling with the subhuman forces of unreason). Both believed that life, although beautiful at times, was fundamentally bad and cruel. Both, apparently, thought the ordinary man was helpless and pitiful or contemptible, fit only to be ruled or redeemed by heroes. And both, it should be mentioned, had a profound distrust of women: recognizing the irresistible power of woman's beauty, they hated woman for her treachery and cruelty, perhaps despised her for her weakness. But Nietzsche was a smaller, shriller man than Spitteler, and he insisted on this more savagely, with something of that imbalance which was at last to ruin him. It would seem that both Spitteler and Nietzsche drew much of their thought from Jacob Burckhardt, who in turn had partly derived it from Schopenhauer and partly worked it out in his own meditations on the meaning of art and history. When

Nietzsche's mind finally failed, he asked to be taken back to two people: Cosima Wagner, whom he loved, and Burckhardt, who had taught him some wisdom.

But it would be wrong to suggest that most of Spitteler's ideas were derived from any other philosopher or poet. He thought hard and long before reaching his mystical creed: at first while he was studying for the Christian ministry, then when he was resolving to abandon it, and later during the eight long years he spent as a tutor in Russia. He continued to think throughout his life, with something of the slowness and the irresistible power of his own mountains and glaciers. The chief merit of *Olympian Spring* is a very rare and great one: like an Alpine landscape, it not only feeds our imagination but raises our thought to a new level above the noise and dust of the workaday world.

*The Book of Miracles*

―――――――――

ONE of the most famous and most amusing books in the whole of European literature got off to a very bad start. Its author was condemned to exile for life before it was published. He burned his manuscript in agony and despair. But fortunately some of his friends had copies, and they got it published for him. It was an instantaneous success, and has been read and enjoyed by hundreds of thousands of people ever since. It was one of William Shakespeare's favorite books, and gave him lots of ideas. The French philosopher Montaigne said that when he was a little boy of seven or eight he used to hide in order to read it without being disturbed. The stern Milton and the still sterner Dante were both devoted to it. It has provided subjects for dozens and dozens of artists, from Botticelli to Picasso. It is a delightful imaginative poem about miracles, by the Roman poet Ovid.

Its official title is *The Metamorphoses*, which means *The Transformations*. In plan, it is a history of the world from creation down to the death of Julius Caesar — or rather of all the miracles, and in particular all the miraculous changes of form, which happened during those long centuries. But most of the time, as we read it, we are scarcely conscious of the plan; we see the poem simply as a long and fascinating string of surrealist stories, fantastic legends — some beautiful and sad, some grotesquely comic, some harsh and horrible, but all easy to read and hard to forget. And furthermore, all are told by a man who was a master storyteller as well as a skillful poet. Practically every tale he relates is as impossible as the *Arabian Nights*. His legends appeal not to the cool, reasoning, logical mind, but to the daring and creative imagination; not to our sense of reality, but to our subconscious, which prefers the strangest things to the most ordinary, the impossible to the everyday, fiction to fact.

Fortunately, this is one of the classical poems which have been really well translated. There is a good brisk eighteenth-century version in couplets, 'by divers hands'; and quite recently the American poet Rolfe Humphries has published a gay, brisk, and epigrammatic rendering in modern English (Indiana University Press). By the way, the first large English book written in America was a translation of the poem by George Sandys, the treasurer of the Virginia Company: it appeared in 1626, and was much admired.

The best thing in the poem is its enormous wealth and variety of stories. Many of the legends which have become an essential part of our Western literature and thought were first told by Ovid, or were best told by Ovid. It was he, for instance, who dug up the story (virtually unknown before his time) of the two Babylonian lovers who could speak to each other only through a narrow chink in the wall dividing their houses. They arranged a secret meeting outside the city at midnight. The girl reached the meeting place first. As she waited, she saw a lion which had been out killing cattle. In terror, she ran off and hid. The lion found her scarf on the ground, and with its bloody teeth chewed it and tore it. Soon afterward, the young man arrived . . . to find his sweetheart's scarf lying on the ground covered with blood and surrounded by the tracks of a wild beast. In despair he killed himself with his own sword. Then, as the body turned cold, the girl returned. She kissed his dead lips. She saw the veil and the sword; she understood; and, rather than be separated from him by the wall of mortality, she used the sword upon herself. That is the tale of Pyramus and Thisbe. It was adapted from Ovid to become one of the first poems in the whole of French literature, and something of its pathos and its desperation went into the story of Romeo and Juliet.

There was a miraculous transformation connected with that legend, as with all Ovid's tales, but it was a small and unimportant one. The two lovers died under a mulberry tree; their blood stained its berries, and ever since then the mulberry tree has had dark blood-red fruit. (White mulberries were a later importation from the Far East.) Sometimes in Ovid's tales the human interest is paramount and the miracle is subsidiary; sometimes the miracle itself is the center of interest and is deeply symbolic.

Such is the adventure of King Midas, who has offered a miraculous gift by a divinity — a gift of power. He chose it himself. He asked that everything he touched should turn to gold. The power was conferred on him; but he had forgotten that he must eat and drink. The food changed to solid metal when it touched his lips; the wine as it entered his mouth became liquid gold. Likely to die of thirst and starvation, he could only ask the same divinity to take back the gift and restore him to humanity. Such, too, is the sad story of Orpheus, whose young wife died suddenly. He went to the underworld to find her. There he made such exquisite music that the King of the Dead allowed him to take Eurydice back to life, provided only that he did not look on her face before they reached the upper world. But he was in love, he was anxious about the sad silent shape which followed him on the long climb, he turned to reassure himself — and this time he lost her forever. And there is the story of Narcissus, the handsome youth who fell in love with his own reflection in the water and pined away, gazing at it, until nothing was left except a flower with a drooping head looking into the forest pool. Then there is the terrible story of Tereus and his outrage on his wife's sister Philomela, and his wife's ferocious revenge; there is the tale of the first men to fly through the air, Daedalus and Icarus; and the wild adventures of Hercules, and Medea, and a dozen other legendary figures.

What is important about stories such as these is that they do not appear to be merely inventions. They appear to be symbols of profound psychological truths which cannot be properly expressed through logical utterance. For example, the story of Pyramus and Thisbe — which is so like the story of Romeo and Juliet and the story of Tristan and Isolde and many others — appears to symbolize some strange connection between violent love and violent death (not death through cruelty, but death through devotion and self-immolation); and also some hidden link between ardent young love and utter self-forgetfulness; and much more which we can feel, but can hardly discuss except in poetry and music.

The meaning of the myths and miracles goes deeper yet. The Swiss psychologist Jung could write a marvelous commentary on the whole of Ovid's poem, both on its central theme and on every one of its separate myths. Jung tells us that in the unconscious mind — not of any single extraordinary individual, but rather of all humanity — there are many patterns through which we interpret the world and ourselves. These patterns, he believes, are just as universal and necessary to us as the structure of our eyes or the dexterity of our fingers. One set of these patterns he calls the Archetypes of Transformation. They appear in dreams. They appear in situations which particularly impress us and in which we participate (for instance, certain religious and social rituals such as initiation ceremonies). They appear in recurrent themes of drama, fiction and myth — such as the long and partially subterranean journey, the quest for a magical or divine talisman, the ordeal in which a soul is tested by hostile or supernatural powers, and the miraculous transformation. In dreams or visions shaped by these archetypal patterns we may see ourselves being transformed, or we may watch strange metamorphoses in process: a tree altering its shape and nature; a human being changing into an animal; a mysterious bird speaking intelligible words. These (says Jung) are not merely confused and meaningless fantasies produced by a brain which is sick or exhausted; and the legends in which they appear are not merely ingenious distortions of reality designed to amuse and to astonish. They are symbols of psychical growth. They are descriptions of what we experience as we explore our own subconscious — that task on which we all, whether we know it or not, are continuously engaged. And (I think I should venture to add) they are interpretations of some of the great emotional and mystical experiences through which all of us must pass. Therefore, it is because these legends — eccentric or absurd as they may superficially seem to be — reflect truly universal human experiences that they have survived for so long, fascinated so many poets and provided subjects for so many artists and musicians.

The stories are the important thing in Ovid's poem. It is a one-volume manual of Greek and Roman mythology. However, it has been enjoyed for a number of other reasons too. Ovid was a brilliant psychologist, at least as far as women are concerned, and his book contains several astonishing monologues in which women, tense with love and despair, analyze their own feelings and try to overcome their conflicts. He did not care much about philosophy, but he knew much more about it than the average writer does today; so he gave a surprising amount of space to the teaching of that mysterious figure Pythagoras, and worked in an exposition of his doctrine of transmigration and his treatment of the paradox of change within permanence. And, strangest of all, during the Middle Ages Ovid himself was thought of as a great authority on cosmology, because, while the standard account of the creation of the world was of course to be found in Genesis, Ovid at the opening of his poem gave a much more detailed description of the process, which was scarcely ever in direct conflict with

Scripture and often appeared to supplement it, even explaining some of the things the Bible leaves unexplained. Like Vergil, he was thought to be one of the few pagan poets who had been partially inspired by the spirit of true religion. I do not for a moment believe he was; but then, if you are a skillful technician, you can convince most people that you are sincere.

And he was a skillful technician, a smooth and consummate craftsman: he was the Mozart, or at least the Rossini, of Latin poetry. He began writing verse when he was only twelve years old, and his first book was a tremendous success when he was about twenty-two. *The Metamorphoses* is one of the easiest and most pleasant of the Roman classics to read — it ought to be taught in schools and colleges before the youngsters approach the somber and thoughtful Vergil — and its lightness and rapidity are not accident, but the result of practiced art and long experience. Rolfe Humphries's translation is not quite so melodious as the original Latin, but it has nearly all of Ovid's liveliness and speed. Here is his version of the climax of the famous tale about the first men who flew. Daedalus, wisest of inventors, the man who built the Labyrinth, was imprisoned on the island of Crete: so he constructed wings for himself and his son Icarus, and escaped on them. Off the two flew, through the middle air.

> Far off, far down, some fisherman is watching
> As the rod dips and trembles over the water,
> Some shepherd rests his weight upon his crook,
> Some ploughman on the handles of the ploughshare,
> And all look up, in absolute amazement,
> At those air-borne above. They must be gods!
>         ... And the boy
> Thought *This is wonderful!* and left his father,
> Soared higher, higher, drawn to the vast heaven
> Nearer the sun, and the wax that held the wings
> Melted in that fierce heat, and the bare arms
> Beat up and down in air, and lacking oarage
> Took hold of nothing. *Father!* he cried, and *Father!*
> Until the blue sea hushed him, the dark water

Men call the Icarian now. And Daedalus,
Father no more, called 'Icarus, where are you?
Where are you, Icarus? Tell me where to find you!'
And saw the wings on the waves, and cursed his talents.*

Good poetry — as light as the feathers which bore up the two fliers. Ovid himself had a disastrous fall: he soared too high, and crashed down, and cursed his talents. Yet the work of his ebullient imagination survived, and is still flying on through the upper air of myth and poetry.

---

* Ovid, *Metamorphoses*, 8.217.34

## *The Epic of a Crime*

---

OVER a battlefield strewn with corpses soar hundreds of vultures: from their claws fall fragments of bone and decaying flesh. A soldier marching through the north African desert is bitten by a venomous snake; his body is horribly distended by the poison, and swells up until it becomes unrecognizable. On the coast of Egypt a great general, in flight from his victorious enemy, is murdered and then beheaded, while his wife watches in horror. A group of soldiers surrounded and outnumbered determine never to surrender; they stab one another to death. At midnight a witch takes a dead body, and by drugs and spells brings it back to life so that it can foretell the future.

Is it possible that these ghastly incidents could ever be made into poetry? that they could become elements in a true work of art? We are tempted to reply 'No' at once. Surely there has never been a poet who was capable of using such hideous scenes, of making them into something above the level of Grand Guignol. But there was. He died when he was only twenty-five; but he had already written enough to make him famous not only in his own time but for many centuries after his death. His chief work, which alone survives, is a poem some six thousand lines in length. It has been called a masterpiece; and it has been called noisy and perverted rubbish. Both descriptions may well be true. It is a mingling of true horror with false grotesqueries like Shakespeare's *Titus Andronicus,* or even his *King Lear.* When it is bad, it is atrocious; when it is good, it is marvellous; certainly it is unlike any other poem in the whole range of literature.

It is an epic poem in Latin, called *The Civil War.* Its subject is the war which Julius Caesar waged against the republic of Rome, the war for which he prepared and which he provoked so that he might become dictator and monarch of a once free community. Its author was a young man who was born in Spain of Roman or Romanized parents: his name, Lucan. Into his twenty-five years of life he crowded more work and more dramatic experiences than most men see in a long career.

He was born in the year 39 after Christ, which made him two years younger than the emperor Nero. Not long after coming to the throne, Nero began to exalt his own powers as a poet and aesthete. He inaugurated a new festival competition in poetry and music (and called it, characteristically, the Neronia). One of the chief prizes was won by Lucan, who was still very young, perhaps nineteen or twenty. At once he became a favorite of the youthful emperor, who gave him several very unusual honors and obviously admired his work. With this encouragement, he started to write an enormously ambitious epic poem. The subject, the civil war which had devastated Rome and most of the western world a century or so earlier, was brand new; it had been described in many prose histories, but never in poetry; it was a challenging theme — as important and exciting as the American Civil War is to us, at the same remove of time; and Lucan's hard, hot, brilliant style was admirably suited to it. He plunged into it with all the passion of a young genius.

When Lucan was about twenty-two or twenty-three, the first three books of his poem were published. They were a huge success; and indeed it is difficult, even now, to read the first five hundred lines without instantly realizing that their author was, even if immature, a genius. Unfortunately, it is also apparent that he was, as many other prodigies have been, something of a fool, and either genuinely misled or else hopelessly insincere, for the first three pages contain such appalling and revolting flattery of the youthful emperor that no modern reader can escape feeling perfectly nauseated. Lucan equates young Nero with God, and begs him, after his life on this earth is ended, to ascend to the very center of heaven, because, so great is his majesty and might, if he moves to one side or the other he will distort the entire universe.

Fortunately, even this gross and monstrous adulation was not enough for Nero. Conceited idiot that he was, he read Lucan's poem as far as it had gone, saw its undoubted brilliance, observed the success it was having with the public, and grew jealous. He himself was to be the outstanding artistic genius of his generation, not some upstart from the provinces. He determined to sabotage Lucan's career. He began by a public insult. While the young poet was reading his work to a large audience, Nero suddenly rose and walked out, on the pretext of having official business to attend to; naturally, the recital had to be discontinued. Shortly after that, Nero positively forbade Lucan to publish any more poetry, or even to give readings in private to his friends.

To a young man seething with ambition, absolutely certain of his own bright genius, devoted to a new and daring subject, and already rewarded by public admiration, this was absolutely unbearable. It is hard enough on Russian composers and writers when they are compelled to write party-line propaganda, and, if one of their works shows traces of non-conformity, to withdraw it and publicly apologize for it; but this was worse. Lucan's career was ended almost before it had begun. Driven almost mad with rage and repression, he continued to write, though not, of course, to publish. He completed six more books of his epic and started a seventh — now without any flattery of the ruler, but filled with the most virulent hatred of all emperors, for the entire system of absolute monarchy, and for the man who, by bringing the tottering Roman republic to its knees and then stabbing it in the back, had degraded it into a dictatorship and become its first ruler, Julius Caesar. In addition, Lucan wrote a savage satire on Nero, which he circulated to his friends. He never ceased to deride his former patron, and even administered the extreme insult of using a phrase of Nero's own poetry to comment on an indecorous incident in a public lavatory. At last, when other Romans who shared his loathing for the absurd and criminal vices of the emperor formed a conspiracy to assassinate him, Lucan joined it, and became one of its most ardent leaders.

The conspiracy was discovered. All its leaders, and most of those connected with them, were either executed or forced to kill themselves. (Nero seized the opportunity to rid himself of his old tutor, the philosopher Seneca, and of one of his former friends, the Epicurean Petronius — both of whom, in different ways, had tried to mold his character and to suppress or sublimate his lust and cruelty.) Lucan was allowed to select his own death. He chose the least painful and the most natural, having his veins opened in a warm bath, so that he could bleed slowly and quietly to death. With a characteristic touch of vanity and extravagance, as he died he repeated some of his own poetry, a passage describing the heroic death of a soldier who collapses under many wounds, so that life leaves him by a hundred gates.

The historians tell us that, before he died, he tried to save himself by accusing other members of the conspiracy, and that one of the people he denounced was his own mother. They add, however, that in spite of this he still had to commit suicide, while nothing whatever happened to her. What are we to think of that report? It is possible, of course, that the young man who had flattered Nero so basely in his first book would basely cringe before him when the soldiers of the praetorian guard surrounded him with their short sharp swords. But is it not more probable that he knew such a vile act (if it ever occurred to him) would be perfectly useless? that an elderly lady would be highly unlikely as a conspirator? and that the entire story was made up and circulated after Lucan's death, by Nero? Remember that Nero was painfully jealous of Lucan's reputation; he had tried to kill his poetry; now he would endeavor to kill his moral reputation; and how? By accusing him of the very crime that Nero himself had committed; for Nero himself, five or six years before, had sent his bodyguard to stab his own mother to death. It was, he thought, part of his emancipation into perfect liberty.

Lucan had a beautiful young wife, who was not involved. She survived both Lucan and his executioner Nero, who himself was overthrown and committed suicide three years later. After the tyrant's death, she published the rest of her husband's poem — that is, as much as he had finished when his life ended: seven more books, the last obviously incomplete, making ten in all. It survived; it was both admired and criticized in ancient times; it came through the Dark Ages and was much read in the Middle Ages — Dante, for example, loved it dearly, placed Lucan in Limbo as one of the six great poets of the world, and adapted the *Civil War* in several of his own finest passages. Since then it has always been a powerful stimulus to some readers and to others an outrageous affliction. Shelley, rebel that he was, preferred it to Vergil's *Aeneid*, and put the poet into his splendid elegy *Adonais*, the lament for the premature death of John Keats: there Lucan appears as one of the predecessors of Keats, the 'inheritors of unfulfilled renown.' The eccentric English poet, Robert Graves, has recently published a prose translation of the epic, called by the wrong name, *Pharsalia*, with the wrong subtitle, *Dramatic Episodes of the Civil Wars* (Penguin, 1957). Like other poets, Graves both enjoys the energy of the poem and loathes its occasional vulgarity and crudity; he compares Lucan to Rudyard Kipling, calling them 'prodigiously vital writers with hysterical tendencies.'

What of the poem itself? It is both great and silly, both vulgar and noble, false and true, cheap and magnificent. It is impossible to read many of its passages without disgust and contempt. It is impossible to think of the entire poem — unfinished as it is — without admiration. This is largely due to the fact that Lucan was too clever too soon: he had the faults of so many youthful prodigies, over-confidence, ostentation, over-emphasis. Nevertheless, he chose a first-rate subject, and he had what most young writers (particularly today) do not have, a perfectly firm and solid substructure of thought. He had been well trained in philosophy before he started writing. His uncle was the Stoic philosopher Seneca, and his own teacher was the distinguished Stoic philosopher Cornutus. Therefore he has no moral doubts, no vagueness about principles. Once finished with the initial flatteries to Nero (which he would certainly have removed if he had lived to finish and revise the poem), he describes the entire civil war as something not like our own Civil War, in which both sides had much right and some wrong to defend, but rather a deliberately planned and coolly executed murder: the slaughter of a republic, the assassination of an ideal.

Can we explain the huge and obvious faults of the poem? Can we understand how they could coexist with its powerful central plan, with its many grandeurs, and with the ultimate integrity of its author? In one way, and in one way only. It is not possible to dismiss Lucan as a charlatan who would do anything to gain public attention and admiration. One does not write book after book of difficult poetry (and his poetry demands a high degree of intellectual concentration), poetry filled with bitter opposition to the system under which one has been brought up, without the hope of seeing any of one's work published, unless one is absolutely convinced that one's cause is right. Therefore Lucan, while writing most of his poem, was sincere. He was also a powerful rhetorician and an inventor of great imaginative gifts. But why the initial flattery? why the all-pervading cruelty, and exaggeration, and shrillness? why the lapses from intense nobility to vulgar violence, as though we were passing from Milton or Dante to Mickey Spillane? The faults of Lucan's poem are a proof of his own thesis. This is a thesis which has often been advanced since his time, and is now, at this very moment, obviously and urgently true. It is impossible to write truly and to create harmonious art under a dictatorship. In a totalitarian state, the ordinary man is benumbed, anaesthetized, plunged into random epicureanism or passive melancholy. The sensitive creative man or woman is either corrupted or distorted. He becomes vicious, or cynical, or melancholiac, or, like Lucan, a sufferer who feels himself going mad, and who strives, not always with success, to keep a grip on reality, as frail and as diminishing as that of the mountain-climber on the icy face of the bitter mountain.

# The Elegy in a Country Churchyard

<hr />

When a poem, or a piece of music, or a painting becomes famous and remains famous, for year after year, then for generation after generation and then from one century into another, we might as well stop arguing. It is a good piece of work. We may not like it, or we may not like all of it; but we ought to try to understand it: by making the effort, we may well increase our own powers of appreciation. We should certainly start by admitting that it is a good work. It will have its faults: the Fifth Symphony is too loud and single-minded: Botticelli's *Spring* is sentimental; *Hamlet* is crazy. The faults are trifles. The thing itself is great.

The most famous poem in the English language is probably *An Elegy Wrote in a Country Church Yard*, published in 1751 by a quiet don at Cambridge University named Thomas Gray. For over two hundred years it has been read and remembered and reprinted. It has been fairly deeply felt, in fragments, although I should not say that it has been thought about (unless by scholars). There are some moving stories about how it has been loved; for instance, the noble but often distorted tale of General Wolfe repeating the *Elegy* just before the battle of

Quebec, in which he was killed. Quotations from the poem are in everybody's mind, whether their source is known or not: *far from the madding crowd, born to blush unseen, mute inglorious Milton, shut the gates of mercy, kindred spirit,* and (most famous of all) *the paths of glory.* Its subject — quiet life, quiet death, peaceful rest in a green graveyard among ancient trees — remains in the mind of anyone who has even glanced at the poem: lingers, with a strange mixture of melancholy and pleasure, a mellow, autumnal, smoky sweetness. Its mood is expressed so memorably that — although most of us have only a vague notion what general literary forms really mean — anyone who was asked about elegiac poetry would think at once of Thomas Gray's *Elegy Wrote in a Country Church Yard.*

Whenever I read it, I seem to hear strains of music: Chopin's Étude in E, Bach's Air for the G String. Of all the arts, poetry is closest to music, and this particular poem is filled with music of its own: not boldly dramatic music like many of Shakespeare's sound effects, nor extravagantly romantic Berlioz-music, as in Shelley, but gentle, subdued, subtle strains, like those in some of the odes of John Keats. Gray himself was a fine singer, though his voice was small; and he was taught to play the harpsichord by the younger Scarlatti. In his poem the music is there, but it is harpsichord music; to hear it, you must be still.

Take the famous first stanza, describing the hour of sunset:

> The Curfew tolls the knell of parting day,
> The lowing herd wind slowly o'er the lea,
> The plowman homeward plods his weary way,
> And leaves the world to darkness and to me.

In the first line, we actually hear the swinging strokes of the evening bell in the double liquids: 'to*ll*s the kne*ll*.' In the second, we hear the voices of the cattle in the long O's: 'the l*ow*ing herd wind sl*ow*ly *o*'er the lea.' In the third there are the heavy footsteps of the tired laborer in the thick, moist earth: 'the *pl*owman homewa*r*d *pl*ods.' In the fourth line, there are no audible sound effects; but the peculiar shape of the line seems to image the gradual closing-in of evening, the narrowing of vision as light leaves the air, until what was once a bright, varied landscape has become nothing but a tiny spark of awareness in the center of quiet, black night: 'leaves the world to darkness . . . and to me.'

That is the essential music of elegy, that minor cadence, that dying fall; and in stanza after stanza throughout this fine poem we can trace how emotion rises and expands, only to diminish again and fade away — as though, in anxiety or protest or hope, our lungs were filled with generous, energetic air, and then sank down again in a melancholy sigh of resignation.

The elegiac movement is particularly marked in those passages of the *Elegy* where the poet draws a contrast between the farmers and villagers who lie buried in the country churchyard, and the haughty gentlemen and ladies of the baroque age who believed that they alone were truly human, while the peasantry were little better than cattle.

> Let not Ambition mock their useful toil,
> Their homely joys, and destiny obscure;
> Nor Grandeur hear with a disdainful smile

— and now an exquisitely light line composed of small and unpretentious words, like a tiny cottage built beside a magnificent palace —

> The short and simple annals of the poor.

In the next quatrain, Gray turns against the aristocrats, rich, handsome, and powerful. He makes their mastery of this life swell out exuberantly for a while, and then, as it must, fall away and perish: and he shows this by using grand, sonorous, rhetorical phrases, which are succeeded by plain words, brief but irresistibly telling, irresistibly somber.

The boast of heraldry, the pomp of power,
 And all that beauty, all that wealth e'er gave,
Awaits alike the inevitable hour;
 The paths of glory lead but to the grave.

The *Elegy* has one quality which is almost forgotten in much modern poetry, as in much modern painting: it has a firm and clearly perceptible structure. It is no easy thing to build a long poem into a shape which is not monotonous and not static, to give it a movement which is regular and comprehensible and appropriate to its meaning. The most famous poem in modern Western literature, Eliot's *The Waste Land,* is full of unforgettable things, but it is almost a heap of ruins and fragments. Ezra Pound's *Cantos* are approaching complete incoherence. In a better known and more conventional American poem, *John Brown's Body,* Stephen Vincent Benét made a determined effort to bring the massive and confused story of the Civil War into a single structural scheme, but I cannot believe that he succeeded. If Gray had been meditating in a graveyard today, he might have produced a shapeless and irregular outpouring of emotion in no steady rhythm and with no firmly perceived relationship between the whole poem and its parts.

But he was writing in the eighteenth century, the age of orderly music and firmly designed pictures and largely planned architecture. Therefore he poured his feelings into firmly molded stanzas, regular in form though subtly varied in sound and movement; and he devoted a group of stanzas to each phase of his developing emotion. The first three describe sunset and nightfall; the next four evoke the dead countryfolk lying buried in the little churchyard; the following four defend them against the sneers of the nobility and gentry, who would not consider being buried anywhere but in a cathedral; and then, in a fine movement of eight stanzas, Gray reflects that, but for their poverty, some of these poor forgotten peasants might have been great and renowned, mighty poets, orators, statesmen. Yet, as they could not be famous for worthy achievement, so they were delivered from the temptation to become either tyrants or the flatterers of tyrants.

> Far from the madding crowd's ignoble strife
>> Their sober wishes never learned to stray;
> Along the cool sequestered vale of life
>> They kept the noiseless tenor of their way.

This orderly development of a deeply felt emotion is something which we know best, nowadays, through music: we feel it in the slow movement of Mozart's Piano Concerto in A; in the Allegretto of Beethoven's Seventh Symphony; and (in our own generation) in Samuel Barber's Adagio for Strings.

Thomas Gray composed his poem very slowly; in stages separated by long periods of silent brooding; cautiously; hesitantly; tentatively — at least in English. He wrote poetry in Latin much more quickly and readily; and I believe that more of his poems are in Latin than in English. Both in Latin and in English he was sustained by one strengthening force which some modern poets lack: tradition. He was always aware that he, although original and individual, was one poet in a long line of creators, and that he could and should learn from them. Therefore he sometimes used the ideas, occasionally the very words, of elder poets, remolding them so that they seemed to be original. Take the famous stanza from this elegy on the dead villagers:

> For them no more the blazing hearth shall burn,
>> Or busy housewife ply her evening care;
> No children run to lisp their sire's return,
>> Or climb his knees the envied kiss to share.

The emotion of loss and bereavement could scarcely be more sincere; yet the entire stanza is an elaboration of a celebrated passage in the Roman poet Lucretius, on the finality of death:

> Never again your happy home will greet you, never
> your loving wife and darling children run to meet
> your kiss, and thrill your heart with sweetness unexpressed.*

---

* Lucretius, *De Rerum Natura* 3.894-6

If we do not know this, we still feel Gray's lines to be somberly beautiful. If we do, our enjoyment is enhanced by hearing the echo of the voice of the melancholy Roman. And so throughout the poem. Gray was a widely and deeply read scholar; even those who have read only half as much as he will have great delight in tracing those resonances from other poems, Greek, Latin, and English. In a few stanzas toward the end of the poem, Gray evokes several famous scenes from Shakespeare and Milton, and yet blends them perfectly into his own imaginative picture.

The end of the poem.... What is the end of Gray's *Elegy*? Everyone knows the opening, with its tolling bell and its gathering gloom; but the conclusion?

The conclusion is a surprise, and not wholly a successful one. After twenty-three stanzas, nearly a hundred lines, of noble meditation on the village dead who lie buried around him, Gray turns unexpectedly to speak of someone else, someone quite different: a young man who loved the countryside and wandered through its fields and forests, but who was not a laborer or a farmer. He was solitary, his life was purposeless, and (quite unlike the villagers who kept the noiseless tenor of their way) his emotions were so disorderly that he looked deranged, laughing to himself, lying in catatonic silence, or drooping with sad melancholy. He died of this disorder (if he did not kill himself), and he is buried in the churchyard. The *Elegy* ends with an epitaph for this youth, 'to Fortune and to Fame unknown.'

Who is this young man? He is identified only in the most awkward stanza in the entire poem.

> For thee, who, mindful of the unhonoured dead,
>   Dost in these lines their artless tale relate;
> If chance, by lonely contemplation led,
>   Some kindred spirit shall inquire thy fate....

It is contorted and hampered in expression, as though Gray found it difficult to say what he meant: here his emotions were so strong that for once he could not put them into clear words.

> For thee, who, mindful of the unhonoured dead,
> Dost *in these lines* their artless tale relate...

'These lines'? They can surely be nothing else than the *Elegy* itself, the poem which Gray (unlike most other poets of his time) dedicated not to the rich but to the poor, and in which he told the simple story of their lives, 'their artless tale.' Therefore (if this is correct) the young, melancholy man who is soon to die is Thomas Gray himself. When he began the poem, Gray was twenty-five. He was thirty-three, the crucial age, when it was published; and he lived to be fifty-four, although he was seldom strong or healthy. He did have a dear friend, Richard West, who after a painfully unhappy life died young; Gray actually sent West a copy of one of his early odes without knowing that his friend was in his final illness. Clearly the end of the poem might have been partially inspired by the misery and waste of his friend's life; but, even through the perplexed phrases and emotions of the transitional stanza, it is clear that Gray is thinking chiefly of himself. He was a man of immense talent, with generous emotions and vast ambitions, but with very little will-power. As a don at Cambridge University, he had a small, safe livelihood, but (as things were then) nothing more. He had no pupils; he had no colleagues who cared for philology and science as much as he did; and he dared not face a great world in which power and wealth meant so much, while a poet could only

> heap the shrine of Luxury and Pride
> With incense kindled at the Muse's flame.

He wished for death. He felt that his essence, his spirit, his expanding mind, had already died young; and he looked forward to his own grave.

To us, who know him only through this and perhaps two or three other poems, it seems strange that Gray should have been so afflicted by melancholy and despair so early in life; many a young man would gladly sell his future happiness if, in exchange, he could be sure of writing poems which would earn him a reputation as sure and invincible as that of Gray. But what he felt, and here tried (not altogether successfully) to express, was that he might have done much more. When he died, he was described as 'the most learned man in Europe.' Within that small, unhealthy body there was a brilliant mind. Within that gentle, timid bookworm there was the shriveled chrysalis of a magnificent, broad-winged genius. Within the poet whose *Elegy* closes with his own epitaph, there was the reluctant corpse of a successor to Shakespeare, a Milton more eloquent, and even more glorious.

## The Madness of Hamlet

———————————————

TOGETHER with his best friend, his only friend, Prince Hamlet enters a churchyard. He watches a man digging a grave, and tossing skulls out of it, and singing. After a time he speaks to the fellow, asking how long he has been a gravedigger. Without recognizing him, the man replies:

> Of all days in the year I came to it...the very
> day that young Hamlet was born; he that is mad.
> (5.1.154f.)

The scene, one of the most wonderful in all drama, goes on with grim jokes and puns and obscenities, until the skull of the jester Yorick is thrown up. Hamlet talks to it, gloomily and meditatively; but not madly. Yet a few minutes later he is in the grave himself, wrestling with Laertes; and then standing beside it raving and shouting like a lunatic; finally, after a horrible display of feverish violence, he rushes wildly off, babbling nonsense (5.1.313-14). It is a fearfully difficult scene to act — because the player must, within a very few minutes, pass from a tone of courtly wit (remember, Hamlet was a poet and a humorist as well as many other things) into elegiac

melancholy and ironic bitterness; and then, after a long pause
of almost complete silence while he sees his sweetheart's body
carried in for burial, into masterful princely energy (5.1.281-5),
and thence into shocking yells and rants and imprecations,
ending at last in a few vague sentences, half pathetic and half
crazy. Difficult as it is to act and harrowing as it is to watch,
this scene contains some of the essential problems of the play,
and it epitomizes the most absorbing of them. The gravedigger
says Hamlet is mad. Hamlet behaves very strangely and furiously toward the end of the scene. Is he mad, or not?

It is a subtle and enthralling problem. It haunts nearly
everyone in the drama: they keep worrying about it and talking of it, each in his own way. It fascinates nearly everyone
who sees the play or acts in it — although Sir Laurence Olivier
apparently never thought about it one way or the other, and
introduced his handsome but stupid version of it by calling it
'the story of a man who could not make up his mind.' The
connection of madness and sanity concerned Shakespeare himself very deeply: nearly every one of his plays has either an
extreme eccentric, or a half-wit, or a melancholic in it somewhere; and, in his other great tragedies, Lady Macbeth goes
slowly mad and Macbeth is threatened with madness, Timon
of Athens is a hopeless psychotic, while *King Lear* is a play
filled with lunacy feigned and real, cruel and innocent. But
in these dramas there is no doubt, although there is grief and
horror. We know who is mad, and who is sane. In *Hamlet*, we
do not know. The plot and the character of the hero are a mystery. They fascinate us both with puzzlement and with a
strange mixture of terror and delight. Dozens and dozens of
critics have written brilliantly about the mystery, and still it
remains a darkness, shot with flashes of light that blind us.

Of course we shall not expect to find a complete solution for
it. One of the essences of character-drawing like Shakespeare's,
and one of the foundations of tragic poetry, is insolubility. Life
is not logical, and logic neither controls nor explains life.
Much of the finest art is built on an unanswerable *Why?*

Yet surely we can solve some of the mystery if we read the

play carefully. It was one of Shakespeare's most deeply felt works, revised much more extensively and written with far more detailed attention than most of his others. (His only son, who died in childhood, was called Hamnet.) Since he thought about it so intensely, he intended us to think about it. Hamlet himself, in those incomparable dying words, asks his friend to live on so as to explain him to the world.

Was he mad, then? I have heard it said that if Hamlet had been mad there would have been no play. That is not quite true. The spectacle of a powerful man — prince or giant or genius — transformed into a dangerous maniac does make an exciting drama; but it is a play of a different type from *Hamlet*, and of a different pattern. The essence of this play is doubt. If we knew all along that the hero was hopelessly mad, there would still be tension, but of a more obvious, an external kind.

Contrariwise, Hamlet is not sane. He is intelligent, but he is not 100 per cent sane, a wily man merely pretending to be a lunatic in order to plot in safety against a usurping king. That was the original story of Hamlet the Dane, the viking's son — a bloody and primitive saga from the Dark Ages. But although Shakespeare's Hamlet often speaks of pretense and carries out several cunning stratagems, his main adventure is not one of disguise, conspiracy, and successful revenge. His most elaborate plots are fruitless or needless, and the killing of his enemies — Polonius, Laertes, Claudius — is accomplished almost by chance: Horatio calls it 'accidental judgments, casual slaughters' (5.2.396).

Let us look inside the play. What do the people there think of Hamlet?

The simpler souls all believe he is mad through and through. (Simple people generally believe that complicated people are mad.) The gravedigger says so; poor Ophelia is convinced of it; so (with a few misgivings) is her father, Polonius, and so is Hamlet's own mother, Gertrude. They think that his insanity comes and goes by spasms of violence; they find it hard to suggest any real origin for it, except love, in which they do not wholly believe; but on the whole they are sure Hamlet is not responsible for his actions.

His friend Horatio always treats him as perfectly sane — although very excitable. He restrains him now and then (1.4.69-78, 1.5.133-5, 5.1.226), but he never doubts him, he is dedicated to him, and he even attempts to die with him.

The king? Ah, the king. One of the best things in the play is that duel between the king and Hamlet, between the Machiavellian usurper and the brilliant amateur. Claudius is a noble villain, every inch an autocrat, and with any other opponent he would have won the contest and survived victorious. He speaks to Hamlet with imperturbable courtesy, with wise firmness when necessary, and even with what looks like affection; while Hamlet consistently ignores or insults him, adding ironic provocations which would make a lesser man lose his control. The king swallows every insult with perfect composure, except the actual re-enactment of his crime. But he watches Hamlet constantly. He sees him first of all as a disturbing element, a silent protest; later as a man incalculable but dangerous, and therefore sane, in the strategic essentials of purpose and planning.

And Hamlet himself? Does he think he is mad? Surely that is one of the major keys to the play. We are so well accustomed to seeing sane and harmonious characters, full of conviction, that we somehow assume a hero must be sure of his own sanity. But when we watch Hamlet alone and listen to his thoughts, seeing him twice contemplating suicide (1.2.129f., 3.1.56f.) and twice reproaching himself bitterly for the unnatural, incomprehensible faults of his mind and will (2.2.584f., 4.4.32f.), hearing him talk (2.2.638) of his own 'weakness and melancholy,' or warn himself against murdering his own mother; or when we see him in a more level mood, speaking to others of his 'bad dreams' and his 'madness,' we recognize a special and a rare tragedy — that of the brilliant man who fears he is losing his mind, and who, nevertheless, subtly enjoys it. He cannot do what he ought to do. He cannot act when he should act. He cannot feel what he ought to feel. His life is divided into two main periods, one of profound gloom, which he knows as melancholy, and the other of wild excitement in which he acts almost without thinking; and these two phases of his life are almost wholly separate from each other.

Yet there are between-times, when he is calm, balanced, energetic, extremely intelligent. No trace of madness then. He is a good (though severe) critic of the drama, a brilliant social satirist, a thoughtful moralist, a wit in the best Renaissance fashion. Alone on ship, he spies on the agents who are commissioned to have him executed, alters their Top Secret orders so that they will die instead of him, then leads a counterattack on a pirate cruiser, is captured, talks his way out of captivity and ransom, and thus survives both a merciless conspiracy and a sinister chance.

Hamlet suffers, then, from intermittent madness. As we would say nowadays, he is 'mentally disturbed'; and his disturbances occur only in certain limited situations. When we first see him, his life has been dislocated by the sudden smooth maneuver through which his uncle has slipped onto the throne of Denmark and made him, once the rightful heir, now a pretender or a hanger-on, almost a displaced person. He is sullen. He is trying to get away, back to the university where he met his friend Horatio. Later, he learns that his father did not die naturally but was murdered, and that his mother committed adultery and incest with Claudius before the murder — so that all those closest to him are victim, criminal, and accomplice. In particular, his mother, after giving birth to him, has now unmade him by abolishing his father and his own existence as heir to the throne. Henceforward, whenever he is brought face to face with this central set of facts, his father's murder, his uncle's treachery, and his mother's guilty folly, he alternates between profound gloom and raving excitement. At those times he distrusts and insults almost everyone who crosses his path, even his own sweetheart. He is sane only when he is away from the court, when he is not faced with that problem which he finds too brutal even to contemplate, far less to solve. Within that prison, he is like a trapped bird, now fluttering wildly, now (as his mother says, 5.1.308-10) passive and drooping.

This is a pattern which *we* know too: we call it manic-depressive. Shakespeare knew it both from life and from books. In particular, the young Earl of Essex behaved in a manner very close to manic depression, alternating crazy excitement and illogical daring with periods of timeless silence and lethargy. (Essex was executed in 1601, and *Hamlet* was produced about 1602.) But there are literary prototypes, too, for the moody madness of heroes faced with insoluble problems. Shakespeare certainly knew the tragedy of the mad Hercules (by Seneca); he may well have heard of Orestes, who killed his mother for planning the murder of his father, and then went mad; he also remembered the criminal and crazy life of Nero, who killed both his mother and his adoptive father.

Hamlet's tragedy has many roots. His mother's vice and his uncle's crime are two of the central roots, but there are others, deeply buried. The English psychologist Ernest Jones has suggested that Hamlet is also in part Oedipus, that he has long contemplated the crimes of parricide and incest and is maddened and paralyzed by the fact that they were committed *for him*. But the main truth is clear. It is this. Hamlet is not a weakling; he is not a neurotic; he is not a sensitive plant too tender for this world, as Goethe imagined him, or a cynical eccentric, as Laforgue portrayed him. Nor is he a solid, thoughtful type surrounded by uncomprehending eccentrics and sinister plotters, as Olivier apparently imagined him. Like Lear and Macbeth and Othello, he is *both* strong *and* weak — or weakened, or wounded. (That is why the perfect actor would have to be both Maurice Evans and John Gielgud, with touches from other disparate characters also; and perhaps Barrymore was most like him of all.) He is *both* mad *and* sane. His suffering, like that of Macbeth and the others, is that his wound betrays him, it takes him out of himself, so that he sees his once excellent mind partly overthrown. A really weak man would have surrendered at once, or degenerated rapidly, like Bonnie Prince Charlie after his defeat. But one of the highest and deepest forms of tragedy is the losing struggle of the light self against the incalculable self which is dark. There are some magnificent dramas on that theme: but none has ever surpassed the play in which a prince sits beside the grave dug for his own sweetheart, and talks with love and horror to the jester's skull.

# ELIOT'S *'CORIOLAN'*

## *An Unfinished Poem*

AMONG modern poets writing in English, T. S. Eliot is certainly the most daring experimenter. Everything he has written brings his readers the shock of the unexpected; his meanings are often painfully obscure; and sometimes it is not easy even to make out what form he is writing in.

In his collected works there is a strange little section subtitled simply 'Unfinished Poems.' These are evidently experiments which he could not carry through to a conclusion. He thought the fragments were worth publishing nevertheless, and he was right. They are extremely interesting. One group of them — to judge by the number of times it is quoted — has already become famous: two scenes from a grim fantasy about light ladies and coarse men, the coarsest being the tough apelike Sweeney. The piece is called — parodying the title of Milton's only tragedy — *Sweeney Agonistes*. It is set out with speeches, songs, and choruses. Eliot calls it a melodrama in the style of Aristophanes. Quite clearly it was meant to be a play, although a very unusual one: something like the French shocker *Ubu Roi,* something perhaps like *The Threepenny Opera*.

Next to it come two short bits of very free verse, linked

under the single title 'Coriolan.' The first is subtitled 'Triumphal March' and the second 'Difficulties of a Statesman.' No further explanation is given. The fragments cover less than four pages. In tone, they are comical and serious, commonplace and highflown. We should like to know more about them, but it is unlikely — at least during Mr. Eliot's lifetime — that we shall. What do the fragments themselves tell us?

First, the title. 'Coriolan.' Far back in Roman history there was a general and a statesman called Coriolanus. He was a highly efficient general, and an arrogant, brutal, ultimately treasonous statesman. Rome was then a republic, trying to become a democracy. Coriolanus hated democracy, loathed the people. He denied their right to share in the country's government. When he had to be elected to an office for which he was obviously the right man, he hated to degrade himself by asking for their votes. At last he left Rome, joined her enemies, and led them against his own country. The story says that his mother and wife went out to his headquarters, and implored him not to attack the city which had nursed him. He gave way; and he died in exile, or (in another version of the story) returned to Rome and was then assassinated. Shakespeare built a splendid tragedy upon this theme, in which Sir Laurence Olivier triumphed during the summer of 1959. We might wonder why Eliot uses the form Coriolan instead of Coriolanus. Probably in order to remind us of the majestic overture which Beethoven wrote for a more modern version of the tragedy; possibly because he likes the fine clanging sound, CORIOLAN; and certainly because he wishes to make this, not a Roman piece, but something universal, free from date and place.

Now, the fragments. Here is the first of them.

## TRIUMPHAL MARCH

Stone, bronze, stone, steel, stone, oakleaves, horses' heels
Over the paving.
And the flags. And the trumpets. And so many eagles.
How many? Count them. And such a press of people.

We hardly knew ourselves that day, or knew the City.
This is the way to the temple, and we so many crowding the way.
So many waiting, how many waiting? what did it matter, on such
    a day?
Are they coming? No, not yet. You can see some eagles. And hear
    the trumpets.
Here they come. Is he coming?
The natural wakeful life of our Ego is a perceiving.
We can wait with our stools and our sausages.
What comes first? Can you see? Tell us. It is

      5,800,000 rifles and carbines,
        102,000 machine guns,
         28,000 trench mortars,
         53,000 field and heavy guns,
I cannot tell how many projectiles, mines and fuses,
         13,000 aeroplanes,
         24,000 aeroplane engines,
         50,000 ammunition waggons,
    now 55,000 army waggons,
         11,000 field kitchens,
          1,150 field bakeries.

What a time that took. Will it be he now? No,
Those are the golf club Captains, these the Scouts,
And now the *société gymnastique de Poissy*
And now come the Mayor and the Liverymen. Look
There he is now, look:
There is no interrogation in his eyes
Or in the hands, quiet over the horse's neck,
And the eyes watchful, waiting, perceiving, indifferent.
O hidden under the dove's wing, hidden in the turtle's breast,
Under the palmtree at noon, under the running water
At the still point of the turning world. O hidden.

Now they go up to the temple. Then the sacrifice.
Now come the virgins bearing urns, urns containing
Dust
Dust
Dust of dust, and now
Stone, bronze, stone, steel, stone, oakleaves, horses' heels
Over the paving.

> That is all we could see. But how many eagles! and how many
> trumpets!
> (And Easter Day, we didn't get to the country,
> So we took young Cyril to church. And they rang a bell
> And he said right out loud, *crumpets*.)
> > Don't throw away that sausage,
> It'll come in handy. He's artful. Please, will you
> Give us a light?
> Light
> Light
> *Et les soldats faisaient la haie? ILS LA FAISAIENT.**

Now, there is no single continuous sense in this poem: obviously. It is not a straightforward description.

The subject is clear enough. There is a parade, watched by an enormous and simple-minded crowd. The parade contains a large army with much military equipment; several civilian groups; and one single important figure, on horseback. He must be a military victor, because the parade is full of symbols of triumph such as flags, eagles, and trumpets, and because it contains relics of the dead soldiers ('urns containing dust').

The subject is clear, but the manner is not. The tone changes abruptly from the accents of common conversation ('We can wait with our stools and our sausages') to the dry style of a newspaper report ('5,800,000 rifles and carbines, 102,000 machine guns...') and then again to sudden notes of high lyrical ecstasy:

O hidden under the dove's wing, hidden in the turtle's breast †

We are seeing a parade from several different points of view, as though we were listening to a radio reporter moving through a crowd with a portable microphone and occasionally interpolating his own statistics and his own factual descriptions; and as though, after his report was finished, a poet had commented on it.

---

* 'And did the soldiers line the streets? THEY LINED THE STREETS.'

† 'Turtle,' as in 'the voice of the turtle' (*Song of Solomon* 2.12), of course means 'turtle-dove.'

Therefore the poem is part of a drama, written with quick and vivid impressionist technique. It could easily be produced, with a number of different speakers — not on the stage, but on the radio or on a phonograph record. With voices fading out and fading in, what appears enigmatic on the printed page would be both realistic and poetic drama when spoken and heard. The only difficulty would be that of varying the voices so as to make the mood and background of each perfectly plain, like this from the beginning of the fragment:

| | |
|---|---|
| A (hopefully): | Are they coming? |
| B (watching): | No, not yet. |
| C (encouraging): | You can see some eagles. |
| D (confirmatory): | And hear the trumpets. |
| B (affirmative): | Here they come! |
| A (eagerly): | Is *he* coming? |

Then a sentence which no human crowd could ever utter, but which, from a higher intellectual level, states the truth about a crowd of spectators.

ABCD (in a solid impersonal voice): The natural waking life of our Ego is a perceiving.

Then the same thing in common language.

ABCD (genially, as though to one another): We can wait with our stools and our sausages.

This is a scene from a collective drama. Eliot has endeavored to convey *all* the feeling of a triumphal procession, or almost all. There is the crowd. There are the vehicles and the marching units. There are the nice beribboned civil groups. The crowd is sometimes a being which speaks as though it existed all in one collective personality, and sometimes an assemblage of little people with family provisions and family troubles and family jokes, about how the boy misbehaved in church, and family economies ('Don't throw away that sausage, it'll come in handy'). There is a press agent, an impersonal publicity-manipulator, who handles facts and numbers. There is a poet,

who observes, and who thinks intensely about the central figure and about the dust of the dead. It is a superb idea, but it is
no wonder that it got away from Eliot, so that he could not
finish it.

A drama on a historical subject has usually some predecessor.
Eliot, who has always had high ambitions, chose the subject
used by Shakespeare and the title used by Beethoven. We
should therefore look at Shakespeare for an earlier treatment
of the same subject. The first act of his *Coriolanus* shows us the
general fighting and conquering. In the second act, he returns
to Rome, a victor. Shakespeare could not, or would not, show a
triumphal procession, but he has his hero pass across the stage
towards his triumph; and then, in terms very like the envious
Casca describing Julius Caesar's almost-coronation, the democratic officials, disgusted, report the triumphal march of
Coriolanus.

> All tongues speak of him, and the bleared sights
> Are spectacled to see him: your prattling nurse
> Into a rapture lets her baby cry
> While she chats him: the kitchen malkin pins
> Her richest lockram 'bout her reechy neck,
> Clambering the walls to eye him: stalls, bulks, windows
> Are smothered up, leads filled, and ridges horsed
> With variable complexions, all agreeing
> In earnestness to see him.*

This fragmentary scene by Eliot is an on-the-spot description of a triumphal procession similar to that evoked by an
observer in Shakespeare's *Coriolanus*.

Yet Eliot's scene is not a Roman triumph, or not principally
a Roman triumph. It contains some symbols which were originally Roman: oak-leaves, eagles, urns containing dust. The
ascent of the procession to the temple, with a sacrifice — that
too is Roman. The crowd bringing stools to sit on, and sausages
to eat while waiting, might be an ancient Roman crowd or a

---

* *Coriolanus* 2.1.224-32

modern Mediterranean crowd: in some ways the difference is small. But the crowd is also modern English: 'young Cyril,' by his name, is lower-middle-class; when he heard a bell in church he was at an Episcopalian service; and he remembered the muffin-and-crumpet seller who used to go through the English streets ringing a bell. The technological part of the parade is indefinitely European, and dated fairly accurately to the 1920's or 1930's. The civilian groups who take part in the parade are both English ('Mayor and Liverymen') and French (the 'gymnastic club of Poissy' comes from a factory town near Paris).

Therefore this fragment is part of the initial triumph of a soldier and statesman, not in any particular country nor living at any special time: an heir of the Romans, in the same way as all modern triumphators have been heirs of the Caesars, but in some important ways fully modern. And it marks the vast gulf between him and the people. They wait, with their stools and their sausages. He alone lives, and is inspired.

Two puzzles remain. One is the burst of extreme lyrical ecstasy about the triumphant general:

O hidden under the dove's wing, hidden in the turtle's breast,
Under the palmtree at noon . . .

Competent victorious generals are rare indeed, but need they be spoken of in terms which would suit a saint, or Christ entering Jerusalem?

The other is the final line, the question and answer in French. I could not solve this problem myself, but I found the answer in F. O. Matthiessen's *Achievement of T. S. Eliot* (Oxford, 1947). Mr. Matthiessen too was baffled, but he found a lead, followed it up, and traced the sentences to a book called *The Future of Intelligence,* published in 1927 by the royalist anti-democratic author Charles Maurras. They come from a mocking description of a republican ceremony, and they show what Maurras most disliked in these big public parades was the uncritical enthusiasm of the mobs that lined the streets. After World War II, Maurras was sentenced to life-imprisonment for becoming a traitor to his native country, and siding with the enemy — like Coriolanus.

Now we can see the subject of Eliot's unfinished play, 'Coriolan,' and we can divine why he never finished it. The subject was the conflict between the great statesman and the humble people; the lonely man who takes responsibility, and the crowd which sits and watches and waves. This conflict is carried further in the second fragment of his abandoned play, called 'Difficulties of a Statesman': it is evidently a spiritual monologue by the ruler of a country, who is faced with great issues and little problems, great ideals and petty committees to realize them. Now, in the 1920's and 1930's, only the dictators, Stalin, Franco, Hitler, solved the conflict, crushed the people down. Mr. Eliot could not sympathize with that solution.

There is also a technical reason. The method in which he was experimenting was too difficult — at least too difficult for straight printed prose. Perhaps — if the BBC had been intelligently guided during those years — he might have completed 'Coriolan' as a drama of the mass against the hero, and had it beautifully produced.

Nevertheless, there may be other solutions to the technical problem of spacing out the speeches and orchestrating the choruses: 'Coriolan' might yet be produced. But the problem of the relation between the leader and the mass — perhaps Eliot missed the inwardness of that because he never saw F.D.R., with his crippled frame and his saintly face, driving through an adoring crowd. Sometimes I wish that Mr. Eliot had stayed in America, from which he has got so much of his inspiration.

# Shakespeare's Dreams and Dreamers

EVERYBODY who sleeps, dreams — even if after waking he does not recall what he dreamed. If he is excited or ill, he is more likely to dream vividly and to remember his dreams than in normal conditions; but the experts say we all dream during sleep. One third of our lives is given up to that strange activity, the play of the imagination, sometimes quite uncontrolled and sometimes directed by mysterious and masterful emotions. Although the work done by the great psychologists of the last two generations has produced new insight into our life during sleep, there are many kinds of dreams which are still unexplained, at present inexplicable. Some help us, some appear to warn us, many terrify us, and many are merely puzzles: secrets made by our own mind, yet incomprehensible to our understanding.

Many distinguished authors, when writing about men and women under severe emotional strain, have described their dreams — or, even more effectively, have made the characters themselves describe their own dreams and try to interpret them. There is something terribly painful and yet intensely human about watching a man over whom you know some agonizing doom impends, as he paces anxiously to and fro, recalling his last night's dream with horror, and usually shrinking from the meaning which stares him in the face as clearly as the open eye-sockets of a skull.

The profoundest observer of the human soul who has ever written dramatic poetry was William Shakespeare. He created not only scores of characters who live with the most intense and compellingly vivid life, but many profound psychological situations, far beyond the scope of most other playwrights. In his plays there are a number of powerful dreams; through them we look into another world, a world which no playwright can show in three solid dimensions to his audience.

The most painful dreams are those inspired by the two destructive emotions: fear and guilt. Perhaps a truly callous criminal never has guilt-laden dreams that trouble him. It is difficult to believe that Heinrich Himmler's rest was ever disturbed by phantoms of remorse, although he surely did fear at times for his own physical safety. But a man or woman who has strong impulses of virtue, and who commits some great and irrevocable evil without paying for it, is usually tormented by the sense of guilt. One of the noblest speeches in Shakespeare's early dramas, filled not only with somber images but with radiant poetry, comes from the tortured heart of a traitor and an assassin. George, Duke of Clarence, is imprisoned in the Tower of London. He dreams — as so many prisoners do — that he has escaped, and is free, safely on board a ship sailing toward France. Free and safe, for a time: but, in what appears to be a mere accident in the dream, his brother knocks him overboard. He sinks into the sea.

> Lord, Lord! methought what pain it was to drown:
> What dreadful noise of water in mine ears!
> What sights of ugly death within mine eyes!
> Methought I saw a thousand fearful wrecks;
> A thousand men that fishes gnawed upon;
> Wedges of gold, great anchors, heaps of pearl,
> Inestimable stones, unvalued jewels,
> All scattered in the bottom of the sea. . . .

As he tells the story, the warder asks him how, while he was drowning, he could see all this.

> Had you such leisure in the time of death
> To gaze upon these secrets of the deep?

'Methought I had,' says Clarence, with a painful reflex of his deeply constricting guilt,

> Methought I had, and often did I strive
> To yield the ghost; but still the envious flood
> Stopped in my soul, and would not let it forth
> To find the empty, vast, and wandering air;
> But smothered it within my panting bulk,
> Which almost burst to belch it in the sea.

This was, for him, the agony of death; but it was not the final agony, for then he entered 'the kingdom of perpetual night.'

> The first that there did greet my stranger soul
> Was my great father-in-law, renowned Warwick,
> Who cried aloud, 'What scourge for perjury
> Can this dark monarchy afford false Clarence?'
> And so he vanished; then came wandering by
> A shadow like an angel, with bright hair
> Dabbled in blood; and he shrieked out aloud
> 'Clarence is come, false, fleeting, perjured Clarence,
> That stabbed me in the field by Tewkesbury.
> Seize on him! Furies, take him unto torment.'
> With that, methought, a legion of foul fiends
> Environed me, and howled in mine ears
> Such hideous cries that with the very noise
> I trembling waked, and for a season after
> Could not believe but that I was in hell,
> Such terrible impression made my dream.*

Clarence was not only feeling the agonizing pressure of his guilt; he was anticipating his own imminent death. And he has scarcely finished his terrible narrative before the two dark men enter who have been sent by his brother the king to murder him.

---

* *Richard III* 1.4.1-63

Others there are in Shakespeare's plays who look back unwillingly upon their crimes. Lady Macbeth, braver and more determinedly brutal than her husband during the murder of their guest and monarch Duncan, nevertheless suffers more acutely from remorse when it at last attacks her. At night she cannot bear to lie in darkness: 'she has light by her continually, 'tis her command'; * and she cannot sleep, but walks at night, with her eyes wide open and their sense shut, to relive the horrible moments when old Duncan's blood dyed her hands, when she said, with callous certainty, 'A little water clears us of this deed,' † and when she tried again and again to wash off the damned spot, the stain of guilt which had become part of her flesh. 'Here's the smell of the blood still: all the perfumes of Arabia will not sweeten this little hand. Oh! oh! oh! . . . .' ‡ She sighs bitterly in her dream, and moves back into the bedroom which is her own torture chamber, where she is soon to die of exhaustion and madness.

Meanwhile, by one of Shakespeare's most marvelously natural contrasts, her husband Macbeth, originally weaker and more reluctant to crime than she, has been first to complain of

> the affliction of these terrible dreams
> That shake us nightly.**

And later, wide awake among his own subjects, he sees the apparition of one of his own victims, murdered that same day by his orders, his former friend Banquo, blood-boltered, silent, glaring-eyed. This is the most terrible of all dreams, the dream which invades waking life as the projection of a haggard and terrified conscience. But because a woman such as Lady Macbeth gives way sooner than an active fighting man, he grows stronger as she grows weaker, until finally he is completely callous, an animal in armor, sneering at life as

---

\* *Macbeth* 5.1.25-6
† *Macbeth* 2.2.68
‡ *Macbeth* 5.1.55-7
\*\* *Macbeth* 3.2.18-19

> a tale
> Told by an idiot, full of sound and fury,
> Signifying nothing.*

The innocent also dream dreams which image some threatening disaster. So in the tragedy of Julius Caesar, the dictator himself had no anticipations of his death, but his wife, on the night before he was to be murdered, dreamed she saw his statue running blood like a fountain, while

> many lusty Romans
> Came smiling, and did bathe their hands in it. †

The reality which was too horrible for her to conceive was only a few hours away, when his assassins stooped over his still-warm corpse, and bathed their hands in blood up to the elbows.

However, not all dreams are dreams of guilt and terror. Many are visions, manufactured by ourselves, of the pleasures for which — whether we admit it or not — we long night and day and night. These are what psychologists call the dreams of wish-fulfillment. Even the most hideous and repulsive monster in Shakespeare has such dreams. Caliban, on the enchanted island of *The Tempest*, tells his visitors that it is full of sweet music and voices that used to lull him to sleep:

> and then, in dreaming,
> The clouds methought would open and show riches
> Ready to drop upon me; that, when I waked,
> I cried to dream again.‡

And one of Shakespeare's most delightful characters, Mercutio, the gay conscienceless gallant who almost steals the play of *Romeo and Juliet* from its hero, anatomizes many of the chief

---

* *Macbeth* 5.5.26-8
† *Julius Caesar* 2.2.78-9
‡ *The Tempest* 3.2.152-5

wish-fulfillment dreams in a speech as charming as a solo from Mozart: the speech evoking Queen Mab, who at night gallops

> Through lovers' brains, and then they dream of love;
> O'er courtiers' knees, that dream on curtsies straight;
> O'er lawyers' fingers, who straight dream on fees ...*

each imagining his own chief felicity.

Yet there are some dreams which are apparently pure fantasy, the idle play of the imagination turning reality upside down and inside out. Shakespeare, with his prolific and almost uncontrollable imagination, loved to talk about this kind of dream; and once, in the most exquisite of his comedies, he attributed it to pure magic. There a lovely spirit, almost a light invisible wraith, is besotted for a time by a gross lump with the head of an animal, and two pairs of lovers almost forget their true loves in the enchanted confusion of a mid-summer-night's dream.

In his greatest play, Shakespeare touched twice, very strangely, on a dreamer and his dreams. Actors and producers and critics have long disputed whether Prince Hamlet was mad, or sane and pretending madness, or perhaps wildly excitable but fundamentally sane. Now, there are mysterious connections between dreams and mental instability; and I have always been very deeply impressed by two things which Hamlet says. Once, emphatically and bitterly, he tells two associates, 'I could be bounded in a nutshell and count myself a king of infinite space, were it not that I have bad dreams.' † And once, in the famous soliloquy in which he contemplates suicide, he uses an argument which is truly extraordinary. He does not say that suicide is wicked. He says that it is attractive and even logical to kill oneself as a cure for heartache — except that death is a sort of sleep, and then it might be filled with dreams: endless, terrible dreams. The man who fears his own dreams in this strange compulsive way is a man

---

* *Romeo and Juliet* 1.4.55-104
† *Hamlet* 2.2.264-6

who is not yet mad, but who feels his reason is giving way under an awful, intolerable strain.

Shakespeare himself may well have passed through crises as terrible as that which wrecked the life of Prince Hamlet; but at last he reached serenity. In his last play of all, he presents himself as a magician, still powerful, but aging and exhausted. He calls up noble and beautiful spirits 'to enact his fancies,' and then, in an immortal speech, dismisses them and all human existence together as a dream.*

> These our actors,
> As I foretold you, were all spirits and
> Are melted into air, into thin air;
> And, like the baseless fabric of this vision,
> The cloud-capped towers, the gorgeous palaces,
> The solemn temples, the great globe itself,
> Yea, all which it inherit, shall dissolve
> And, like this insubstantial pageant faded,
> Leave not a rack behind. We are such stuff
> As dreams are made on, and our little life
> Is rounded with a sleep.

* *The Tempest* 4.1.148-58

# A BROWNING DRAMATIC MONOLOGUE

## That's My Last Duchess

---

EIGHTY or ninety years ago, Robert Browning was an avant-garde poet. Societies were formed to discuss and interpret his works; he was freely quoted, often recited in public. As usual, this fashion obscured some of the poet's real merits. Then, when it died away, it tended to carry with it some of the genuine interest in his poetry, and to kill the whole thing. By nature, Browning was an eccentric poet. He did not found a school — although he has at least one modern pupil, Auden. He stood rather outside our poetic tradition, and he cannot be fitted into any easy category. Now he is unjustly neglected: although erratic, he was a fine poet.

There is one type of poetry which he practiced more intensely and successfully than others. This is a form of drama: the dramatic monologue. In it, one single character speaks. As he speaks, he reveals his mind (both on its conscious and on its unconscious levels), tells us something of his life-history, and sketches his own era and his surroundings. Not deliberately, of course. Usually he is talking of something else, something which is of great concern to him; but in speaking of that, he reveals all the rest.

Here is one of Browning's little masterpieces in this manner. It is called *My Last Duchess*, with the subtitle *Ferrara*.

Ferrara is a city in north central Italy, where there were dukes from about 1470 until about 1590: therefore the subtitle tells us that we shall be hearing of one of the noble families of the Italian Renaissance. These four words have already outlined a setting for us, and faintly sketched a figure or two. Then the figures come to life. Here is the poem, only fifty-six lines in length. I have punctuated it by spacing, in order to make its dramatic structure clearer: this is how a good actor would speak it.

That's my last Duchess painted on the wall,
Looking as if she were alive. I call
That piece a wonder, now: Frà Pandolf's hands
Worked busily a day, and there she stands.

Will 't please you sit and look at her?
                                        I said
'Frà Pandolf' by design, for never read
Strangers like you her pictured countenance,
The depth and passion of its earnest glance,
But to myself they turned
                            (since none puts by
The curtain I have drawn for you, but I)
And seemed as they would ask me,      if they durst,
How such a glance came there;
                                so, not the first
Are you to turn and ask thus.
                                Sir, 'twas not
Her husband's presence only, called that spot
Of joy into the Duchess' cheek: perhaps
Frà Pandolf chanced to say, 'Her mantle laps
Over my lady's wrist too much,' or 'Paint
Must never hope to reproduce the faint
Half-flush that dies along her throat:'
                                        such stuff
Was courtesy, she thought, and cause enough
For calling up that spot of joy.
                                She had
A heart — how shall I say? — too soon made glad,
Too easily impressed: she liked whate'er

She looked on, and her looks went everywhere.
Sir, 'twas all one! My favor at her breast,
The dropping of the daylight in the West,
The bough of cherries some officious fool
Broke in the orchard for her, the white mule
She rode with round the terrace — all and each
Would draw from her alike the approving speech,
Or blush, at least.

          She thanked men, — good! but thanked
Somehow — I know not how — as if she ranked
My gift of a nine-hundred-years-old name
With anybody's gift.

          Who'd stoop to blame
This sort of trifling? Even had you skill
In speech — (which I have not) — to make your will
Quite clear to such an one, and say 'Just this
Or that in you disgusts me; here you miss,
Or there exceed the mark' — and if she let
Herself be lessoned so, nor plainly set
Her wits to yours, forsooth, and made excuse,
— E'en then would be some stooping;

          and I choose
Never to stoop.

      Oh sir, she smiled, no doubt,
Whene'er I passed her; but who passed without
Much the same smile?

      This grew; I gave commands;
Then all smiles stopped together.

          There she stands
As if alive.

     Will 't please you rise? We'll meet
The company below, then.

         I repeat,
The Count your master's known munificence
Is ample warrant that no just pretence
Of mine for dowry will be disallowed;
Though his fair daughter's self, as I avowed
At starting, is my object.

        Nay, we'll go
Together down, sir.

Notice Neptune, though,
Taming a sea-horse, thought a rarity,
Which Claus of Innsbruck cast in bronze for me!

A short poem. But what a powerful effect it produces! The first impression we get is that of a strong, cruel, family-obsessed, arrogant nobleman, with an indomitable will. Through that there emerges the outline of a terrible story in his past, an atrocious episode in which he grew to disapprove his wife: not because she was vicious, but because she was kind and gracious, too warm-hearted to be proud. He had her murdered. And finally, we see the future. He is a widower, and has been receiving a messenger from another nobleman — a Count, rich evidently but less exalted than a Duke — whose daughter he expects to marry, and to bring back to the palace which still has the dead Duchess painted on the wall.

If we reread the poem, its people come more sharply into focus. The speaker, being a Duke, has the highest of all ranks of nobility below princes and kings. He says he has a nine-hundred-years-old name, so that he can trace his family (genuinely or fictitiously, although he would strike us down for suggesting any doubt) back through the Dark Ages almost to the Romans. He lives in Ferrara, and he has a magnificent palace, for he has been showing the visitor round it and describing his works of art. When does all this happen? We are not intended to know precisely — although Browning may have had a particular nobleman in his mind; but the story is placed in the early Renaissance by the facts that the Duke possesses a rare bronze group showing Neptune taming a sea-horse,* and that his wife's portrait was painted by an artist priest, Brother Pandolf. It is a true touch of the Renaissance that the entire poem is framed in a discussion of works of art, with the story emerging only as comment.

As we look, through the Duke's eyes, at the portrait of 'my

---

* A similar theme appears in a splendid sixteenth-century Venetian door-knocker, reproduced in Plate X of the article Bronze Work in the *Encyclopaedia Britannica*.

last Duchess' (the phrase is intensely patronising), we learn
something about her. She was beautiful. She enjoyed life. She
would respond with a lovely smile to a rich sunset or a small
compliment, a handsome docile animal or a word of admiration. The Duke disapproved. He thought that for her to be his
wife, his Duchess, was sufficient happiness; and that she should
have felt and shown enjoyment in nothing else. No other experience, he believed, was comparable to that. And let us not
believe that he is in the slightest degree exaggerated. He had
an English parallel, Charles Seymour, the sixth Duke of Somer-
set, the premier peer of the realm, who behaved as though he
were a monarch. Once, when his second wife tapped him on
the shoulder with her fan, to attract his attention, he turned
on her indignantly and said, 'My first Duchess was a Percy, and
she never dared to take such a liberty!'

Evidently, as this Italian Duke continued cold and impassive
and proud — he tells his visitor that he was unable to explain
what he felt, and that he would not condescend to argue — the
woman's heart, chilled on one side, found warmth elsewhere.
Not in a love affair: that is not even hinted; but simply in the
beauty of the world and the kindness of ordinary humanity.
This the Duke found intolerable.

So, he had her killed. 'This grew. I gave commands. Then
all smiles stopped together.' Is there perhaps a moment's remorse, or at least regret, in the brief sentence with which the
Duke dismisses the subject? 'There she stands . . . as if alive.' Is
he looking at her portrait and regretting something, her beauty
which went with such a warm heart, the duty to his family
pride, which led him to destroy such a sweet creature? Do we
feel perhaps that he himself is dead, and that she is more truly
alive? And when the new wife, 'the count's fair daughter,' ar-
rives in his haughty palace and begins to die too, will he
hasten her death with the same regretful compulsiveness, like
a vampire?

Yes, a fine poem. Other poets in Browning's time wrote
these dramatic monologues — think of Tennyson's *Ulysses* and

Arnold's *Empedocles*. But those by Browning are deeper and more varied. This monologue is very short. There are others, much longer and more complex: for instance, a strange exposition of primitive man's religion, called *Caliban upon Setebos;* a wonderful piece on a Renaissance prelate, *The Bishop Orders his Tomb;* two analyses of nineteenth-century twisters, *Mr. Sludge the Medium* and *Bishop Blougram's Apology;* many more. The greatest of Browning's works, *The Ring and the Book,* centers on a seventeenth-century murder case, making its chief characters, the lawyers, the public, and the Pope himself, all speak separately, and all reveal both the truth (at least, in part) and the workings of their own souls.

What kind of poetry is this? Is it an unusual, an inverted way of telling a story? It might be. In each of these monologues there is enough material for at least a short story, and some of them could clearly be expanded into a novel. Browning himself is said to have offered the story of *The Ring and the Book* to a novelist, before he started turning it into poetry.

Yes, it is storytelling; it is drama; but it is more. Browning was more interested in human character than in the tales told about it; because character is the root, the stories are only the leaves. His main interest was the revelation of the human soul. And we can understand Browning's technique best by comparing it with another art to which he was devoted: namely, with painting.

Look at some of the great portraits carved and painted during the Renaissance. Look at El Greco's wonderful picture of the Grand Inquisitor, Cardinal Nino de Guevara. First you see only a sumptuously dressed figure in red satin with a rich lace garment showing beneath it; then you look at the face; and then you look again. Within all this wealth, the satin and the lace, there appears a cold, grim, humorless, determined elderly man. His beard is greying. He sits in a heavily decorated chair, grasping one arm as though he had just taken some serious decision. His eyes, behind heavy spectacles, do not look at you. They are sidelong eyes under heavy eyebrows:

they are thinking of something else, and yet somehow watching you too. The Cardinal de Guevara: the Grand Inquisitor; a powerful and dangerous man.

Or look at the portrait of Innocent X, painted by Velasquez after he had studied El Greco's picture of the Cardinal. Here an even loftier figure, the Pope himself, wearing even more magnificent robes and sitting in a chair like a throne, frowns at the beholder with an air of authority and shrewdness, shot through with uncertain wariness, which tells us as much about him as we could learn from a biography several hundred pages long. Such also is the portrait of Paul III, by Titian; earlier, such is the Bellini portrait of the proud Doge Loredano, and the Verrocchio statue of the commander and condottiere, Bartolommeo Colleoni.

Now, poetry is an art which depends on time. It takes several minutes to read and understand even a short poem. Painting is often supposed to be an instantaneous art, because you can see a whole picture in less than a second. But really to understand the character-portrayal which is implicit in these fine Renaissance portraits takes time; it takes study; it takes the realization of many separate details and the understanding of their relationship to the face of the central figure, and to his soul. So, when Browning created these dramatic monologues, in which the frame is set up and the outline sketched by a few words, and then, detail by detail, significant phrases are uttered and unconscious revelations are made, and memories long hidden come to light and half-comprehended plans for the future begin to show themselves, until, just as the poem closes, a complete man stands before us, visible through to his innermost heart — surely, when Browning conceived and completed these gripping poems, he was attempting to rival, in poetry, the portraiture of the Renaissance painters. His brush-work may not always have been so subtle, nor his line so graceful; but his conceptions were as important, and his penetration was not less profound.

## GOETHE'S *FAUST*

### Man and the Devil

ONCE upon a time there was a wise man, who sold his soul to the devil. In return, the devil gave him the power to perform miracles, such as flying through the air. At last the term of his contract expired, and the devil came and carried him off to hell, where he is now.

It is a well-known story, invented during the late Middle Ages. It was current in Germany during the late sixteenth century. Thence it reached England, where it was turned into a fine though unequal play by the brilliant rival of Shakespeare, Christopher Marlowe, who called it *The Tragical History of Doctor Faustus*. Some time after the play was produced, a troupe of English actors took it back to Germany on tour. There it was made into a show for the puppet theater, and held the stage for an amazingly long time.

In the mid-eighteenth century a boy who lived in Frankfurt saw the puppet show, and loved it. The story of Doctor Faustus stuck in his mind because it looked both probable and impossible, both true and incredible. His name was Johann Wolfgang Goethe. He spent the rest of his long life thinking from time to time about the man who sold his soul to the devil. Goethe became the most eminent poet in Germany, and his most ambitious work was his dramatization of this late medieval legend. In the opinion of most Germans, it is the finest creation of poetry and imagination in the German language; many of them believe it to be the highest achievement of all modern literature. Goethe began writing it when he was twenty-four. He finished its first part when he was over fifty; and he did not complete the work till he was eighty-two. It haunted him. Like the fiend haunting Dr. Faustus, the story possessed him; and eventually it gave him the power to work miracles.

It is a very strange masterpiece, Goethe's *Faust,* far more difficult and heterogeneous than the poetic masterpieces of other languages — English, Greek, French, Latin, Spanish, Italian. Although technically a drama, it cannot be performed on any normal stage, since it is full of the most ferocious difficulties of production, and there are important gaps and wild superfluities in the plot, which Goethe leaves quite unexplained. It would make a magnificent motion picture, if produced by some genius with infinite amounts of money, great technical skill, soaring poetic imagination, and an absolutely first-rate cast. It should rather be thought of as a dramatic poem, written so that, when we read it, it can be played on the stage of our mind, like our own dreams and visions. (The best parallels in English are the almost equally unproduceable *Prometheus Unbound* of Shelley and Hardy's *Dynasts.*)

The plot of this dramatic fantasy is a collection of apparently disconnected adventures, with a mystical prologue and a mystical conclusion. Only after several readings do we see how the adventures all fit into a gigantic plan.

In the prologue — evidently modeled on the Book of Job — Almighty God, enthroned among his angels, is visited by the devil, here called by the grotesque name of Mephistopheles. They talk of Faust, the thoughtful, ambitious, doubting servant of the Lord on earth. God permits the devil to tempt him, but declares that, nevertheless, Faust will justify himself.

> A good man, struggling onwards in the dark,
> Still knows, or feels, the way of righteousness.

After this, Faust is shown, learned beyond all other men, but dissatisfied with his learning, hating his old age after a life wasted on books, philosophy, and science, and contemplating suicide. As he swings between hope and despair, Mephistopheles appears to him, offering to be his servant and do anything that Faust wishes *here* — provided that Faust will do the same for him *there*. Yet the bargain is not so simple as it was in the old legend. Faust does not want external things. He wants spiritual satisfaction. For that, only for that, will he surrender himself. So the contract is drawn on this condition: that if he is ever so happy that he can hope for nothing more, if he ever finds any single moment of experience so delightful that he can wish it to continue for ever, then he will become the slave and the chattel of the devil. Otherwise, the contract will not be fulfilled. *Faust* is such a deep book that we can read many meanings into it. Therefore we can think of this satanic contract as the reverse of the vows of a monk or a nun. In order to find perfect happiness, a postulant contracts with God to leave this world and to surrender his soul to heaven. In order to find perfect happiness, Faust contracts with the devil to surrender his soul to hell, provided he can once fully enjoy this world.

The remainder of the first part of the poem shows the adventures of Faust, now restored to youth and granted illimitable earthly power. He plays a little with magical tricks. Then he turns to pursue beauty and to experience love. With the devil's help — because of the devil's help — he attains them in the wrong way. He seduces a simple and beautiful girl called Margaret, wrecks her life, brings death to her brother and mother, and finally — after attending a wild witches' sabbath where he sees Margaret as a ghastly living corpse — visits the prison to which she has been condemned (for murdering their child), witnesses her final despair, and leaves her to perish. So ends the first part of *Faust,* in misery, death, madness, damnation.

The second part of *Faust* (completed during Goethe's amazingly prolonged middle age) is quite different. Formerly Faust's adventures were silly and vicious, but still youthful, naïve, realistic. Now they become complex, mystical, symbolic. Faust visits the court of the Holy Roman Emperor, and, at his command, summons up the beautiful Helen of Troy. Here Goethe abandons the original legend — in which the magician, since he could do anything and fulfill any human wish, possessed the most beautiful woman of all ages and all lands. When Helen appears before Faust, Faust rushes forward to embrace her; but he does not possess her. There is a violent explosion and she disappears, leaving him unconscious. By his own simplicity and violence, he has destroyed a vision. (Germans sometimes do this.)

When Faust recovers, he sets out through a fabulous region inhabited by the weirdest supernatural beings of ancient Greece to find Helen again. At last, by delivering her from a tyrannous husband and defending her as a conqueror, he can possess her; and they have a son, called Euphorion, which means something like 'Gay Energy.' Almost as soon as born, the son bursts into wild activity, leaping and dancing, always higher and more dangerously, until at last he tries to soar up into the sky, falls, and dies. With his death, Helen vanishes into the clouds. Another of Faust's adventures is over. But we are left asking: What does Helen symbolize? Who was the miraculous child? Why did he live in such a way as to die? (Goethe gives us an enigmatic clue by saying that, when Euphorion's body disintegrated, his features looked for a moment like 'a well-known face'; and we are given to understand that Goethe was thinking of the doomed prodigy Byron. Byron, the son of Goethe and Helen of Troy?)

Two more adventures remain. Faust becomes a victorious general, in a short war, satirically described. Military fame is brittle and transitory. Then he turns to helping mankind, by reclaiming land from the sea and making it fit for cultivation. Although, in the process, an old farmer and his wife are burned to death in their little cottage, still, they were obstacles to Progress. Now at last, although grown old again and hitherto never satisfied, Faust sees satisfaction within his grasp: the happiness of helping others, of making something out of nothing, of self-forgetfulness . . . and at that moment he dies. The devil instantly claims him. But he is rescued by angels, because he loved much and because his betrayed mistress Margaret loved him even more. The poem ends with a chorus of divine beings drawn from the Roman Catholic mythology proclaiming his salvation. The final words are either very shallow, or very deep:

> Eternal womanhood
> Still leads us on.

An astonishing poem: almost as astonishing as Johann Wolfgang Goethe himself, who, at the age of seventy-two, could still fall in love with a beautiful young woman and write her Oriental poems of passion; who was not only a poet and a courtier, but (like Faust) a scientist, working on optics and on botany; who looked so calm and sure and proud, yet was so painfully unstable, so vitally unpredictable.

Clearly *Faust* is a symbolic poem. Like all good symbolic poems, it conveys not one single truth, but a number of truths, which could not possibly be conveyed all together (and possibly not separately) in logical terms.

It is an allegory of man's life. From the early energies of youth — sensual, blind, and pleasure-loving, selfish and remorseless — it moves through the larger ambitions of maturity to the interwoven selfishness and selflessness of old age.

Then again, it is a symbol of what we are told is our inalienable right, the pursuit of happiness. In his way through life, Faust pursues every kind of happiness, but he finds them all unsatisfying. Like the Preacher, he always has to say:

> All the rivers run into the sea; yet the sea is not full; unto the place from whence the rivers come, thither they return again. All things are full of labor; man cannot utter it: the eye is not satisfied with seeing, nor the ear filled with hearing.*

Here the most fascinating symbol is surely Helen of Troy, who repels and stuns the vulgar modernist Faust when he tries to clasp her brutally, but later, after he has worked hard to win her, lets herself be conquered, while conquering her conqueror — as Greece conquered Rome and as Greco-Roman culture conquered the barbarians.† She represents the beauties of art — and in particular the beauties of Greco-Roman art, literature, thought, and landscape. She cannot therefore be captured by a brief assault. She must be revered. She must be admired. But even when she is achieved and understood, the results of the union, though beautiful, are short-lived.

We might also say that Goethe was thinking of a different kind of experience: the search for companionship. Most great men live solitary lives, even when they are surrounded by people. Poets, composers, philosophers, inventors, scholars largely live alone. In their loneliness they are often companioned by beings who are not fully human — spirits of health and goblins damned, ideals and wizards, seraphim, ghosts, muses, fauns, dybbuks, Doppelgänger, entities as strange as the 'angels' on the radar. In *Faust* there are actually more superhuman beings than real people. These, and many others whom we cannot know, were the companions of Goethe's remote life.

On a higher level still, *Faust* represents man's search for his true relation to God. And it is here that it is least satisfactory. The main body of the poem almost ignores the Creator, sel-

---

* Ecclesiastes 1.7-8
† 'Captured Greece took prisoner her savage conqueror': Horace, Ep. 2.1.156

dom mentions the Redeemer, and often ignores Christian moral standards and their sanctions — at least in relation to Faust himself. The play is an assertion of Goethe's belief in humanism, his faith that religious prohibitions were artificial, that human standards alone were meaningful, and that individual aspirations ought to be fulfilled, at whatever cost. The essentials of religious life are therefore omitted from *Faust*, except at the beginning and the end. This is a notable contrast to *Job*, which is almost one long argument about religion, first with orthodox pietists, and later with Almighty God himself. The drama concludes with the assertion that Heinrich Faust, dying 'with all his crimes broad blown, as flush as May,' will go straight to heaven without remorse or repentance. Dante, for one, and Milton, for another, would have sent him elsewhere; and they might have called the entire drama a paean of praise to the favorite idol of humanity, Selfishness.

Even so, it is a moving and thoughtful poem. It is not easy reading — as life is not easy living. It is a constant struggle. Most of it is not idealistic rhapsody, but bitter, cynical, humorous, even grotesque poetry. It is full of slang; in the first sentence uttered by its hero, there is a joke — or at least a sneer. Jokes of all kinds, many of them almost unprintable and some of them sharply topical and satirical, spice the entire play, so that it is less like Aeschylus and Shelley than *Don Quixote* or Rabelais. It is like a Gothic cathedral, where the altar is hidden and gargoyles grin down from every corner. Yet, intermingled with the jests, there are lovely passages of pure lyric poetry, dreamily mystical meditations, and dark speeches pregnant with wisdom.

This blend of the beautiful, the grotesque, and the incomprehensible is what most new readers find hardest to appreciate and to accept in *Faust*. They would like it to be uniform. Instead, it is a restless swirl of discordant elements, like the physical universe, like the life of man.

As we range through the phantasmagoria of Faust's career, we realize one more, perhaps the most important, of the many truths which Goethe intended to convey in his drama.

Throughout his poetry, bizarre humor and noble lyricism are woven inextricably together. In his plot, Faust and Mephistopheles are linked more closely than Don Quixote and Sancho Panza, more closely than Pantagruel and Panurge, far more closely than Job and his afflicter Satan. Goethe meant that these two could scarcely exist separately — at least on this earth; and that he himself, like us, was both the sneering negative devil and the optimistic demanding man.

# The Waste Land

THE WASTE LAND is certainly the most famous and influential poem published in English during the last two generations. It came out in 1922, when its author, T. S. Eliot, was thirty-four years old, an American immigrant living in England, and very little known except to a small circle of experimental writers and critics. One of the things which helped to launch it into the publicity it has since enjoyed was that it was awarded an annual prize for poetic excellence, instituted by what was then a highly influential journal of poetry and poetic appreciation, *The Dial*. But it would have succeeded without any boosting, although perhaps more slowly. It was so deeply original, so full of hauntingly beautiful and penetratingly terrible images, so weirdly and passionately eloquent. It was helped even by the fact that it was so fabulously difficult to understand. For this, it came at the right time. In an epoch where people think they know the answer to most questions, poetry can, and perhaps should, speak with perfect clarity and decision. In a period of doubt and dismay like the 1920's, a poem will make a far deeper impression if it is hesitant, groping, obscure. Obscure *The Waste Land* certainly was, and is. Perhaps if it had been longer it might have been less opaque. There is a story that, under the advice of Ezra Pound,

Mr. Eliot took out one third of the original version and threw it away. But possibly that extra material might have added to the formidable complexity of the poem and deepened its inspissated obscurity. Mr. Eliot himself knew that his magnum opus was excessively resistant to understanding, for he added four pages of notes, naming some of the diverse sources from which certain of its ideas were drawn, and citing the original dramas and poems which it adapted and parodied. Nevertheless, they do little to clear up the chief problems of the poem. There have been a number of commentaries on it, but I know very few which give anything like a complete explanation of the poem's meaning.

In one way it was strange that *The Waste Land* should become so popular so soon. In 1922, when it came out, and in the years after that when it was making its reputation, most sensitive people were anxious about four phenomena. These were: the horrors of world war and the need to prevent their recurrence; unemployment and economic dislocation; revolutionary violence leading toward anarchy; and an abrupt decline in morality, particularly sexual morality. One would have expected that any poem which became influential at that time would deal with all these painful themes. *The Waste Land* did not. True, one of its principal subjects was the misuse of sex. Also, in his notes, Mr. Eliot explained that some of it dealt with 'the decay of eastern Europe,' by which he presumably meant the rise of Bolshevistic communism and its organized destruction of religion; but, frankly, that was not apparent from the text of the poem, and still is not. Unemployment, poverty, starvation, economic decay were not even mentioned. The war was only a piece of background, not tragic, but tedious.

> Think of poor Albert,
> He's been in the army four years, he wants a good time,
> And if you don't give it him, there's others will, I said.*

It looked, in fact, as though *The Waste Land* deliberately refrained from treating public themes. It seemed to be a purely

---

* *The Waste Land* 147-9

personal poem about a complex group of private torments, never described explicitly, and, as far as could be judged, very dissimilar to the anxieties and agonies which most people were suffering in the 1920's.

Yet the power of a poem does not depend wholly on its subject. Think how many hundreds of thousands of people have been enraptured by the beauties and intricacies of the tragedy of *Hamlet,* when they were in fact quite unmoved by its central problem, a young prince's revenge on the usurper of his throne. The general tone of *The Waste Land* was almost exactly right for its time: disillusionment, profound world-weariness and self-hatred, abandonment of faith in mankind, loss of Christian belief and a search for some other creed, fascination with trifles and vulgarities, something very like anarchism in the spiritual and intellectual realm, and an ethos which nobody else has ever captured so brilliantly and sensitively, combining the tragic, the jocular, and the bitterly cynical. I was just growing up when *The Waste Land* was published, although I did not hear about the poem until it had been out for three or four years; I remember that, at the time, that was exactly how many people felt and talked. Private it may have been, but it spoke for half the world.

True, but what did it say? What was it about? What is it about? It is constantly being quoted; it has elicited dozens, scores, of imitations and parodies; but scarcely anyone seems able to describe its theme. Of course you can always say (and many critics do say) that it is impossible to explain what a poem is about — any more than you can state what a piece of music or an abstract painting is about. But this is surely mistaken. The first movement of the Fifth Symphony is not about plaintive melancholy or fragile impressions of nature. Piet Mondrian's paintings are not about chaotic disorder or rebellious and impulsive lust. We all know perfectly well what activities of the human soul these works of art express, although it may be impossible to put everything they say into words. Therefore we can and should ask what *The Waste Land* is about. We know that this can be done, because Mr. Eliot has populated the poem with symbolic figures, taken from famous myths and even from his own earlier poems: these symbols convey a group of meanings which can be elucidated and analyzed. Also, he has packed it (almost too full) with vivid quotations from books both famous and obscure. There are fragments of the *Confessions* of St. Augustine, bits of a sermon by Buddha, a stanza from Wagner's *Tristan and Isolde,* a line of Baudelaire and a line of Verlaine, a parody of a Goldsmith song, an imitation of a Greek funerary epigram, pieces of classical and later Latin, memories of the Bible, and a few words of Sanskrit. Although it requires a good deal of reading and a long memory to recognize them all, they can be traced (Mr. Eliot's notes help) and they all carry strong and intelligible meanings.

Take the first of all, three lines of Latin mingled with Greek which are printed (without author's name or explanation) just after the title and before the first words of the poem. They come from the Roman satirist Petronius.* They are about the Sibyl, the ancient prophetess who lived near Naples, and who, although she was nearly a thousand years old, shriveled and shrunk into the size of a grasshopper, still could not die. In the body of the poem we meet another prophet, Tiresias, who is also very old, is now a spectator and a sufferer rather than an actor, blind, impotent, and almost dead although still able to think and perceive. Therefore one of the main themes of the poem is hatred of life and the wish for death — not because of poverty or physical pain or the more usual incitements to despair, but rather because of the exhaustion of the spirit which makes it old long before the body is worn out. When Mr. Eliot published the poem he was thirty-four and he was surrounded by 'Bright Young People' and the frenetic assertion of youth; yet he was writing about someone who felt infinitely old and was only waiting for death.

* See a perceptive article called 'The Sibyl in the Bottle,' by Helen H. Bacon, in *The Virginia Quarterly* 34 (1958) 262-76

This theme is carried all through the poem in another symbol: the waste land itself, the desert longing for water, dead trees, hot sun beating cruelly down, dry rocks, earth cracked and parched, thirst which cannot be assuaged. Such an existence is neither life nor death, but a numb suffering, what the Ancient Mariner and his shipmates, crazed with thirst, saw as 'the Nightmare Life-in-Death.' That is why the poem begins with the unforgettable paradox that spring — the season which normal people love so dearly and which lovers welcome with rapture — is hateful, because it revives the life of the cataleptic soul.

> April is the cruellest month, breeding
> Lilacs out of the dead land, mixing
> Memory and desire, stirring
> Dull roots with spring rain.*

This, then, is one of the main subjects of *The Waste Land*: the agony of a single human soul which has grown prematurely old, which has been transformed into a desert, which loathes life but cannot die.

Another theme, so important that it gets one of the five main sections of the poem to itself and is expressed in a reminiscence of an earlier poem by Mr. Eliot (a mysterious affair written in French, and full of sinister implications, *Dans le Restaurant*), is the unusual theme of Death by Water: the drowning of a young man, tall, handsome, and bitterly regretted — a young man who haunts more intimately the memory of someone who loved him than Lycidas haunted the memory of John Milton, and indeed with the magical power of one of Shakespeare's most bewitching fairies, Ariel, whose actual song is quoted in *The Waste Land*:

> Those are pearls that were his eyes.†

The drowning of this young man helped, it appears, to numb and to age the suffering soul which has become a waste land.

---

* *The Waste Land* 1-4
† Shakespeare, *The Tempest* 1.2.396; *The Waste Land* 125

Sex, sex mishandled and cheapened, is another principal theme of the poem; but it is expressed in a set of symbolic scenes very hard to connect and interpret. A rich and beautiful woman brushing her hair in an exquisite candle-lit bedroom talks to a man with whom she cannot communicate: she is painfully nervous, longing for love or at least companionship, afraid of going mad, living the life of a wealthy neurotic, while the man with her feels as though he were already dead, cannot talk to her, and remembers the drowned youth. The two live like a zombie and an invalid. They are as distant as two chess players, competitors rather than friends, rivals, and not lovers.

> 'What is that noise?'
>                     The wind under the door.
> 'What is that noise now? What is the wind doing?'
>                     Nothing again nothing.
>                                             'Do
> 'You know nothing? Do you see nothing? Do you
>             remember
> 'Nothing?'
>
>     I remember
> Those are pearls that were his eyes.*

That is the most intense and the most fully developed scene between a man and a woman. The others are little dramas showing how cheap and vulgar heterosexual love can become: a Cockney woman in a pub beginning to explain how she took another woman's husband away after the wife was exhausted with childbearing and abortion, a typist being seduced almost without emotion by a vulgar and pimply young man, whose

>         vanity requires no response,
>     And makes a welcome of indifference.†

But it is strange to learn from the poem that the aged seer, Tiresias, whom Mr. Eliot describes (in the Notes) as the princi-

---

* *The Waste Land* 117-25
† *The Waste Land* 241-2

pal character, not only sees this little seduction but, as partly a *woman* 'throbbing between two lives,' experiences it passively, with a repugnance close to torment.

In shape, the poem called *The Waste Land* is like its subject: chaos, a shattered, barren desert. It is incoherent. I can think of no poem in any Western language — apart from the babblings of the Dadaists and the later *Cantos* of Ezra Pound — which is so far from making continuous logical sense. It is — from one point of view — an impressionist drama, with many different voices emerging from a background of confused interior and external noise, being heard for a few moments, and then sinking into silence again. A man who was going mad, with a wonderful memory and a painfully active imagination, might hear such a drama playing itself out in his head, and hope for the final deliverance of those claps of thunder which sound through the end of *The Waste Land*.

The shape and the leading themes give us an idea of the subject of the poem. It is an attempt to describe the mind of a man whose life has been fearfully, fatally dislocated by the death of a beloved youth through drowning, whose marriage and spiritual life have been turned into a desert, and who is trying to save himself from going mad. How? By taking refuge in the one unassailable citadel of certain sensitive souls — the beauties of poetry and music and art, which are at least fragments he can 'shore against his ruins' * — and by hoping, however distantly, to find the peace of release and annihilation in an ascetic religion, some creed such as Buddhism, whose highest ideal, Nothingness, is the most that such a tormented spirit can hope for: death within life, but deliverance from desire and pain and memory, a paradoxical state to be achieved only through a miracle beyond merit and beyond prayer.

---

* *The Waste Land* 430

# Values

# *What Use Is Poetry?*

CHILDREN ask lots and lots of questions, about religion, about sex, about the stars. But there are some questions which they never ask: they leave grown-ups to ask them and to answer them. Often this means that the questions are silly: that they are questions about nonexistent problems, or questions to which the answer is obvious. Sometimes it means that the questions *should* be asked, but that the answer is difficult or multiplex.

So, children never ask what is the good of music. They just like singing and dancing, and even drumming on a low note of the piano. In the same way, they never ask what is the use of poetry. They all enjoy poems and songs, and very often come to like them before they can even talk properly; but it never occurs to them that they ought to find reasons for their enjoyment. But grown-ups do inquire about the justification of poetry: they ask what is the point of putting words in a special order and extracting special sound effects from them, instead of speaking plainly and directly. And often — because they get no adequate answer, either from the poets or from the professors — they conclude that poetry is only a set of tricks like conjuring, or a complicated game like chess; and they turn away from it in discouragement... until, perhaps, a poetic film like *Henry V* shocks them into realizing something of its power; or, as they grow older, they find that a poem learned in childhood sticks in their mind and becomes clearer and more beautiful with age.

What is the use of poetry?

There must be a number of different answers to the question. Just as a picture can be meant to give pleasure, or to carry a puzzle, or to convey information, so poems are meant for many different things. We can begin to get some of the answers if we look at the poetry that children themselves naturally enjoy, and then see how it is connected with the most famous grown-up poems.

The first pleasure of poetry is the simplest. It is the same pleasure that we have in music — the pleasure of following a pattern of sound. Everyone loves talking, and most people like what might be called doodling in sound. So, if you look through the *Oxford Dictionary of Nursery Rhymes*, you will find several tongue-twisters, like this:

> Peter Piper picked a peck of pickled pepper;
> A peck of pickled pepper Peter Piper picked;
> If Peter Piper picked a peck of pickled pepper,
> Where's the peck of pickled pepper Peter Piper picked?

On a grown-up level, many a famous poem is little more than a pattern of sound: for instance, Shakespeare's love song:

> It was a lover and his lass,
>   With a hey and a ho and a hey nonino,
> That o'er the green cornfield did pass,
>   In the spring time, the only pretty ring time,
>     When birds do sing, hey ding a ding ding;
>     Sweet lovers love the spring.*

---

* *As You Like It* 5.3.18-23

Much of the best poetry of Swinburne is pattern-making in sound, with a very light core of meaning. Here are four exquisite lines which really mean very little more than the sound of spring showers:

> When the hounds of spring are on winter's traces,
>> The mother of months in meadow or plain
> Fills the shadows and windy places
>> With lisp of leaves and ripple of rain.*

Small meaning, but lovely rhythm and melody.

There is a second pleasure in poetry. This is that it is sometimes better than prose for telling a story. It even gives authority to a story which is illogical or incredible, or even gruesome. That is one reason children love the poem that tells of the tragic fate of Jack and Jill. There is an interesting variant of it: the cumulative story, in which one detail is piled up on another until the whole story has been set forth with the simple exactitude of a primitive painting: for instance, 'The House That Jack Built,' and the funeral elegy, 'Who Killed Cock Robin?' and the famous old Jewish rhyme, 'Had Gadyo,' about the kid bought for two pieces of money — which is said to symbolize a vast stretch of the history of the Jewish people. Another variant is the limerick, which is simply a funny story in verse. Many a man who would protest that he knew no poetry, and cared nothing for it, could still recite eight or ten limericks in the right company.

In serious adult poetry there are many superb stories, including the two oldest books in Western literature, the *Iliad* and the *Odyssey*. Every good collection of poems will include some of the most dramatic tales ever told, the English and Scottish ballads, which are still occasionally sung in our own southern states. One of the strangest things about the stories told as ballads is their terrible abruptness and directness. They leave out a great deal. They give only a few details, a name or

---

* Swinburne, *Atalanta in Calydon,* 1st chorus

two; they draw the outlines, harsh and black or blood-red, and they concentrate on the actions and the passions. Such is the ballad about an ambush in which a knight was killed  by his own wife's brother. It is called 'The Dowie Houms of Yarrow' (that means the sad fields beside the river Yarrow, in the Scottish borders), and it opens immediately with the quarrel, almost with the clash of swords:

> Late at een, drinkin' the wine,
>   And ere they paid the lawin',
> They set a combat them between,
>   To fight it in the dawin'.

Within only a few verses, the knight has been surrounded, and treacherously murdered, fighting against heavy odds; and when his widow goes out to find his body, her anguish is described in one of the most terrible stanzas in all poetry:

> She kissed his cheek, she kamed his hair,
>   As oft she did before, O;
> She drank the red blood frae him ran,
>   On the dowie houms o' Yarrow.

That story in poetry and a few others like 'Edward, Edward' — in which a mother persuades her son to kill his own father, and drives him mad — are absolutely unforgettable.

But besides storytelling, poetry has another use, known all over the world. This is mnemonic. Put words into a pattern, and they are easier to remember. I should never have known the lengths of the months if I had not learned:

> Thirty days hath September,
> April, June, and November;
> All the rest have thirty-one,
> Excepting February alone,
> And that has twenty-eight days clear
> And twenty-nine in each leap year.

This is certainly four hundred years old, for it occurs in an English manuscript dated about 1555, and there is a French poem, with the same rhyme scheme, written three hundred years earlier. (It might be easier to change the calendar, but mankind is by nature conservative.) On a simpler level there are many nursery rhymes in every language which are designed to teach children the very simplest things; for instance, counting and performing easy actions:

> One, two,
> Buckle my shoe,
> Three, four,
> Shut the door.

And even earlier, before the child can speak, he is lucky if his mother can recite the poem that goes over his five toes or fingers, one after another:

> This little pig went to market,
> This little pig stayed at home,

up to the comical climax when the child is meant to squeak too, and to enjoy staying at home.

Adults also remember facts better if they are put into verse. Nearly every morning I repeat to myself:

> Early to bed and early to rise
> Makes a man healthy and wealthy and wise.

And nearly every evening I change it to Thurber's parody:

> Early to rise and early to bed
> Makes a male healthy and wealthy and dead:

or occasionally to George Ade's variant:

> Early to bed and early to rise
> Will make you miss all the regular guys.

This is the source of what they call didactic poetry, poetry meant to teach. The best-known example of it is the Book of Proverbs in the Bible, which ought to be translated into rhythmical prose, or even verse. The third oldest book in Greek literature, not much younger than Homer, is a farmer's handbook all set out in poetry, so that it could be learned off by heart and remembered: it is the *Works and Days* by Hesiod. To teach has long been one of the highest functions of the poet: great poetry can be written in order to carry a message of philosophical or practical truth — or sometimes an ironical counsel, as in the strange poem by Sir Walter Scott:

> Look not thou on beauty's charming;
> Sit thou still when kings are arming;
> Taste not when the winecup glistens;
> Speak not when the people listens;
> Stop thine ear against the singer;
> From the red gold keep thy finger;
> Vacant heart and hand and eye,
> Easy live and quiet die.*

There is one peculiar variation on the poem that conveys information. This is the riddle poem, which tells you something — but only if you are smart enough to see through its disguise. There are some such riddles in the Bible: Samson created a good one, about the dead lion with a hive of wild bees inside it. Legend has it that Homer died of chagrin because he could not solve a rather sordid poetic puzzle. The nursery rhyme 'Humpty Dumpty' was really a riddle to begin with (before Lewis Carroll and his illustrator gave it away). We are supposed to guess what was the mysterious person or thing which fell down, and then could not possibly be put together again, not even by all the king's horses and all the king's men, and nowadays by all the republic's scientific experts: the answer is an egg. There is a beautiful folk song made up of three such riddles: the cherry without a stone, the chicken without a bone, and the baby that does not cry. It is at least five hundred years old, and yet for four hundred years it was passed on from one singer to another, without ever being printed.

Again, there are some famous and splendid poems that deal with mystical experience in riddling terms, phrases which have two meanings, or three, or one concealed: these are also

---

* Lucy Ashton's song, from *The Bride of Lammermoor* c. 3

didactic, informative, and yet riddles. One such poem, by an American poet, deals with the paradox of God — the complete God, who includes all the appearances of the universe, both the appearance of good and the appearance of evil.

> If the red slayer think he slays,
>     Or if the slain think he is slain,
> They know not well the subtle ways
>     I keep, and pass, and turn again.
>
> Far or forgot to me is near;
>     Shadow and sunlight are the same;
> The vanished gods to me appear;
>     And one to me are shame and fame.
>
> They reckon ill who leave me out;
>     When me they fly, I am the wings;
> I am the doubter and the doubt,
>     And I the hymn the Brahmin sings.
>
> The strong gods pine for my abode,
>     And pine in vain the sacred Seven;
> But thou, meek lover of the good!
>     Find me, and turn thy back on heaven.*

This is a riddle which is meant not for children but for adults. There are similar riddles in the Bible, sometimes equally beautiful. Such is the meditation on old age at the end of that mysterious and rather unorthodox book called *Koheleth*, or *Ecclesiastes*:

> Remember now thy Creator in the days of thy youth,
>     while the evil days come not, nor the years draw nigh,
>         when thou shalt say, I have no pleasure in them;
>     while the sun or the light or the moon or the stars be not
>         darkened, nor the clouds return after the rain;
>
> in the day when the keepers of the house shall tremble,
>     and the strong men shall bow themselves,
>     and the grinders cease because they are few,
>     and those that look out of the windows be darkened,

---

\* Emerson, 'Brahma'

and the doors shall be shut in the streets,
 when the sound of the grinding is low,
 and he shall rise up at the voice of the bird,
 and all the daughters of music shall be brought low,
also when they shall be afraid of that which is high,
 and fears shall be in the way,
 and the almond tree shall flourish,
 and the grasshopper shall be a burden,
 and desire shall fail:
  because man goeth to his long home
  and the mourners go about the streets;
or ever the silver cord be loosed,
 or the golden bowl be broken,
 or the pitcher be broken at the fountain,
 or the wheel broken at the cistern.
Then shall the dust return to the earth as it was;
and the spirit shall return unto God who gave it.*

All these enigmatic and memorable phrases are descriptions of the symptoms of the last and almost the bitterest fact in life: old age. An old man, growing decrepit, is compared to a house or a city gradually depopulated and deserted. The 'keepers of the house' are his arms and hands. The 'strong men' who 'bow themselves' are his legs, once straight and now insecure. The 'grinders' are his teeth and 'those that look out of the windows' are the sight of his eyes. The 'daughters of music' are the once flexible chords of his voice. The 'fears' which emerge are those which all old people suffer. The 'almond tree' is the grayish-white hair on the head of age; and the grasshopper is a burden because old people are so frail that they cannot bear the slightest noise or weight. The images at the end are more difficult, but probably they are images of death: the 'silver cord' is the thread of life, and the 'golden bowl' our head or our heart which contains our life. If this is correct, then the whole passage means that, even before the dissolution which is final death, old age is a slow dying.

---

* *Ecclesiastes* 12.1-7

If we do not see fully through these moving images, the whole passage still makes memorable poetry; if we do understand them, they will remain with us all our lives. Some poetry is a riddle which life itself solves.

Such poetry is unusual. Or rather, its manner is unusual, while its subject is a fact of common experience. It is possible for poets to speak frankly and plainly about everyday life; and that is one more of the uses of poetry — one of the best known. Poetry can express general experience: can say what many men and women have thought and felt. The benefit of this is that it actually helps ordinary people, by giving them words. Most of us are not eloquent. Many of us — especially in times of intense emotion — cannot say what we feel; often we hardly know what we feel. There, in our heart, there is the turmoil, be it love or protest or exultation or despair: it stirs us, but all our gestures and words are inadequate. As the emotion departs, we know that an opportunity was somehow missed, an opportunity of realizing a great moment to the full. It is in this field that poetry comes close to religion. Religion is one of the experiences which the ordinary man finds most difficult to compass in words. Therefore he nearly always falls back on phrases which have been composed for him by someone more gifted. Many, many thousands of times, in battles and concentration camps and hospitals, beside death beds, and even on death beds, men and women have repeated a very ancient poem only six verses long, and have found comfort in it, such as no words of their own would have brought them. It begins, 'The Lord is my shepherd; I shall not want.'

If we look at poetry or any of the arts from this point of view, we shall gain a much greater respect for them. They are not amusements or decorations; they are aids to life. Ordinary men and women find living rather difficult. One of their chief difficulties is to apprehend their own thoughts and feelings, and to respond to them by doing the right things and saying the right sentences. It is the poets who supply the words and sentences. They too have felt as we do, but they have been able to speak, while we are dumb.

Not only that. By expressing common emotions clearly and eloquently, the poets help us to understand them in other people. It is difficult to understand — for any grown-up it is difficult to understand — what goes on in the mind of a boy or girl. Parents are often so anxious and serious that they have forgotten what it was like to be young, and vague, and romantic. It is a huge effort, rather an unpleasantly arduous effort, to think oneself back into boyhood. Yet there are several poems which will allow us to understand it, and even to enjoy the experience. One of them is a fine lyric by Longfellow, called 'My Lost Youth':

> I remember the gleams and glooms that dart
>   Across the schoolboy's brain;
> The song and the silence in the heart,
> That in part are prophecies, and in part
>   Are longings wild and vain.
>     And the voice of that fitful song
>     Sings on, and is never still:
>     'A boy's will is the wind's will,
> And the thoughts of youth are long, long thoughts.'
>
> There are things of which I may not speak;
>   There are dreams that cannot die;
> There are thoughts that make the strong heart weak,
> And bring a pallor into the cheek,
>   And a mist before the eye.
>     And the words of that fatal song
>     Come over me like a chill:
>     'A boy's will is the wind's will,
> And the thoughts of youth are long, long thoughts.'

If you have a young son who seems to be woolgathering half the time, and who sometimes does not even answer when he is spoken to, you should read and reflect on that poem of Longfellow.

This function of poetry is not the only one, but it is one of the most vital: to give adequate expression to important general experiences. In 1897, when Queen Victoria celebrated her Diamond Jubilee, the Poet Laureate was that completely inadequate little fellow, Alfred Austin; but the man who wrote the poem summing up the emotions most deeply felt during the Jubilee was Rudyard Kipling. It is called 'Recessional.' It is a splendid poem, almost a hymn — Biblical in its phrasing and deeply prophetic in its thought:

> The tumult and the shouting dies;
>     The captains and the kings depart;
> Still stands Thine ancient sacrifice,
>     An humble and a contrite heart.
> Lord God of Hosts, be with us yet,
> Lest we forget — lest we forget!

However, as you think over the poems you know, you will realize that many of them seem to be quite different from this. They are not even trying to do the same thing. They do not express important general experiences in universally acceptable words. On the contrary, they express strange and individual experiences in abstruse and sometimes unintelligible words. We enjoy them not because they say what we have often thought but because they say what we should never have dreamed of thinking. If a poem like Kipling's 'Recessional' or Longfellow's 'Lost Youth' is close to religion, then this other kind of poetry is close to magic: its words sound like spells; its subjects are often dreams, visions, and myths.

Such are two most famous poems by Coleridge: 'The Ancient Mariner' and 'Kubla Khan.' They are scarcely understandable. They are unbelievable. Beautiful, yes, and haunting, yes, but utterly illogical; crazy. Coleridge himself scarcely knew their sources, deep in his memory and his subconscious — sources on which a modern scholar has written a superb book. Both of them end with a mystical experience that none of us has ever had: 'The Ancient Mariner' telling how, like the Wandering

Jew, he must travel forever from country to country, telling his story with 'strange power of speech'; and 'Kubla Khan' with the poet himself creating a magical palace:

> I would build that dome in air,
> That sunny dome! those caves of ice!
> And all who heard should see them there,
> And all should cry, Beware! Beware!
> His flashing eyes, his floating hair!
> Weave a circle round him thrice,
>   And close your eyes with holy dread,
>   For he on honey-dew hath fed,
> And drunk the milk of Paradise.

Not long after those fantastic verses were written, young Keats was composing a lyric, almost equally eccentric, which is now considered one of the finest odes in the English language. It ends with the famous words which we all know, and which few of us believe:

> 'Beauty is truth, truth beauty', — that is all
> Ye know on earth, and all ye need to know.

It is the 'Ode on a Grecian Urn'; but how many of us have ever stood, like Keats, meditating on the figures that surround a Greek vase? and, even if we have, how many of us have thought that

> Heard melodies are sweet, but those unheard
> Are sweeter?

It is a paradox. The entire ode is a paradox: not an expression of ordinary life, but an extreme extension of it, almost a direct contradiction of usual experience.

Most modern poetry is like this. It tells of things almost unknown to ordinary men and women, even to children. If it has power over them at all, it is because it enchants them by its strangeness. Such is the poetry of Verlaine, and Mallarmé, and Rimbaud; of the difficult and sensitive German poet Rilke; in

our own language, such is most of Auden's poetry, and Ezra
Pound's; and what could be more unusual than most of T. S.
Eliot — although he is the most famous poet writing today?
This can easily be tested. Let us take something simple. Spring.
What have the poets said about the first month of spring? Most
of them say it is charming and frail:

> April, April,
> Laugh thy girlish laughter;
> Then, the moment after,
> Weep thy girlish tears! *

That is Sir William Watson; turn back, and hear Shakespeare
talking of
> The uncertain glory of an April day; †

turn forward again, and hear Browning cry

> Oh, to be in England
> Now that April's there! ‡

And hundreds of years earlier, see Chaucer beginning his
*Canterbury Tales* with a handshake of welcome to 'Aprille,
with his shoures sote.' Indeed, that is what most of us feel
about April: it is sweet and delicate and youthful and hopeful.
But T. S. Eliot begins *The Waste Land* with a grim statement
which is far outside ordinary feelings:

> April is the cruellest month, breeding
> Lilacs out of the dead land, mixing
> Memory and desire, stirring
> Dull roots with spring rain.

And the entire poem, the best known of our generation, is a
description of several agonizing experiences which most of us
not only have never had but have not even conceived as possible. Yet there is no doubt that it is good poetry, and that it

---

\* Watson, 'April'
† *Two Gentlemen of Verona* 1.3.85
‡ 'Home-Thoughts, from Abroad'

has taken a permanent place in our literature, together with other eccentric and individual visions.

But some of us do not admit it to be poetry — or rather claim that, if it is so extreme and unusual, poetry is useless. This is a mistake. The universe is so vast, the universe is so various, that we owe it to ourselves to try to understand every kind of experience — both the usual and the remote, both the intelligible and the mystical. Logic is not enough. Not all the truth about the world, or about our own lives, can be set down in straightforward prose, or even in straightforward poetry. Some important truths are too subtle even to be uttered in words. A Japanese, by arranging a few flowers in a vase, or Rembrandt, by drawing a dark room with an old man sitting in it, can convey meanings which no one could ever utter in speech. So also, however extravagant a romantic poem may seem, it can tell us something about our world which we ought to know.

It is easier for us to appreciate this nowadays than it would have been for our grandfathers in the nineteenth century, or for their great-grandfathers in the eighteenth century. Our lives are far less predictable; and it is far less possible to use logic alone in organizing and understanding them. Therefore there are justifications, and good ones, for reading and memorizing not only what we might call universal poetry but also strange and visionary poetry. We ourselves, at some time within the mysterious future, may well have to endure and to try to understand some experience absolutely outside our present scope: suffering of some unforeseen kind, a magnificent and somber duty, a splendid triumph, the development of some new power within us. We shall be better able to do so if we know what the poets (yes, and the musicians) have said about such enhancements and extensions of life. Many a man has lived happily until something came upon him which made him, for the first time, think of committing suicide. Such a man will be better able to understand himself and to rise above the thought if he knows the music that Rachmaninoff wrote when he, too, had such thoughts and conquered them, or if he reads the play of *Hamlet,* or if he travels through Dante's *Comedy,* which begins in utter despair and ends in the vision of

> love, that moves the sun and the other stars.

And even if we ourselves are not called upon to endure such extremes, there may be those around us, perhaps very close to us, who are faced with situations the ordinary mind cannot assimilate: sudden wealth, the temptations of great beauty, the gift of creation, profound sorrow, unmerited guilt. The knowledge of what the poets have said about experiences beyond the frontiers of logic will help us to sympathize with them in these experiences. Such understanding is one of the most difficult and necessary efforts of the soul. Shelley compared the skylark, lost in the radiance of the sun, to

> a Poet hidden
> In the light of thought,
> Singing hymns unbidden,
> Till the world is wrought
> To sympathy with hopes and fears it heeded not.

To create such sympathy is one of the deepest functions of poetry, and one of the most bitterly needed.

# INDEX

Byron, 11, **22**, (33), 44 means that Byron is mentioned on pages 11 and 44, that he is discussed in detail on p. 22, and that on p. 33 he is alluded to but not named; 33 n. means the note on p. 33.

Abelard, 63
Ade, George, 327
Aeschylus, 321
Agathon, 220
allegory, 261, 319
alliteration, 5-10, 156, (279-80)
Altick, Richard, 56 n.
America and the Americans, 23, 53, 81, 96, **98-113**, 129-30, 136, 147, 158, 159, 161, 247, 249-50, 265, 272, 300, 323, 335; American literature, 27, **98-113**, 129-34, 137, **143-50**, 155, 162, 207, 210-11, 212-19, 281, 339, 345; *and see under individual authors*
Anacreon and the Anacreontics, **174-82**, 206
anapaestic rhythm, 21, (22-3)
Anderson, Judith, 131
Anon, 175
Apollo, 243, 252, 257, 258
*Arabian Nights (Thousand and One Nights)*, 88-9, 265
Ariosto, 86, 253, 258
Aristobulus, 175
Aristophanes, 220, 293
Arnold, Matthew, 52, 313
assonance, 157
Auden, W. H., 30-31, **167-73**, 212, 308, 345; *Age of Anxiety*, 184; *Birthday Poem*, 31; *Mundus et Infans*, **167-73**; *Songs and Other Musical Pieces*, 6; sonnets, 191, 194-5
Austin, Alfred, 343

## B

Bacchus and bacchanalia, 239, 240, 241, 242, 243
Bach, 239, 279
Bacon, 52
ballads, 107-11, 115, 116, (124), 192, **197-204**, 229, 335-6
Barber, Samuel, 213, 282
Barnes, William, 29
Barrymore, John, 291
Basho, 186
Baudelaire, 326
Beethoven, 20, 278, 282, 294, 298, 325
Belleau, Remi, 176
Bellini, 314
Benét, Stephen Vincent, 281
Bentley, E. C., 217
*Beowulf*, 248
Berlioz, 84, 279
Bible, 137, 202, 248, 326, 338, 339, 343; Old Testament, 99, 175, 248; Genesis, 59, 268-9; Job, 316, 321, 322; Psalms, 341; Proverbs, 209; Ecclesiastes, 320, **339-40**; Song of Solomon, 296 n.; Gospels, 59, 70-71, 156; Acts, 68; Revelation, 155
Bishop, Morris, 214, **215**, 218
blank verse, 12, (**13-20**), 131
Boadicea, 24-5
Boccaccio, 220
Böcklin, 262
Book of Kells, 156
Boswell's *Life of Johnson*, **75-6**

INDICE COMPLETO SALTAT SCRIPTOR PEDE LAETO